FINDING, SELECTING, DEVELOPING, AND RETAINING DATA PROCESSING PROFESSIONALS THROUGH EFFECTIVE HUMAN RESOURCES MANAGEMENT

VNR VAN NOSTRAND REINHOLD COMPANY

NEW YORK   CINCINNATI   TORONTO   LONDON   MELBOURNE

1 Barbara Dalton
2 John DeMarino
3 John Tangney
4 Charles LaBelle
5 Michael Krawetz
6 Susan Bookbinder
7 Lynette Mayne
8 Denise Kreiger
9 Len Smith

About the Authors

Charles D. LaBelle is Vice President of Human Resources, The Operations Division of Manufacturers Hanover Trust, one of the country's leading commercial banks.

Susan M. Bookbinder is Vice President in charge of Human Resource Advisory and Implementation Services Operations Division at Manufacturers Hanover Trust.

John W. DeMarino is Vice President of Human Resource Development for Manufacturers Hanover Trust's Operations Division.

Michael Krawetz is a human resources communications consultant who has written extensively about computers.

Denise V. Kreiger, also with Manufacturers Hanover Trust, is Manager of Computer-Based Training, Human Resources, Operations Division.

Barbara Dalton is Vice President in charge of Human Resources for the Metropolitan Corporate Banking Division of Manufacturers Hanover Trust.

Lynette Mayne, manager of a Manufacturers Hanover Trust information center, is a member of the Business Forum at New York University.

Leonard P. Smith is an independent consultant specializing in human resources and data processing.

John T. Tangney, Assistant Vice President in charge of Resource Planning for Manufacturers Hanover Trust, has had extensive experience in the recruiting and placement of data processing professionals.

FINDING, SELECTING, DEVELOPING, AND RETAINING DATA PROCESSING PROFESSIONALS THROUGH EFFECTIVE HUMAN RESOURCES MANAGEMENT

Charles LaBelle

with

Susan Bookbinder · Barbara Dalton
John DeMarino · Denise Kreiger
Lynette Mayne · Len Smith
John Tangney · Michael Krawetz

VNR VAN NOSTRAND REINHOLD COMPANY
NEW YORK CINCINNATI TORONTO LONDON MELBOURNE

Library of Congress Catalog Card Number: 83-3513
ISBN: 0-442-26012-1

Manufactured in the United States of America

Published by Van Nostrand Reinhold Company Inc.
135 West 50th Street
New York, New York 10020

Van Nostrand Reinhold Company Limited
Molly Millars Lane
Wokingham, Berkshire RG11 2PY, England

Van Nostrand Reinhold
480 Latrobe Street
Melbourne, Victoria 3000, Australia

Macmillan of Canada
Division of Gage Publishing Limited
164 Commander Boulevard
Agincourt, Ontario MIS 3C76, Canada

15 14 13 12 11 10 9 8 7 6 5 4 3 2 1

Library of Congress Cataloging in Publication Data

LaBelle, Charles.
    Finding, selecting, developing, and retaining
data processing professionals through effective human
resources management.

    Includes index.
    1. Electronic data processing departments—Personnel
management. 2. Electronic data processing personnel—
Training of. I. Bookbinder, Susan. II. Title.
HF5548.2.L22   1983   658.3′044   83-3513
ISBN 0-442-26012-1

Figure 6-1 © by Manufacturers Hanover Trust

To
Manufacturers Hanover Trust
For Allowing Us the Latitude to Creatively
Explore New Concepts in Human Resource Management

And

David Larson, Jack Evans and Allan Proske
Without Whose Managerial Support and Guidance, We
Would Not Have Succeeded

Preface

The data processing (DP) environment of the 1980s is marching to a new rhythm orchestrated by human resource leaders who have created people-oriented organizations that a modern workforce can respond to.

Our book is written for the DP human resources leader who needs to be in the forefront of dealing with the challenges posed by changing technology and its subsequent impact on the modern workforce that helped develop it.

The 1980s DP human resources leader has been entrusted with a mission to challenge traditional concepts of what management should be—and then to produce a better way to help run an organization.

There is no choice but to succeed. Failure in the new decade—already riddled by a declining population base and a seemingly unending national appetite for skilled computer industry workers—will create havoc for the unprepared DP human resource executive.

We publish our new guidebook for all DP human resource leaders—whether in industry, government or academia, or those serving as consultants—who want to create a better and more successful way of managing in the present and future DP human resources environment.

Examine the workforce and the marketplace around you to grasp at the fully documented reality of the DP environment for the remainder of this decade:

- You're up against a new workforce that asks more for its services—and demands less repetitive assignments.
- You're being challenged by non-traditional competitors who will meet the needs of an emerging workforce that rejects corporate benefits in lieu of salary increases.

- You're dealing with a changing workforce that rejects the old-line corporate manager, repudiates employer inflexibility and makes the pursuit of leisure as significant as career-pathing.

OUR BLUEPRINT FOR DP WINNERS

Don't read any further in this book unless you're a committed human resources professional in the DP environment who wants to emerge as a winner—and provide your successors with that same opportunity for the remainder of this century.

Follow us throughout these carefully-documented pages and we'll show you how to maintain a data processing/human resources equilibrium while you cope with staying within your recruitment budget, adjust to personnel transfers, reorganizations and DP burn-out.

Our book will not provide you with any hollow or short-term strategies. We didn't set out to produce a bandage. We produced a new DP/human resources leader's handbook.

We suggest that our guidelines—successfully implemented in the DP environment in Manufacturers Hanover, the nation's fourth largest financial institution—can help you to be the leader in demand for the 1980s.

We'll show you how the correct management decisions are made in an organization's human resources approach to the acquisition, retention and career-path development of the DP professional. We'll show you how to successfully operate within the competitive pressures of the DP marketplace. And if you're a frontline human resources manager who will be called upon to help develop the strategies to tackle and implement the critical DP productivity issues, you'll see how good management will help you produce those results.

If you're ready to be part of the cutting edge of human resources change in the DP environment for the 1980s—and want to create a better and more successful working blueprint for the future—our first lesson is on "Learning How to Break With the Past."

Introduction

"It was the best of times; it was the worst of times." Those were the words that Charles Dickens aptly used to portray the era of the turbulent French Revolution.

In reality, the situation once described by Dickens could easily be used to paraphrase many periods of mankind's history—including the present.

Dicken's classic observation tends to characterize the extremities, omitting the lesser gradations of good and bad. That tendency is carried with each generation—including our own.

As we leapfrog into the 1980s, the "best of times" is represented by the extended period without a *major* world conflict. It also includes the advanced standards of living that exist in many parts of the world—and the potential for growth promised by the future. For the 1980s, the "worst of times" denotes the major political and economic uncertainties surfaced by continued East/West political tensions and a spiraling crime rate both in the U.S. and abroad. It is also evidenced by the presence of loosened moral values and their accompanying impact on society.

Whatever the case, all problems and solutions lay within the attitudes and motivations of the world's official and non-elected leaders. To this end, we must recognize the dilemmas and provide answers. History has taught us that the world survives; nations and cities may not. In truth, Tennyson's line from "Passing of Arthur" was quite prophetic:

"The old order changeth, yielding place to new, and God fulfills himself in many ways."

Thus, we move into the opening pages of our book with the understanding that today's rapidly changing nature of events will not permit the "meek to inherit the earth" in the literal sense.

The past has been written. We can only learn from it and, it is hoped, benefit by it. In the truest sense, we must break from the past because the old ways simply will not suffice. Let us now see why, by examining the graphic chart in Figure I-1 below that shows the origins of pressure on a contemporary business organization.

PRESSURES ON THE ORGANIZATION

Figure I-1 illustrates those factors which are impacting an organization, its work and its people. Peter Drucker in his latest book, *Managing in Turbulent Times,* states, concerning population dynamics, that "the most important change is not the much discussed 'population explosion' in the developing countries, massive though that is. The truly important and yet unperceived development ahead is the imminent labor shortage in the developed countries, and especially the shortage of young people available for traditional jobs in manufacturing and services."

This speaks to the first long-range factor which will profoundly affect organizations in the U.S., namely a declining population base. This, linked with an increasing demand on the work side for skilled labor, portends a demand supply situation fraught with increasing shortages of people and rising prices for their services.

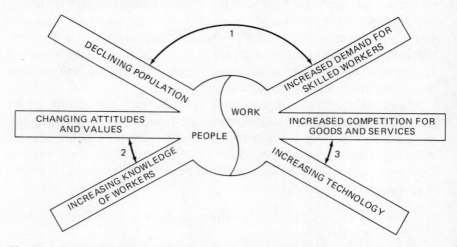

Fig. I-1. The above chart shows the factors which are impacting an organization, its work and its people. The computer field will be hit hard by the upcoming labor shortage and the future will pose a severe challenge for the DP human resources executive.

This is especially so in the computer field, irrespective of the coming labor shortage. We need not belabor this fact, only crystallize it in terms of the future.

Regarding the intellectual makeup of the emerging workforce, Drucker adds, "The labor force of the 1980s is one in which an increasing number of young people have had an advanced education." If Drucker is on target—as he usually is—his warning poses a challenge for organizations, not only about the nature of work that employees will be willing to accept, but also the conditions under which those employees will cooperate in applying their efforts. Many companies today are either unable or unwilling to accept this unalterable fact.

In addition to the dilemma brought on by increased knowledge, there is the added social tinderbox of the changing attitudes and values of today's emerging workforce. Alvin Toffler's prediction in his bestseller, *The Third Wave,* is that "work will grow less, not more, repetitive. Work will become less fragmented, with each person performing a somewhat larger, rather than smaller, task. Flextime and self-pacing will replace the old need for synchronization of behavior. Employees will be forced to deal with more frequent changes in their tasks, as well as experience a blinding succession of personnel transfers, product changes, and reorganizations.

"What 'Third Wave' employers will increasingly need to insure the continued momentum of their organizations will be men and women who accept responsibility and who understand how their work dovetails with others. Employers will seek out workers who can handle even larger tasks, who adapt swiftly to changed circumstances, and who are sensitively tuned in to the people around them."

If key hiring officers across the U.S. take into consideration the sometimes clashing attitudes and values of the emerging workforce that is highly critical of corporate life and then add Toffler's augery of the future, it is evident that they and the organizations they represent have a tall order ahead of them.

Meanwhile, the third combination of forces that is creating havoc with today's business world is the powerful thrust being paved by technology. That thrust is mainly generated by the computer industry, along with the competition of worldwide companies for products and services. Organizations that don't keep up with technology's thrust are doomed. Even if those organizations do, they may still be priced out of the world markets. And short-term profit strategies don't work. They have proven to be only temporary bandages on a much larger wound.

In the face of the multiplicity of pressures, many managerial decisions must be made. Our book concentrates on those conditions that relate to an organization's human resources. Our book provides a set of strategies that will accent the "care and feeding" of the highly mobile and sometimes egocentric data processing professional. Its strategies will show industry peers the human resources success story, which spelled out is: "We care about you in a real way—and we will demonstrate this by actions and not just by words."

However, other factors besides caring are also involved. These new human resource strategies must also take into consideration the fast-paced accelerating technologies, competitive marketplace pressures, the critical productivity issue and lastly the realization and willingness to do what is necessary to enact change.

However, implementing these strategies and solutions is management's responsibility. Only management has the power and ability to make the difference. Recent progress on defining productivity solutions and a growing respect for modern Japan's results has, for example, shed new light on that subject. And the evidence continually points to management's new 1980s role in its relationship with its employees.

From an additional perspective, the New York *Times* reports that W. Edward Deming, the American statistician whose work in Japan in the late 1940s fathered the productivity boom there, concludes that 85 percent of all productivity problems can be traced to management leadership while only 15 percent of the productivity problems reflect worker's performance. Deming further adds that productive managers share several common values and practices not found among the less productive managers, which are:

- *Positive outlooks.* Managers believe that most workers are capable and desirous of doing good work.
- *Honest relationships.* Managers are candid and receptive with workers, and do not make power moves or play political games.
- *A sense of partnership.* Managers recognize the usefulness of personal involvement in one's job and create opportunities for subordinates to feel that "the organization's work is my work."

- *Useful work.* Managers know that the work must be stimulating and provide opportunities for workers to grow and test their abilities.

Richard T. Pascale and Anthony G. Athos, in their recent book, *The Art of Japanese Management,* define human resource management as the attempt to manage productively and systematically more of the important aspects of the human flow through corporations from recruitment to retirement. Japanese management is primarily concerned, understandably, with groups of people, and not so much with individuals as such. The fact is of fundamental importance.

The authors further comment on the obsessive Japanese attention to the selection, training and development of its future executives, developed in a divisional structure. This obsession extends down to the staff and the skills employed by management to develop their human resources and pass their skills on to their successors.

The new reality is that all roads lead to the effective management of our human resources. That is the thrust and message of the following chapters.

Contents

1
The Role of the Human Resource Organization in Your Company

The term "human resources" has many different meanings throughout the U.S. corporate sector.

For every major American business, a different working concept may come to mind. For example, a large food chain might consider personnel administration to be the focus of its area of responsibility; whereas an appliance manufacturer may feel human resources represents training and development. Still another labor-intensive organization may place its emphasis on organizational development.

But the new reality of the term "human resources" for the rapidly changing 1980s refers to the traditional sense of the term—the "people" side of running a business. It means that human resources oversees management, staff, line and clerical administration because every organization needs people in order to operate and subsequently to produce a profit.

Human resources is a relatively new corporate phenomenon brought into the workplace because of changing conditions and marketplace priorities. In the past, the high-expense corporate priorities were attributed to basic material requirements such as raw materials, machinery, building costs, power, furniture and related supplies. In the past, management honed in on developing systems and procedures that would exert better control and facilitate the above-mentioned material needs. Sadly enough, the "people" needs were almost totally ignored by most organizations.

A changing labor-intensive economy quickly put an end to the neglect of the highly skilled American laborforce. At the same time, there was a dramatic shift in the higher expense items from material costs to people costs, especially in the new and mushrooming computer industry field. Computers cropped up everywhere and suddenly there weren't enough skilled workers around to program the essentially required equipment. Old manpower solutions just wouldn't do. A new mandate was issued: Find immediate-action solutions to the problems of attracting, motivating and retaining superior computer talent.

For corporate personnel managers with depleted manpower inventories, fighting back meant finding better ways to meet needs that are universal to all 1980s employees, such as formulating and allowing for:

- Providing competitive marketplace salaries.
- Offering individual education plans for job development leading to new opportunities and challenges.
- Presenting all employees with a career path for advancement in the organization which provides wider career opportunities throughout the entire corporation.
- Offering a progressive benefit program allowing each employee to select from various options such as a comprehensive health and dental care package, day care centers, bonuses, flexible work hours and work week, work at home programs, profit sharing and savings and investment programs.
- Putting into action salary administration practices providing rewards for outstanding laborforce performers paid at a more substantial sum than the average performer.
- Implementing objective performance appraisal mechanisms based on actual performance tied into specific work objectives, instead of counterproductive subjective opinions and performance rating curves.
- Implementing career counseling mechanisms requiring management and employees to talk to each other and plan with regard to the respective employee's short and long-range career goals. This includes providing direction and a commitment to help assist the employee in realizing these goals.

Across the nation, management—especially in the labor-short computer manpower area—found that meeting the above needs was usually an enormous job. Success resulted in minimized turnover, higher productivity and ultimately a boost in company profits. Failure usually represented the inability to find or retain "star-performers" and eventual shortages in computer manpower needs.

What separated the "winners" from the "losers" in the tightly contested data processing human resources endeavors? What were the new guidelines for "playing to win" in this highly competitive businessworld battlefield where data processing salaries skyrocketed annually and data processing specialists made corporate hopscotching their new favorite pastime?

The human resource winners had to counterattack with new strategies. They had to work fast. Their new priorities were to:

1. Develop human resource functions that were required in order to effectively address the human resource needs of data processing personnel.
2. Define and then implement the organizational placement of the human resource function in their respective organizations.
3. Determine the profile of a data processing human resource professional.

HUMAN RESOURCE FUNCTIONS AND THE HUMAN RESOURCE SYSTEM: HOW IT WAS ACCOMPLISHED AND IMPLEMENTED

The new managerial philosophy contended that the human resource function was a composite of all activities necessary to meet all data processing human resource needs. These critically needed functions would include the following:

- Career development: career paths, position descriptions, skill matrixing and education matrices
- Career counseling and performance appraisal
- Resource planning: mobility, hiring, consultant usage
- Education development and training
- Human resource advisory functions
- Personnel and salary administration.

Combining the new data processing (DP) managerial philosophy with long-term employee needs produced a system known as SHURE

(Structured Human Resource Management System). This human resource system would be created not only to assist the human resources department in its efforts, but also to support DP management in effectively utilizing its human resources while also providing an around-the-clock vehicle to help employees enrich their own careers and professional growth.

A structural chart of the entire SHURE process is illustrated on the next page (see Figure 1–1). The next section provides a summary of what is involved in each of these functions from an internal perspective and where and how these functions fit into the SHURE system. More in-depth discussion of those functions will appear in subsequent chapters.

How to Provide Career Development: Career Paths, Position Descriptions, Skills Matrixing and Education Matrices

The career development function represents the roots and mainstay of the entire system. It begins with developing career paths plotting how an employee can proceed in an organization (#1 in Figure 1–1), and includes writing detailed position descriptions of the responsibilities involved in every position (#2). For every job function, a listing of all skills that are needed to perform that job must be created along with levels of proficiency (#3). Beyond the skills glossary is the creation of a skills matrix, which ties skills and their levels of proficiency to each position in a career ladder (#4).

Once this framework has been created, a skills data base and education data base is used to produce a skills and education profile for each employee (#5 and 6). Human resource personnel work with DP management in the use of these profiles to assist in their employees' career counseling and performance appraisal, and as a basis for mobility and promotion.

Implementing Performance Appraisal and Career Counseling

This significant function is involved with on-going monitoring of employee performance appraisal and ensures that the appraisals are conducted as scheduled. In addition, this function ensures that there is consistency between the ratings and salary treatment, and that the

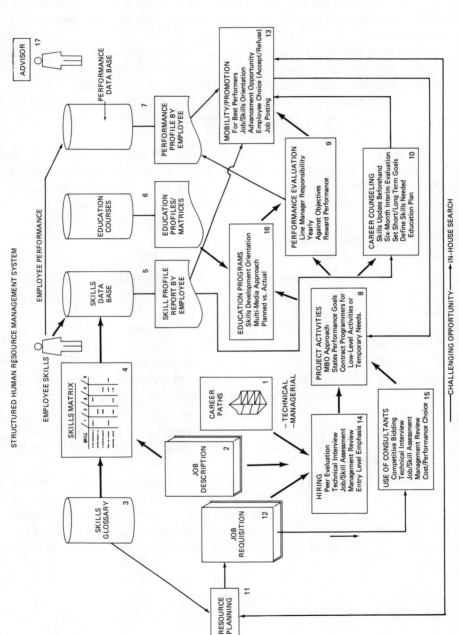

Figure 1-1.   Structured human resource management system.

rating given is based on work objectives and performance goals that tie into a given position. After the performance review, the employee's performance rating is updated, creating an employee profile (#7 through 9).

This procedure also involves the on-going monitoring of employee career counseling to ensure that short- and long-term employee career objectives are being set. It also ensures simultaneously that job position responsibilities are being met in relation to the skills required. The procedure also guarantees ensuring that an individual's skills profile is updated (#10).

In addition to the human resources monitoring, there is an on-going review and modification of the existing performance appraisal and career counseling methodologies. This is conducted to reflect the current needs of the DP organization and its people.

How to Implement Resource Planning: Mobility, Hiring and Consultant Usage

This multifaceted function relates to the identification and placement of qualified candidates, both internal and external, in order to fill open DP job requisitions that detail the job and skills needed (#11 and 12). This method is accomplished in one of three ways: internal mobility of employees, external hiring or use of consultants.

Internal mobility means obtaining qualified internal employees through a job mobility draft list and job posting system (#13). A search is first performed on the existing data base inventory of employees' skills. In the next stage, all qualified candidates—found through the data base search—are reviewed for performance criteria. Outstanding candidates are sometimes produced through this internal search system.

The external hiring process involves obtaining qualified candidates through the use of employment agencies, personnel referrals or newspaper and trade magazine advertisements. This process also means that resumes must be screened, technical and managerial interviews arranged and salary follow-up offers constructed and accepted (#14).

The selection of consultants involves competitive bidding for specific DP projects to assure the best quality manpower for the most reasonable price. The procedure includes choosing the appropriate firms to provide bids, technical interviewing of candidates, cost-effective rate negotiation and final selection (#15).

How to Provide Education Development and Training

This function encompasses providing quality DP education and training at the most reasonable cost (#16). There are two major types of education. The first relates to education linking to skills definition as part of the human resource system. The second major area is the area of project and installation needs arising as a result of the constantly changing nature of DP technology breakthroughs.

To successfully handle this, education analysts interface directly with management in evaluating and implementing the functions of needs analysis, curriculum preparation, course media/vendor selection, course development, course implementation and post-evaluation.

Training is delivered using a multi-media approach that includes classroom, audio-visuals, programmed instruction and computer-based training approaches.

Implementing the Human Resource Advisory Function

The human resources advisory function (#17) takes on a many-faceted role. The advisor is a senior human resource professional dedicated to a group to consult and work with the line management on any human resource issue. This role serves to augment general line management skills and expertise with the defined specialty of human resource development. An analogy can be made that it is similar to utilizing either a controller or marketing specialist. This augmentation is especially critical given some of the considerations in today's market such as the competition for scarce resources, high labor cost, the growing sophistication of the laborforce, increasingly complex and demanding environments and a concern for the improved quality of worklife. These considerations require more involved and focused effort(s) in maximizing the utilization of human resources in the achievement of business goals and objectives.

In terms of the general operating concept of this role, an advisor becomes intimately knowledgeable about each group's business plans, objectives and "culture." This knowledge includes an understanding of any systemic or technological changes that might be planned as well as any organization or reorganization considerations. Based on a knowledge of these so called "directions," an advisor first works with the group management to analyze the implications from a human resource standpoint. These implications ultimately will become a plan of human resource development strategies which will consist of both on-going support activities and defined special projects. An advisor will either be actually responsible for performing or "brokering" out activities to the specialists in the human resource department and/or corporate personnel. Examples of some of the specialists within the human resource department are official salary administration, quality circles, management development, education planning and administration, clerical training and development and personnel administration. Although obviously simplistic in its representation, a line manager can think of these specialists as a "resource pool" that an advisor can draw from to carry out different activities in a group to meet needs.

As a general rule, an advisor typically spends 90 percent of his or her time dedicated to activities directed at the group with which the advisor is aligned, with the remaining time focusing on cross-group efforts for the entire department. Of the 90 percent, approximately 50 percent is devoted to the on-going advisory support activities, such as (but not limited to) mobility, career counseling, ombudsman, and official salary and performance management. The remaining percentage of time is devoted to special advisory projects that are unique to a group based on the mentioned analysis of "directions." Examples of such projects could be a new manager orientation, succession planning or reorganization study.

In all cases, the result of the human resource development strategy for a group is reflected in a group contract. This contract is a formal document that is the end product of a process that is representative of needs identification, prioritization and, in some cases, negotiation between line management and the human resource department of activities to be performed and associated major milestones. This group contract is formally reviewed and updated on a quarterly basis.

Probably the best way to understand the advisor role is to think of it as a series of five sub-roles that are performed during the course of activities. The sub-roles are liaison, diagnostician, implementor, coach counselor and manager.

Fine-Tuning the System:
Personnel and Salary Administration

Although the personnel and salary administration function is not included as a separate entity in the SHURE system, it links all of the human resources functions together for fine-tuning of the human resources computer-based system. It provides the control arms of the overall resource system, and oversees the administrative functions of career development—performance appraisal and career counseling, resource planning, education and training and human resource advising. Most important, it provides the control functions for these areas and incorporates detailed administrative processing procedures for each of the above-mentioned functions.

All of the key human resources monitoring functions are carefully combined into a closely interwoven system. Each part may appear to be a separate element, but a closer examination shows that their interdependence is critical in creating a workable system that serves both management and employees. In addition to the system's data base printouts, the still-crucial human one-to-one approach factor ensures complete success of the system's long- and short-range capabilities.

A simple career counseling session, for example, between manager and employee best illustrates this relationship. A formalized career counseling session can not only result in documenting short- and long-term employee goals (#10) but will incorporate the detailed job descriptions (#2) and skills profile report (#5) to plan specifically for subsequent job experience and skills development.

Since continued state-of-the-art education is a major process for acquiring those skills, a manager and an employee can agree on an individualized education plan (#16). Setting new goals will come into play at the next performance evaluation (#9), resulting in an update of the employee's performance profile (#7). This next stage may ultimately lead to career mobility or promotion in the respective employee's future (#13), the next process providing a result as a search is undertaken for qualified employees with specific skills (#5) and performance (#7) in order to fill a job requisition (#12).

Just about all the parts of this finely-honed human resources system impact each other at some point in the process, and continually create "checks and balances."

HOW TO STRUCTURE THE ORGANIZATIONAL PLACEMENT OF THE DP HUMAN RESOURCE FUNCTION IN YOUR COMPANY

Where does the human resource function structurally fit into the evolving 1980s organization that plans to be around for the next century? What are the key considerations to keep in mind regarding current and future organizational placement? Consider the following realities.

Traditionally, the DP human resource functions were placed in the organizational workplace based upon political issues rather than how these functions could be logically tied together and positioned in the corporate environment to be most effective. Here's a typical example: personnel and salary administration, performance appraisal, and hiring are normally found at the corporate personnel level throughout many nationwide organizations. However, if appropriate, these functions could and should easily be placed within the DP organization.

How and when should the determinations be made to consider one of the above-mentioned situations? What are some of the key considerations required before restructuring action takes place? First of all, the size of the DP staff to be serviced is important. But what is first required is a contemporary definition of a small, medium, large or very large DP staff that is universally accepted. The data processing composition should include all the families of the DP department: systems and programming development, computer operations, software engineering and telecommunications (voice/data). The standardized breakdown of DP manpower is as follows:

- Small   0–100 employees
- Medium   101–300 employees
- Large   301–1000 employees
- Very large   1001 and above employees.

Small DP organizations may not require a dedicated DP human resource department to service their manpower needs. For example,

DP personnel and salary administration could easily be handled at the corporate level. But in a large DP organization—constantly raided by corporate headhunters and ravaged by high employee turn-over—the human resource needs of the DP personnel may well jus-tify a dedicated human resource department servicing all of those needs.

Here's a sobering question to the DP organization in gridlock: *What is the importance of the human resource function in your com-pany?* Is there a new emphasis on productivity improvements and on keeping pace with technological advances? Is it progressive enough to recognize the importance of addressing all of the human resource needs throughout the organization? Has it placed the hu-man resource function at the highest executive level, in either the corporate personnel or DP organization—or is it moving in that di-rection? The answer is that the human resource function must be placed at the highest executive level and be considered a critical func-tion in the organization.

Another primary consideration in moving ahead with the struc-tural development of the data process/human resources function is the scope and magnitude of the human resource capabilities that you decide to implement for the new DP human resource area. The fol-lowing criteria should be strategically resolved in the advanced plan-ning sessions.

Will you include all the human resource functions—resource plan-ning, organizational development, career counseling and perfor-mance appraisal, education development and training, personnel and salary administration and human resource advisory function—within the DP human resource department? And, if so, what will the scope of functions be—either broad or narrow?

By determining in advance whether the above-mentioned human resource functions will be implemented in a "broad" or "narrow" scope, you will then know the exact depth to which each of these functions are due to be performed. An example of this is training. An organization can opt for bringing in consultants to meet its ed-ucation needs or, at a much deeper level, that same organization can execute in-depth education planning, analysis and development.

The following is a guideline for planning the implementation scope of a fully operational human resources delivery mechanism. If the respective human resource organization has a large scope and magnitude, its operation will most likely warrant a dedicated data processing human resource area. However, if the respective organizatioin's scope and magnitude is narrow, that human resources function may become part of corporate personnel or combined with other departments.

By examining the various alternatives from an organizational viewpoint, three operating postures for the DP human resource function are provided to choose from. They are as follows:

- Centralized implementation at the corporate personnel level.
- Decentralized start-up as an independent human resources group.
- Establishing a combined centralized/decentralized human resources group.

Each of the above-mentioned human resources alternatives have their strengths and weaknesses and are detailed in the following pages.

HOW TO IMPLEMENT A DP HUMAN RESOURCE FUNCTION IN A CENTRALIZED CORPORATE PERSONNEL LEVEL

An operational example of how a typical DP human resource function can fit into a corporate function is depicted in Figure 1–2. In this corporate structure arrangement, both the DP and non-DP human resource functions—resource planning, education and training, personnel and salary administration, career development and advisors—are joined together under one corporate direction. The group head reports directly to the executive-in-charge of corporate personnel. However, it should be noted that within each of the above-mentioned functions are sub-functions which are dedicated to servicing either DP or non-DP human resource needs of that respective organization.

Other key operational elements in this corporate organizational structure example are the qualifications and technical capabilities of the personnel who fill the DP human resource positions for each of the individual human resources functions. They must possess the recommended profile, which includes a strong DP background. Subsequent sections discuss in detail the recommended profile for the DP human resource professional to serve in this structure.

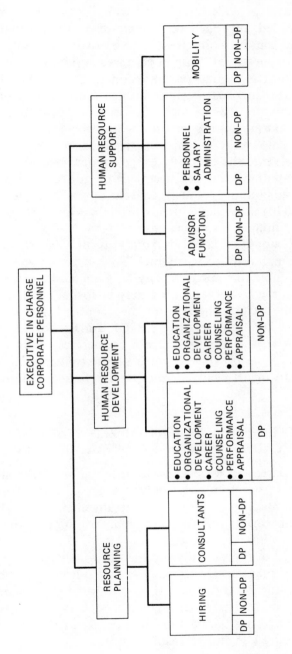

Figure 1-2.   Centralized/corporate personnel.

The advantages provided by this centrally based structure offer a consistent, unified approach to human resources throughout the company which can be maintained. Those advantages not only hold true for the corporate DP human resource functions, but also for augmenting non-DP human resource functions as well. This work arrangement also provides high assurance that all corporate standards and guidelines will be met. The structure also avoids duplication of human resources efforts while delivering high-quality services to all employees and ensuring legal conformity.

At the same time, the centrally based human resources structure provides that all manpower resources can be utilized to meet the entire corporation's human resource goals as opposed to specific functional needs. This arrangement thus offers a wider career path for the participant human resource staff.

However, it should be noted that a disadvantage exists in the centrally based human resources structure. That disadvantage occurs because, while a unified approach may be gained, the close-working network within the DP organization may be lost. That disadvantage comes into play because the DP human resource function does not report into the DP organization, the DP staff's human resources needs may not be sufficiently met nor the services delivered as efficiently or rapidly as possible. It can also lead to increased employee turnover due to insufficient energies being channeled into the DP staff priorities.

HOW TO IMPLEMENT A DECENTRALIZED START-UP AS AN INDEPENDENT HUMAN RESOURCE GROUP

There are two areas in an organization where a decentralized DP human resources function may report: either to DP or directly to corporate personnel. In both reporting arrangements, the DP human resources group carries out the same mandate of all functions associated with "human resources."

Experience from the past decade has shown that the DP human resources department easily becomes an integral part of the DP organization, serving alongside the other traditional DP functions. The DP human resources department manager reports directly to the officer-in-charge and has the back-up support of a full-time staff dedicated to servicing DP human resource needs.

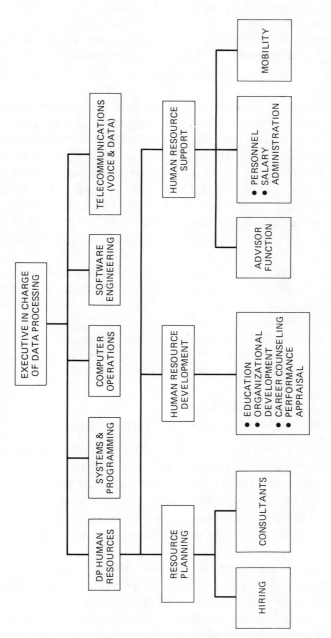

Figure 1-3.   Decentralized/data processing.

In the afore-mentioned arrangement, all of the human resource functions needed to service the DP community are conducted by this user-oriented full-time human resources group. Corporate personnel, in this arrangement, performs similar human resources functions servicing the respective corporation's non-DP human resource needs.

An advantage of this day-to-day working partnership is the direct reporting relationship of the human resources organization, which is in constant tune with the organization's DP human resource needs. The close relationship that develops as a result of daily interaction and involvement in the long- and short-range planning process also yields numerous short-term and long-term benefits. The process provides a close working relationship and reporting structure. That relationship also ensures extremely high quality and timeliness of services to better satisfy all of the human resource needs required by DP personnel.

But there's also a slight drawback that may arise; namely, conflict of interest situations because of the direct reporting relationship to the head of DP. If the foremost objective is to satisfy the DP organization's needs—as opposed to adhering to corporate personnel's standards and procedures—this separation may create inconsistencies and some duplication of effort throughout the corporation.

This organizational structure is depicted in Figure 1-3.

THE DECENTRALIZED/CORPORATE PERSONNEL ARRANGEMENT: HOW IT WORKS

In this structural arrangement, all of the DP human resources functions are decentralized and report to a DP human resources department manager, serving as a prototype of corporate personnel. Overall direction is set by corporate personnel. The satellite organization thus only services the DP day-to-day requirements. Corporate personnel, in turn, provides similar human resource functions servicing all of the non-DP community.

Because the decentralized DP human resources group in this corporate arrangement reports directly to corporate personnel, adherence to corporate standards and guidelines is assured. This adherence—as previously mentioned—avoids duplication of effort, ensures consistency in providing quality services to all organizational

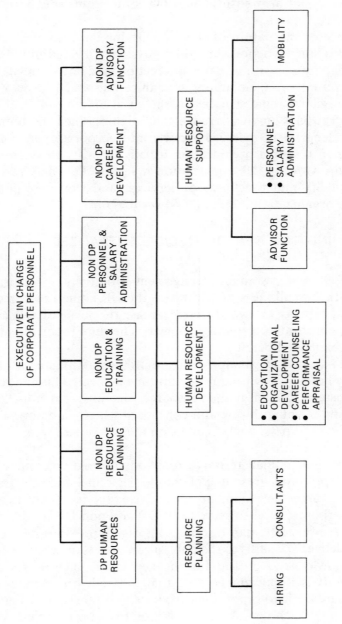

Figure 1-4.   Decentralized/corporate personnel.

employees, and also ensures meeting legal requirements regarding affirmative action.

Because of the nature of this satellite human resources arrangement, this staff function should be physically located in the DP installation, thus ensuring daily interaction and involvement in the short- and long-range planning human resources/DP process.

This organizational structure is shown in Figure 1–4.

The drawback in this arrangement is that, since the human resources department manager reports into corporate personnel, the DP human resource organization usually loses its close on-line relationship with the DP organization it serves. This may result in a lesser quality and timeliness of services, and slower responses to pending organizational DP/manpower logjams.

COMBINING THE CENTRALIZED/DECENTRALIZED HUMAN RESOURCES GROUP

This DP/human resources arrangement is best suited for organizations with a small DP staff. It means the DP human resource function also reports to two different areas: the head of DP and the ranking corporate personnel manager. The dual reporting arrangement is explained below.

If the in-house DP manpower strength is small, that area's human resource needs will not require a full-time dedicated human resource staff. Instead, certain human resource functions—such as DP education and training, hiring and consultant usage—are normally carried out by DP personnel, in addition to their other DP assignments and responsibilities.

In addition, human resource functions normally germane to the entire corporation—resource planning, personnel and salary administration, career development, and advisor services—are conducted at the corporate level to serve both DP and non-DP needs.

This combined human resources approach provides the opportunity to deliver DP skills to the human resource functions where technical knowledge is critical for the key areas, such as hiring and training. It is important to note that in small organizations, it is highly unrealistic to expect the corporate personnel staff to grasp the necessary DP technical skills, in addition to its basic human resource

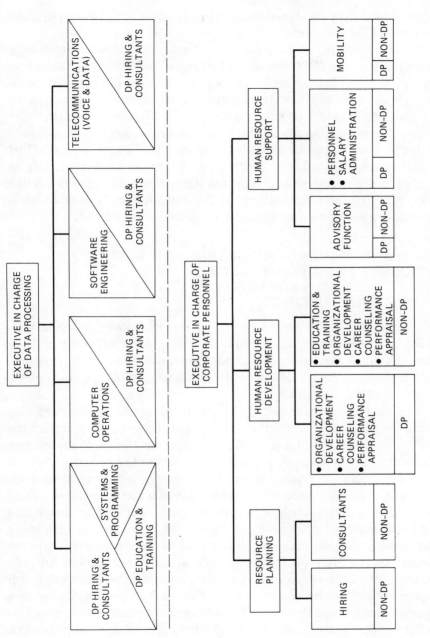

Figure 1-5. Combined centralized/decentralized.

skills. The above-cited option can readily solve the problem created by the lack of DP expertise.

In terms of the disadvantages created by the above-mentioned arrangement, the DP work-related responsibilities usually take precedence over the human resource responsibilities. This condition usually means that the human resource needs may not be met in an on-the-spot response or in a quality manner. It also means that corporate human resource standards and policies may not be adhered to because of a split in reporting structures. Without a joint effort in the planning and implementation of human resource efforts throughout the respective corporation, weaknesses will result when least expected, and they will affect the bottom line if not dealt with.

This organizational structure is pictured in Figure 1–5.

PROFILE OF THE DATA PROCESSING HUMAN RESOURCE (DPHR) PROFESSIONAL: WHAT CATEGORIES ARE HIGHLY CRITICAL FOR SUCCESS?

Why is it important to fill the DP human resource position with skilled personnel who have actual "frontline" DP experience? Why can't a typical human resources administrator—trained in personnel administration, salary and benefits, and having some training knowledge—fill that position?

The answer is that the average human resources administrator today lacks the critical DP technical skills required to properly service the DP community job and marketplace demands. Some organizations attempt to fill this gap by providing their human resources personnel with elementary exposure to the DP field via educational courses. These one-dimensional courses are usually at a very basic level. These introductory courses will not provide the in-depth knowledge and on-the-job experience needed to do the job correctly. Insufficiently prepared personnel assigned to the role of data processing/human resources (DPHR) professional may actually hinder the DP objectives. Here's why: Someone lacking in-depth DP knowledge, for example, will not be able to correctly select the appropriate training courses needed for in-house DP employees who are ready to move to the next stage in their technical career paths. Nor will the non-

DP-oriented human resources administrator be able to understand his or her organization's short- and long-range DP objectives from a technical viewpoint.

In fact, because DP is such a dynamically evolving technology with an overwhelming amount of information, it is far easier to impart human resource skills to a DP person than DP skills to a human resources staffer.

The name of the human resources game for the 1980s is to gain the confidence of the technical user. There are very few second chances. On the whole, DP managers are extremely discriminating, intimidating and highly demanding. They have a language of endless buzz words. They have little patience for "outsiders" who are not privy to their computer jargon. To maintain their objectives, they normally demand someone who speaks their language before that new human resources staffer will be accepted into the fold and obtain the necessary cooperation to get the human resource job done.

What then is the ideal profile and makeup of the 1980s DPHR professional? What should be the human resource and technical criteria for the following categories: DPHR management, DPHR staff responsibilities and DPHR clerical support functions?

SUPERVISORY/PROJECT MANAGEMENT EXPERIENCE— REQUIRED OF ALL DPHR MANAGEMENT CANDIDATES

The typical profile of a DPHR management candidate includes one to five years' management experience. This background involves providing overall direction and management guidance to human resource areas. Ideally, the candidate should have experience in managing personnel in the following human resource areas: DP resource planning, DP education and training, DPHR planning and development and technical programming and analysis.

The candidate's track record should also include a short- and long-range human resource planning background to meet cost-effective organizational goals and oversee the implementation of those plans. This includes utilizing various project control methodology. As far as staff administration, the candidate will eventually become involved in such administrative matters as performance appraisal and salary administration, budget control, professional development of staff, and assignment of personnel to projects. Matching the background with the candidate's delivery capabilities remains the utmost priority.

A LOOK AT THE IDEAL DP EXPERIENCE GUIDELINES

The candidate DPHR manager should typically have from four to six years of DP experience. This person should be completely familiar with the scope and implications of all DP functions including systems and programming development, computer operations, software engineering and telecommunications.

The "hands-on" experience should also include background in systems design and analysis, DP programming, systems documentation, validation, maintenance and support, user interface and computer operations.

It should be noted that DP and HR experience can be interchanged to equal a total of four to six years of work experience. However, the candidate should have sufficient experience garnered from each field so that highly critical in-depth working knowledge is acquired.

HR EXPERIENCE REQUIREMENT
FOR THE DPHR MANAGER

The ideal DPHR manager candidate would typically have from four to six years of human resource experience. This well-rounded background should include complete familiarity with the scope and implications of all HR functions: career development (career paths, position descriptions, skills and education matrices), career counseling and performance appraisal, resource planning (mobility, hiring, consultant usage), education and training, HR advisory function and personnel and salary administration.

Among other experiences, the ideal DPHR manager candidate should have excellent "people" skills. Unfortunately, "people" skills are sorely lacking in America's high-level managerial ranks today. It means that many managers are selected lacking "people" skills, primarily because of an outmoded system allowing the salary and grade level to be associated with a next-in-line management position. That practice is counterproductive to America's long-term corporate and industrial needs.

Are managers with important "people" skills born that way—or can they be trained to receive that key quality? It is difficult to infuse, through training, the necessary people skills to make an individual an effective manager, some leaders say. In the human resource profession, the "people" skills are far more important attributes than required in other managerial positions. The "people" skills can be increased by observing skilled practitioners and participating in workshops stressing one-to-one and group dynamics participation.

Meanwhile, the DPHR manager candidate should possess the following skills, abilities and traits for effective leadership implementation:

- Good writing skills in order to submit plans, reports and proposals to upper management.
- The ability to communicate and promote ideas effectively with management and staff, both inside and outside the organization.
- Strong interpersonal skills and behavioral sensitivity in dealing with management and staff, both inside and outside the organization.
- The ability to provide short- and long-range strategic planning and design skills.
- The ability to organize and facilitate meetings and projects through all phases.
- The capability to identify problems, gather necessary data, evaluate alternatives and recommend and implement solutions.
- The capability to give formal presentations, both inside and outside the organization
- Assertiveness, political sensitivity, and leadership in managing projects and supervising personnel, resolving conflict situations and building rapport.
- Good follow-through and personal time management.
- A high level of expertise in the HR and DP fields by keeping abreast of new developments.

HR Staff Personnel

The typical corporate profile of a DPHR staff candidate may usually include supervisory or project management experience. However, a relatively seasoned senior staff member ideally might have one to two years of project leadership experience and would also be capable of functionally supervising more junior staff members.

DP Experience

The DPHR staff person would normally have from two to six years of DP experience. Like the DPHR manager, these candidates should have a good working knowledge of all DP functions, including systems and programming development, computer operations, software engineering and telecommunications.

It should be noted that DP and HR experience can be interchanged to equal a total of two to six years' experience. However, an individual should have sufficient experience from each field so that an in-depth working knowledge has been acquired.

HR Experience

In addition to the above-mentioned capabilities, the DPHR staff person should normally have from two to six years' "on-line" HR experiences. This individual should additionally have a good working knowledge of all HR functions, including career development, career counseling and performance appraisal, resource planning, education and training, HR advisory functions and personnel and salary administration.

General Skills, Abilities and Traits

Again, just as in the case of the DPHR manager, it is vitally important that a DPHR staff candidate be equally strong in "people" skills. It is a sad commentary to note that the DPHR staff positions are often filled by employees who may be perceived as poor performers. It is even perceived as a corporate "dumping ground"— often the place to send someone for a last chance and thus fulfilling the adage: "Those who can, do; those who can't, teach." This corporate dumping-ground practice works against every organization's best interests. In fact, just the opposite should be the case. The DPHR staff leader should be one who has demonstrated "high performance" in the past accomplishments and has expressed a strong desire to pursue a career in the human resource field.

In addition to the above-mentioned quality and performance standards, the DPHR staff person should possess the following skills, abilities and traits:

- The ability to devote considerable attention to accuracy and completeness in gathering and reviewing information for research.
- The ability to organize time and work efficiently to meet deadlines and recognize work flow priority.
- An enthusiastic approach to work and the willingness to take on responsibility without being told, exhibiting good follow-through and a commitment to task completion.
- A willingness to support management decisions and to readily adjust to changing work priorities or changes in operational procedures, and the ability to accept constructive work criticism and direction.
- The capability to work effectively with minimum supervision, identifying problems and bringing them to the attention of management in a timely way.
- Working well with others and being capable of resolving conflict situations and promoting harmony.
- Good writing skills, providing clear, concise and complete documentation.
- Grasping logical reasoning, research and analytical ability and problem-solving ability.
- The ability to communicate and promote ideas effectively with management and staff, both inside and outside the organization.
- A high level of expertise in the HR and DP fields by keeping abreast of new developments.
- Adherence to personnel policies and procedures, such as absenteeism and punctuality.

PROFILE OF THE DPHR CLERICAL SUPPORT CANDIDATE: SUPERVISORY/PROJECT MANAGEMENT EXPERIENCE GUIDELINES

An extensive DP background does not apply to the DPHR clerical support positions for the most part. Indeed, there are some supervisory personnel in the clerical area throughout nationwide organizations who have a traditional "management" profile for directing clerical level personnel, such as leadership, planning and controls, good communication skills, etc. However, should a candidate exist with a knowledge of either the DP or HR fields, that background would be highly useful, as would an interest in working in the DPHR field.

HR EXPERIENCE GUIDELINES
FOR THE DP CLERICAL SUPPORT PERSON

The typical profile of a DPHR clerical support person should include one to four years in the areas of personnel administration, office administration, word processing and education administration. This background also includes activities such as administration and maintenance of personnel files; administration of hiring, mobility and consultant usage; monitoring HR budgets; preparing statistical reports for the department; monitoring performance appraisal and salary administration; providing word processing services to human resources personnel; and also education scheduling and student registration.

THE CLERICAL ADMINISTRATION FUNCTION
IN THE DPHR GROUP: GENERAL SKILLS,
ABILITIES AND TRAITS EMPLOYMENT GUIDELINES

When examining the clerical administration function in the DPHR organization, corporations make the false assumption that the clerical staff is only capable of conducting menial and rudimentary activities. Quite to the contrary, experience has shown that clerical personnel have the ability to perform in a higher capacity and level than is traditionally assumed—if given the opportunity and the proper training. An organization should always simultaneously strive to fully utilize not only the professional staff but also the clerical support staff. In the ideal situation, the clerical level positions can serve as the entry-level position to a career path into the DPHR field.

The following are general guidelines for the DPHR clerical support person. He or she should:

- Display good organizational skills
- Be tactful, personable and efficient in using the telephone and in personal contact, both inside and outside the organization.

- Have the ability to operate keyboard machinery, such as type-writer, word processor, keypunch and computer terminals, accurately and efficiently.
- Work well with others and be willing to offer assistance to the benefit of the functioning of human resources.
- Maintain good record-keeping and file maintenance to provide human resource staff members easy access to information.
- Ensure that inventory (forms, supplies, etc.) is efficiently managed and available when needed for daily operation of the aligned areas.
- Receive and process incoming and outgoing correspondence and route or deliver to appropriate personnel or location quickly and efficiently.
- Display the ability to apply secretarial skills in spelling and grammar in the preparation and/or editing of correspondence and reports.

The working profile of the DPHR professional requires keeping pace with two worlds: that of the DP and HR field professionals. A summary comparing the three professional categories to the work experiences can be found in Figure 1–6.

		Profile Categories		
		DPHR Management	DPHR Staff	DPHR Clerical
Work Experience	Supervisory/ Project Management	1–5 Years	Normally not Applicable Senior Staff 1–2 Years Project Leadership	Not Applicable
	Data Processing	4–6 Years Combined	2–6 Years Combined	Knowledge and Interest
	Human Resources			Knowledge and Interest
	Clerical Administration	Not Applicable	Not Applicable	1–4 Years

Figure 1-6.   DPHR professional profile summary.

SUMMARY

As stated previously throughout this chapter, it is important to recognize that the "people side" of operating a business has become far more important to an organization than at any other time in modern corporate history. An organization's cost for the staff salaries and benefits continues to climb higher and higher. It won't drop in the future.

That's why it's absolutely necessary for contemporary organizations to create and maintain an HR system dedicated to properly hiring, retaining, motivating, utilizing and developing personnel. That challenge is gladly accepted by the nation's HR staffers. They're playing the game to win. They know the importance and role of the new HR organization. They know that role is not a luxury, but rather a necessity that must be viewed in this regard.

A number of options for the organizational placement of the DPHR function have been provided. They range from a centralized HR function with all of the sub-functions reporting into it, to a decentralized function with the sub-functions reporting to corporate personnel, DP, or a combination of both. It is the reader's decision to implement the best working strategy for each respective organization.

2

HOW TO ORGANIZE AND QUANTIFY YOUR HUMAN RESOURCE SYSTEM

If you're planning to develop your organization's first human resource (HR) system, the first essential strategy involves carefully coordinated corporate groundwork—and some tough self-appraisal.

You'll also need "reality-oriented" feedback from all of the key players the system is designed to serve. Will the line management you serve stand behind the proposed system's debut?

If so, do you also have senior management's "across-the-board" backing in time, money and corporatewide support? Are you staffed with the right "players" to provide the system design, start-up and follow-through?

And if you're still "fence-straddling" because of some last-minute doubts, the appropriate responses to the next set of questions could firm up your subsequent course-of-action:

Are you "sick and tired" of never-ending and always increasing employee turnover in the critically short data processing (DP) field?

Are you concerned about shelling out tens of thousands of dollars—and even more—every quarterly period to "head-hunting" personnel recruiting agencies? How else might you have invested those precious and hard-earned dollars?

Is your organization's DP staff creating a track record of failing to meet project deadlines? Is that reputation now a full-fledged built-in corporate weakness diminishing your organization's productivity effectiveness?

If any one of the above-mentioned workplace stresses—or others you can think of—are a reality in your organization, you're now ready to sharpen your pencils, roll up your sleeves, schedule a smoke-filled conference room for some heavy "brain-storming" and subsequently agree to design, produce and deliver your own custom-tailored HR system.

The first step you'll take after design, strategy and timetables have been agreed upon, is to *organize and then quantify* the HR system being developed. Is it really as simple as it sounds?

It can be—and within easy grasp of any corporate HR team that speaks with one voice. Here's what is meant by "organizing and quantifying" the HR system:

It means that a logical two-step procedure has been initiated by the respective management team to conceptualize—and then map out all of the actual components of the human resource system. It means following through with the logical organization and working environment interrelationship with the project's components. No one component should ever be minimized.

Now if you're a newcomer, you're probably asking about the procedure—"quantifying the human resource"—and wondering: what does it all mean? That's a very good question. "Quantifying the human resource" means that your new HR system will be equipped with the crucial measurement mechanisms necessary to provide a feedback mechanism commonly known as a "check and balances" system. When properly implemented, the "checks and balances" system provides and delivers to management a direct accounting regarding all strengths—and whatever unexpected shortcomings—that may surface during the new system's initial tour of HR duty. Above all, your new HR system must be designed to deliver immediate responses to one and all HR/environmental realities. Here's how that priority is implemented to produce the computer-generated reports that will subsequently deliver management the entire HR scoreboard.

The process begins with the "backbone" of your newly-developed human resource system, officially known as the career development system. Actually, the career development system is really comprised of six components that combined produce the successful computer-generated HR output in the active DPHR environment. The career development system components are as follows and are accompanied by illustrative charts found in this chapter:

- The Career Ladder Component: This is an easy-to-grasp graphic portrayal of the many different career path options that an employee can choose from to advance within the organization.
- The Position Description Component: This is a constantly up-dated and detailed description providing for management and the respective employees the spectrum of all responsibilities, duties and tasks that will be performed in the respective job category linked to the above-mentioned career ladder component.
- The Skills Glossary Component: This part of the career development system consists of a detailed index listing all of the mandatory job skills required and their accompanying associated levels of proficiency called for all presently posted DP positions.
- The Skills Matrix Component: This is an easy-to-read illustration/posting—assembled in a matrix format—that provides the levels of proficiency required for each skill in relation to each respective DP job posted in the organization's DP career ladder.
- The Skills Profile Report Component: This part of the process is the feedback output generated by the computer system. The report will actually depict an employee's current skill levels, the recommended skills level required to upgrade any outstanding skills deficiency.
- The Education Course Matrices: This part of the process consists of the education output generated by the computer. The report produced provides a detailed listing of all courses that are readily available to bolster the in-house proficiency requirements needed for the various job skills.

By reviewing the multi-stage development process found on the HR system flowchart in Figure 2–1, observers can see how readily the career development portion fits into the overall HR system as highlighted in stages #1 through 6 shown on the flowchart.

The career development system produces far-yielding benefits to both management and technical staff members. It works for management because it is an active working tool for short- and long-term education planning and objective performance evaluation and also reinforces the effective utilization of all respective management staffs. For the staff member—or incoming new employee—the system pinpoints an individual's skill strengths, locates job-assignment

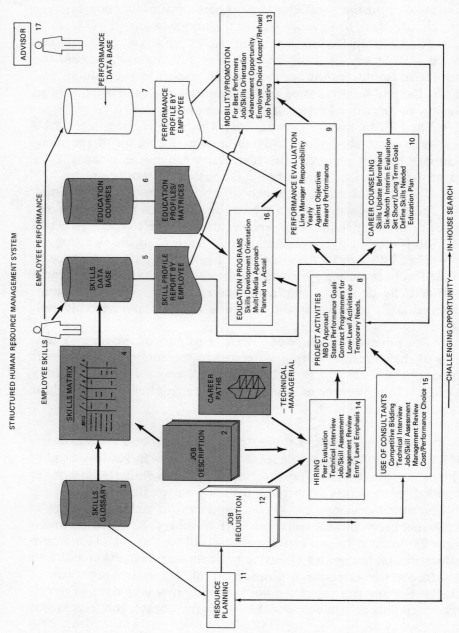

STRUCTURED HUMAN RESOURCE MANAGEMENT SYSTEM

ADVISOR 17

PERFORMANCE DATA BASE

PERFORMANCE PROFILE BY EMPLOYEE 7

EMPLOYEE PERFORMANCE

MOBILITY/PROMOTION 13
For Best Performers
Job/Skills Orientation
Advancement Opportunity
Employee Choice (Accept/Refuse)
Job Posting

PERFORMANCE EVALUATION 9
Line Manager Responsibility
Yearly
Against Objectives
Reward Performance

CAREER COUNSELING 10
Skills Update Beforehand
Six-Month Interim Evaluation
Set Short/Long Term Goals
Define Skills Needed
Education Plan

EDUCATION COURSES 6

EDUCATION PROFILES/MATRICES

SKILLS DATA BASE 5

SKILL PROFILE REPORT BY EMPLOYEE

EDUCATION PROGRAMS 16
Skills Development Orientation
Multi-Media Approach
Planned vs. Actual

PROJECT ACTIVITIES 8
MBO Approach
States Performance Goals
Contract Programmers for
Low-Level Activities or
Temporary Needs.

EMPLOYEE SKILLS

SKILLS MATRIX 4
SKILL

CAREER PATHS 1
— TECHNICAL
—MANAGERIAL

JOB DESCRIPTION 2

SKILLS GLOSSARY 3

HIRING 14
Peer Evaluation
Technical Interview
Job/Skill Assessment
Management Review
Entry Level Emphasis

USE OF CONSULTANTS 15
Competitive Bidding
Technical Interview
Job/Skill Assessment
Management Review
Cost/Performance Choice

JOB REQUISITION 12

RESOURCE PLANNING 11

CHALLENGING OPPORTUNITY ——— IN-HOUSE SEARCH

Figure 2–1.

deficiencies and produces and defines specific job responsibilities. The career development system also identifies potential career paths. Using the career development system is a must for all DPHR personnel who want to remain in the vanguard of the ever-changing technological environment.

The career development system is a time-tested HR process first started in 1973. Since that time, the DP industry has undergone repeated and significant changes. The system has grown and changed with each DP breakthrough.

In fact, extensive revisions and state-of-the-art enhancements have been made concurrent with all late-breaking industry developments. This dedication to growth and change will continue in the future.

CAREER LADDERS; WHY THEY'RE NEEDED

The following section spells out in full step-by-step detail the working of each individual component of the career development system.

Why is there a need for career ladders? Answer: The times demand them!

Every U.S. corporation today faces the challenge: How to hold onto highly qualified in-house workers while also attracting recruits from the outside to keep pace with growing internal needs. One time-tested mechanism to assist in accomplishing this very tough task is providing a visible representation of potential career path alternatives for employees' future growth and career aspirations. This process has repeatedly demonstrated that it is an important strategy in successfully reducing employee turnover. Here's why: In-house personnel—the men and women on the corporate payroll—are interested in knowing not only where they stand today but where they might be in the future, especially elsewhere in the organization in the event they're looking for additional career enhancement apart from their assigned jobs. It is important that every employee be issued his or her own career alternatives. This official distribution thus ensures the standardization of career paths and job mobility to prevent misinterpretations—and eliminates all "grapevine" chatter concerning career growth choices.

Providing a graphic career path to discuss options is an extremely helpful hiring instrument in marketing the corporation's positioning and strengths to a perspective candidate. Because of the career path options shown during the initial interviews, the candidate can easily grasp that the hiring company is people-oriented, logically organized, and equipped to grow with the future. Presenting career opportunities—to all newcomers—is just as important as selling the applicant on the job and the salary and related benefits of the position.

Career ladders by themselves won't alone bring in new employees to fill skilled positions, but they will be helpful in achieving these recruiting goals.

Life in a DPHR environment, however, does not begin or end on the subject of the highly-popular career ladder. They are augmenting the classifications used successfully to deal with DP employee's growth options. The subsequent evolution of the career ladder ushered in the emergence of the "Big Four DP Job Families." You'll meet each of the "families" in the following section.

It is important to know the strengths and individuality of each of the "Big Four DP Job Families" if you're in the DPHR workplace environment to be successful at what you're doing. The "families" are unique and require custom-tailored HR attention, but knowing their individual marketplace demands will avoid future fumblings in the job-staffing process. The "families" are as follows: systems and programming, computer operations, software engineering and telecommunications (voice and data).

THE SYSTEMS AND PROGRAMMING FAMILY: WHAT IT DOES

The systems and programming family interfaces extensively with the respective organization's user community. When a user, for example, has identified a DP-driven business need, the next step is to call upon the services of the "systems and programming family" to evaluate the feasibility of providing and delivering this anticipated need through the use of a computer. Here's the sequence of events that take places to see whether the proposed system need will turn into a workplace reality. It's a five-step process.

Feasibility: This phase determines whether or not a DP
(Step 1)   system is feasible in terms of technical, op-

erational, and economical considerations. This process subsequently results in a systems proposal that outlines in broad terms the recommended approach in meeting the user's requirements.

Functional Analysis:
(Step 2)

This phase determines the exact business functions the proposed DP system will perform from the user's point of view. This intense process involves heavy user interaction and working knowledge of the user's needs providing a grasp on how the system will work, be tested and be installed. This phase moves on to produce functional specifications which summarize the resultant system business functions, input and output file considerations and hardware and software requirements. This agreed-upon package subsequently becomes the contract between the user and the systems and programming family.

Design:
(Step 3)

While the above-mentioned functional analysis is concerned with the capabilities of what the system will do, the subsequent design phase is concerned with "how" the system will do it. This phase produces design specifications which provide detailed information concerning system design, conversion plans and more accurate production time and cost estimates.

Implementation:
(Step 4)

This phase is concerned with the actual system construction. The "systems and programming family" develops the program and tests the business functions performed by the system. As soon as the user is satisfied with the testing results, the system is next turned over to the "computer operations family," where it is again tested in an actual production environment. The system is now officially installed and turned over to the user after this final environmental test.

Maintenance: (Step 5)

This phase deals directly with enhancements or modifications to an operating or previously installed system. Maintenance work implementation bypasses all of the above-mentioned formal phases in order to be performed. Maintenance is an on- going activity and requires constant interaction with the user.

The personnel who perform these programming-related functions are pictured in Figure 2–2 and are part of the systems and programming job family. There are two pivotal legs comprising this career ladder: the programmer analyst leg and a systems analyst leg. Here are the options they provide: At that point in time when the programmer reaches the senior programmer level, a carefully contemplated career choice must be made. The DP staffer who displayed the skill strengths and career goals aligned to the technical "bits and bytes" aspects of developing a system, would naturally move forward on the programmer analyst leg. Likewise, the DP staffer who aspires for a "more people-oriented" and analytical work environment would follow the systems analyst leg. This is the logical strategy because the heavy user interface calls more upon strong communication skills than technical skills in the latter-mentioned job category.

The career ladder—one of the best friends to DPHR personnel—allows for cross-movement within the two legs. Organizations today must recognize that there is nothing wrong—or out of character—with an employee changing career goals within an organization over a span of five, ten or fifteen years. It's the new career path lifestyle of the 1980s. Allowing flexible career paths not only satisfies your internal staff's changing aspirations, but also develops a new cadre of well-rounded DP specialists who will prove to be more valuable to your organization. Never discourage either horizontal or vertical career movement. The crossflow of talent enhancement opportunities will yield many benefits and allow you to hold onto your DP achievers.

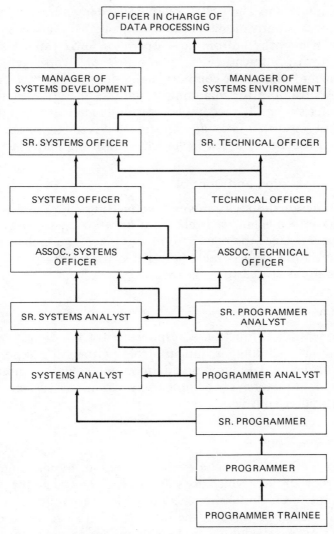

Figure 2-2.   Career ladder: DP systems and programming family.

THE COMPUTER OPERATIONS FAMILY:
WHAT IT DOES

The computer operations family—and its accompanying career path
ladder—is quite similar to other production environments found in
most organizations. And just like in any workplace operation, the

"demanding nuts and bolts" operational demands of the machinery must be constantly monitored and controlled in order to provide and maintain smooth "bottom-line" operation and to minimize machine breakdowns: "downtime," "idle time" or, worse yet, computer equipment failure. The computer operations family is entrusted with the responsibility for maintaining smooth operation of the overall computer system. It's a complex corporate mandate, and here's how the most important tasks are implemented through the computer operations functions, which include the following major activities.

Data Preparation and Control

This functional activity involves converting data from source documents into machine-sensible form by utilizing various data entry equipment. Once the conversion takes place, the input data and resulting output reports must be verified for accuracy and completeness and monitored for timeliness.

Equipment Operation

This operational function is responsible for the direct operation of all computer equipment, ranging from peripheral equipment that is associated with data input and data output, to data communications terminals, to data entry equipment, to computer systems, including the computer console.

Production Control

This pivotal activity includes the scheduling, monitoring, and controlling of DP jobs which are submitted to the system for processing. This function includes the scheduling of the computer resources that will be needed to perform the job, maintain a record of equipment performance, scheduling and logging job input and output and communicating with users on the status of specific jobs.

Production Support

This back-up area supports the computer operations in such areas as maintaining the library of data files, maintaining an inventory of DP supplies, maintaining a library of operations documentation,

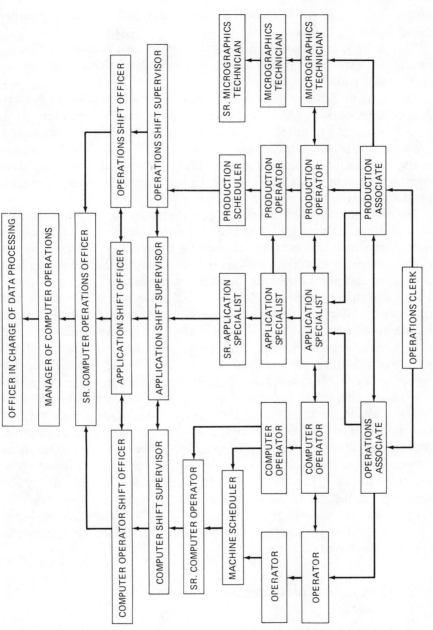

Figure 2-3.   Career ladder: DP computer operations family.

providing security of the computer facilities and distributing computer output.

The skilled staffers who perform these activities in the computer operations family are pictured and strategically positioned in the career ladder shown in Figure 2–3.

Of the four families that make up a DP organization, this operational unit normally has the largest number of DP personnel. It is also important to note that compared to other work assignment areas, the job of operating equipment can become rather monotonous. Carefully documented statistics show that routine, non-complex, boring tasks often result in job disenchantment, lowered productivity and subsequent high turnover.

In order to stem boredom and profit-ebbing employee turnover, it is essential to provide career ladder alternatives that offer cross-movement and job rotation. Reviewing Figure 2–3, for example, it is easy to grasp how the semi-skilled levels on the ladder—machine operator, computer operator, applications specialist, production operator and micrographics technician—can easily move laterally across the board. There is great flexibility that the career ladder offers to all employees to experience different kinds of job alternatives in the computer operations family. This unique semi-skilled career path alternative not only allows employees to gain broad experience, but serves as a powerful and reliable back-up system in the event of illness and unexpected turnover, while it simultaneously boosts employee morale. Proceeding up the ladder, it becomes clearly evident that lateral movement tapers off, due to the technical specialization of the respective positions (see machine scheduler, senior applications specialist, production scheduler and senior micrographics technician). However, the career ladder does provide the opportunity for senior personnel to advance up the ladder—right up to the top—to eventually become officer-in-charge of DP. It's a fantastic long-term career challenge inducement for the aspiring computer operations family career path achiever.

THE TELECOMMUNICATIONS (VOICE/DATA) FAMILY: WHAT IT DOES

Today's "state-of-the-art" DP-related communications is the process of exchange or transmission of high-speed information either orally or in writing. It's been a careful evolution. In the early 1900s, for example, the key communication device was over a one-wire telephone line—known as voice transmission. By the time the mid-1940s arrived, voice channels could then be carried over coaxial cables. Later, a superior generation of microwave chains were developed to carry more electronic channels. In the beginning, these then "state-of-the-art" telecommunications links were mainly designed for handling voice and television signals. Additional transmission breakthroughs continued to unfold in time for DP's emergence. Meanwhile, the need for man and business to quickly process data pushed through even newer developments. Telecommunications would officially be known as the marriage of the engineering of communications to that of the computer industry. The marriage was fruitful and produced new major modifications with existing telephone lines and microwave chains that would now carry computer generated "data," as well as voice. Since then, both private and public sectors have established networks to handle data transmission. In addition, over the last eight years, extensive work has been undertaken to develop another transmission media through the use of satellites for both voice and data communications.

Thus, telecommunications "voice" means the transmission of voice over the various carriers mentioned, and telecommunications "data" means the transmission of computer-generated data.

That's why the need for two distinct career ladders exists in the telecommunications job family, officially known as voice and data. This next section provides an overview of the telecommunications "voice" job family.

The telecommunications "voice" job family is responsible for all aspects of voice communications. The job-task mandate includes the short- and long-range planning, design, installation and maintenance of a voice communications network tailored to an organization's business needs. In order to reflect the various functions and directions, the career ladder consists of five legs. Figure 2–4 depicts a graphic display of voice telecommunications task functions.

The three telecommunications "voice" job family main activities are as follows:

- *Voice Information.* This area is responsible for the corporate telephone directory, telephone user education, telephone billing, telecommunications billing and allocation and telephone operation (operators).

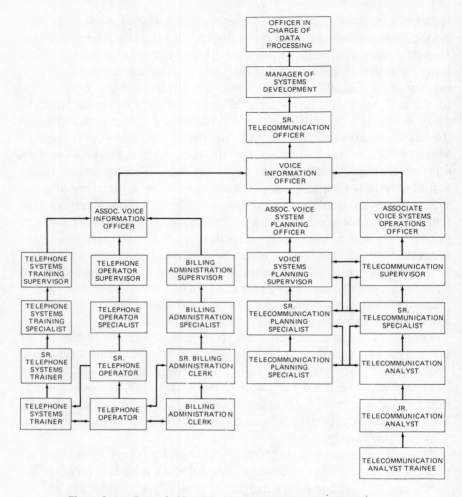

Figure 2-4.   Career ladder: DP telecommunications voice job family.

- *Voice Planning.* This includes short- and long-range voice communication services. The principal responsibilities are the review of existing systems and all aspects of the procurement and use of new voice communication facilities.
- *Voice Systems Operation.* This unit oversees corporatewide installation and maintenance of existing voice communications systems, as well as the analysis and research of proposed systems.

Within the telecommunications voice family, both vertical and lateral career opportunities are provided for staff members, particularly between voice systems planning and voice systems operations where the jobs are closely related.

Guide to the Telecommunications "Data" Job Family

The telecommunications "data" job family is responsible for providing data telecommunications services to the entire organization. In order to conduct its mandate, the telecommunications "data" job family career ladder consists of four legs.

Figure 2–5 illustrates the data telecommunications career ladder. The main activities of the family are as follows:

- *Strategic Planning.* This group is responsible for the long-term future of the data network, including long-term user requirements and the research needed for long-term development through a network plan.
- *Data Communications Development.* This area oversees the control of the delivery and development of the entire software environment, and a wide range of special hardware required to support the data network.
- *Data Communications Engineering.* This area is responsible for providing data communication services to include record, image and radio communications. This includes overseeing the research, systems design, engineering, implementation, maintenance and documentation of data communications services.
- *Data Communications Operations.* This area handles the technical support, maintenance and operation of the 24-hour-a-day, 7-days-a-week data network. It also is responsible for maintaining the smooth operation and speedy repair of problems.

Functions of the data telecommunications job family are somewhat similar in numerous respects to the previously mentioned systems and programming job family because both operations are involved in a full life cycle of feasibility, analysis, design, development, implementation and maintenance.

Movement within this job family—provided by numerous vertical and lateral career opportunities—is more readily available within the strategic planning, development and engineering career legs. However, it is more difficult for the operations career leg to straddle over

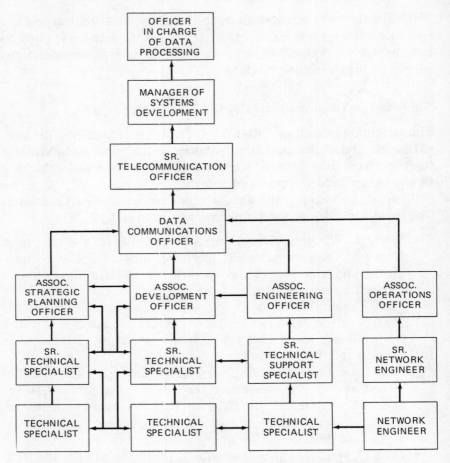

Figure 2–5.   Career ladder: DP telecommunications data family.

to the other three paths because the skills required to perform these jobs are different and more complex. However, it should be noted that the operations leg provides as much career potential to advance as the others.

THE SOFTWARE ENGINEERING FAMILY: WHAT IT DOES

The fourth and final job family is software engineering. There is no direct parallel in terms of job similarities between the software engineering family and the other job families that have been described up to this point.

Complex software normally is supplied by a manufacturer or purchased from an outside software organization. These software systems which are used by the computer (hardware) are referred to as the "operating system." Because of the complexity of technology and the new innovations and releases, operating the system requires continual maintenance and modification to be used efficiently.

The employees responsible for the operating system and its actual maintenance and support of all "operating software" are known as software engineers. Software engineers, meanwhile, are involved in designing software modifications and making operating system modifications. Software engineers also make recommendations on hardware and software modifications necessary to operate the overall computer system efficiently. This includes debugging software problems and consulting with other job family personnel on complex software-related problems. Figure 2-6 shows the software engineering job family. In this working sector, the career ladder is positioned as a vertical career strategy, with only one "leg." That's because the key skills required to perform the tasks associated with each of the software engineering family's job tasks are highly technical, requiring mastery of the varied software and hardware configurations. And in the environmental reality, there is really only one function—systems engineering—with multiple position levels within the family, that actually serves as the career guidelines for that specialty area.

As indicated, movement in the software engineering family is only vertical. Nevertheless, upward career movement can progress all the way to the top of the DP organization for the employee determined to succeed in his or her chosen specialty endeavor.

In all of the previously cited four major DP job families—systems and programming, computer operations, software engineering and voice/data telecommunications, and the various career paths found in each of those families—every employee has the opportunity to "go for the gold": the challenge to rise and become the officer-in-charge of DP. It's not an impossible dream. Here is the recommended workplace career strategy for the rising achiever intent on one day becoming that DP leader:

Ideally, the candidate should have the first-hand experience and knowledge of all four job families. That's the start. The candidate

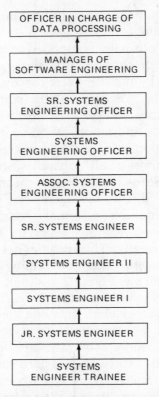

Figure 2–6.   Career ladder: DP software engineering family.

should also have the skills and sensitivity demanded of all good officer candidates:

- Always encouraging his or her employees to improve themselves.
- Providing employees with new opportunities so that they can move forward and accept increased responsibilities.
- Recognizing the good work provided by each individual employee.
- Never snapping or barking at a subordinate or co-worker when attempting to provide feedback concerning the quality of work performance.

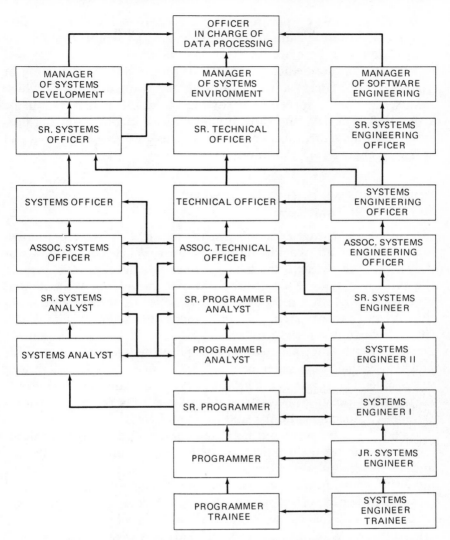

Figure 2-7.   Systems and programming and software engineering: cross movement between families.

- Providing the guidance necessary to enable co-workers or subordinates to carry out the work assignment.
- Displaying at all times the openness to let all employees—regardless of their grades or tasks in DP—to have a full and clear understanding of what is expected.

If your in-house corporate game plan wisely includes the creation of a fertile in-house climate for the grooming of senior-level DP officer candidates, here are the front-line-tested guidelines.

It's not going to be accomplished overnight, but the grooming of high-level DP officers starts by carefully reviewing Figure 2–7, which points out how a career path for high-level DP achievers can be structured. The DP "upward mobility" path incorporates the possible cross-movement between the systems and programming and software engineering job families.

HOW TO DEFINE CROSS–MOVEMENT GENERAL PARAMETERS

It's important to define some general parameters for cross-movement between the two job families shown. When considering employee cross-movement, the strategy taken into account must include the skills and knowledge acquired in one family and the potential usefulness in another job family. If the skills and the knowledge acquired can be transferred, then movement into other families is feasible. Retraining must also be considered. If, with a minimum amount of training, a person can acquire the necessary new skills and knowledge, then movement within families is practical as well as feasible. The third consideration is the salary and position levels. If the salary position levels are comparative, then movement within families can occur without penalizing employees.

As a rule, entry-level and management-level positions are conducive to the above-mentioned parameters. As pointed out in the example, the entry-level programmer and systems engineer positions are easily transferable. Likewise, at the first-line management level (associate officer), cross-movement is possible. At the high-management tiers and the middle-line positions, it becomes evident that cross-movement is not as prevalent. This is due to understandable retraining and salary/position level considerations.

However, there is a definite business need to create movement from a DP family into a non-DP family (and vice versa). Here are some of the important reasons supporting cross-movement of personnel from the two working sectors.

For the remainder of this decade—and heavily into the next century—the dynamic business community will best position itself through integrated growth the cross-migration of DP and non-DP personnel into key leadership roles.

There are strong corporate needs for this cross-fertilization of manpower/skills exchange within the organization. Observers who have studied the strengths and weaknesses of the typical large-scale American corporation, have repeatedly urged the incorporation of a combined DP/business balance in the decision-making processes. This is because these observers point out from experience that most DP specialists have a limited perspective of long-range business reality when it comes to dealing with the true-to-life technical realities required by their respective organizations. Can these technical achievers really distinguish the difference between a new computer system being market-driven or computer-driven in the brutally competitive marketplace? Are they creating computer systems that are technically challenging for the DP personnel involved—but have they forgotten how to create computer systems that are "user friendly" in solving and implementing the organization's day-to-day business needs?

These same observers also point out the advantages of not allowing full input control to originate entirely from the decision made by non-DP executives concerning the direction of computer system growth within the organization. However, there's also another side to this same argument.

Computer system growth strategy must also be coordinated by DP personnel, it is stated, because their non-DP counterparts do not sufficiently participate in the planning and design stages of a computer system. The absence of non-DP personnel in the computer strategy planning usually means that, in the future, changes made to the system—which are costly and prolonged—will follow just because of the non-DP low-profile minimum involvement.

These same observers also point out that another reason why non-DP persons usually like keeping low profiles in providing sorely-needed input during the design stages of a new project is simply that those non-DP persons are intimidated by the mushrooming computer technology.

There is a strong truth to the amount of long-term damage impacting the start-up of a new system because the actions of a non-DP executive—who may wield strong corporate clout—end up resisting the very systems being proposed that could increase the business'

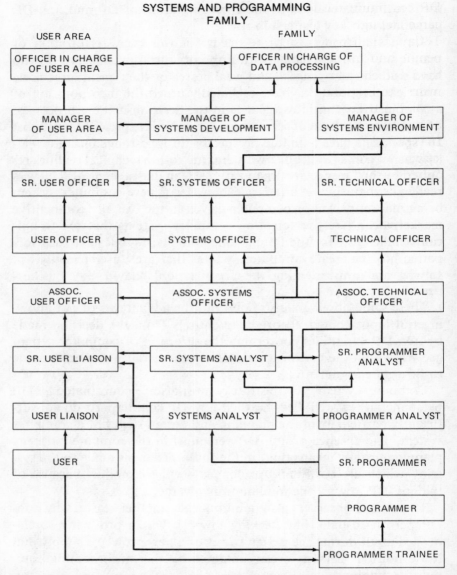

Figure 2–8. Movement from a non-DP family into a DP family and movement from a DP family into a non-DP family.

operating capacity. Synergy and teamwork are the right combination and produce the real corporate winners when cross-over takes place between the DP and non-DP ranks.

Also, until very recently, there was a widespread belief that the

DP community was an exclusive society and that only those who came through its DP ranks could penetrate. This is no longer true. Today's challenge is to make the DP person more attuned to the people and business issues while making the user more attuned to the DP technology. This can be accomplished through cross-movement (see Figure 2–8).

As illustrated, the "user" area itself is also a very good place to acquire new personnel "entry-level" programmer trainee positions. In turn, employees at the systems analyst or programmer analyst positions who are people-/business-oriented may be suited to fill the "user liaison" positions. Both "worlds" (DP and non-DP) have career opportunities to move up the ranks.

Indeed, more progressive organizations are taking people from the user areas and training them to be DP personnel. These organizations are also allowing qualified DP personnel to change their career paths into the user areas at comparable salary and position levels. In addition to career movement, resources are being spent towards the education of the DP person and the user in an attempt to ensure reaching these goals. Information centers and user liaison groups are examples of methods of bridging the communications gaps.

WHY A DP ORGANIZATION NEEDS
POSITION DESCRIPTIONS

Once the "career ladder" strategies have been defined and approved, the next step in the career development system is the preparation of job descriptions for each of positions found in the career ladder— and, ultimately, the entire job family.

There are four good reasons why every organization should maintain DP position descriptions:

1. Position descriptions are used for the assignment of grades and salary ranges to ensure compatibility within the respective organization and also serve as a measuring tool for rating industry compatibility with regards to competitive compensation.
2. Position descriptions are used to communicate job expectations to employees in terms of job functions, responsibilities, organizational relationships and accountability.
3. Position descriptions serve to alert in-house staffers of the selection process used to enlist new job candidates for the soon-to-open new jobs.

4. Position descriptions spell out the full terms of prerequisites to all would-be job contenders. At the same time, the up-front posting of past experience requirements—also listed on the description forms—are used to screen all candidates to determine how well they meet the posted requirements.

The following section will describe and provide the actual components of the position descriptions. Many organizations across the nation utilize the Hay point system to assign grades or salary ranges to positions. The Hay guidelines specifically evaluate jobs in three major categories, which are as follows:

1. *Know-How.* This category represents the sum total of every kind of task/skill required for acceptable job performance.
2. *Accountability.* This category incorporates the measured effect of the job on end-results or its impact on the organization.
3. *Problem-Solving.* This category incorporates the original "self-starting" thinking required by the job for analyzing, evaluating, creating, reasoning and arriving at and making conclusions.

A format that has been found to be highly conducive to effectively presenting all job position descriptions in a clear manner for Hay evaluation is illustrated in Figure 2–9, with explanations of each of the components in the position description.

In most organizations, the assignment of grades to positions—be it through the use of the Hay point system or other methodologies—is a corporate personnel function. The writing of position descriptions, however, can be performed in a combination of ways—either by divisional human resources, corporate personnel, user management or jointly.

To make this process easier, there are two recommended approaches to use when developing job descriptions. They are either directly from the job description form itself or through a position task analysis form. Either process can be used, depending upon the situation at hand. A personnel employee may find it difficult to complete the actual position description form. If that's the case, the personnel representative should require assistance from user management in completing the respective task analysis form, as indicated in Figure 2–10.

In this sequence, personnel interviews the user in identifying all of

TITLE: Indicates formal position title.

REPORTING STRUCTURE: Indicates immediate supervisory level.

GENERAL RESPONSIBILITIES:

Describes the major purpose, objective and function of the position.

I. PREREQUISITES:

  A. Education:

  The minimum educational level, formal degrees or training required for this position.

  B. Experience:

  Describes the minimum amount of work experience and the specific type of work experience necessary to qualify for consideration for this position.

II. RESPONSIBILITIES:

  A. Applications:

  Indicates the number and nature of decisions required by this position, as well as the extent to which these decisions or recommendations are accepted as final or are changed by superiors.

  B. Projects:

  Describes the responsibility of the position for the planning, development, implementation and direction of specific assignments, projects or programs.

  C. Policies and Methods:

  Describes the responsibility and authority for the formulation or interpretation of corporate and divisional policies and methods or systems, where originality and creativity are required because standard guides do not exist.

  D. Relationships:

  Describes the level and type of relationships maintained by individuals within this position in dealing with individuals, organizations or associations, both within and/or outside the corporation, which may include customers, vendors or contract personnel.

  E. Supervision:

    1. Given:

    Indicates the type of subordinates reporting directly to this position and the control exercised over these subordinates.

    2. Received:

    Indicates the extent to which immediate superior initiates and/or reviews the activities of this position.

III. ACCOUNTABILITY—GAIN OR LOSS:

Describes the extent to which the position presents opportunities for producing financial gain or other benefits for the corporation or for preventing financial losses.

Figure 2-9. Position description format.

LEGEND

A – ASSISTS
P – PERFORMS
L –
D – LEADS DIRECTS

POSITION TASK ANALYSIS FORM

	DEPT./FUNCTION																				DEPT./FUNCTION HEAD			
	Senior Systems Analyst				Systems Analyst				Senior Programmer Analyst				Programmer Analyst											
	A	P	L	D	A	P	L	D	A	P	L	D	A	P	L	D	A	P	L	D	A	P	L	D
1. Feasibility Study and Final Report		X																						
2. Functional Analysis and Functional Specifications		X																						
3. Detailed Design Specifications (coordinates)	X	X																						
4. System Test Data Specifications or Plans		X																						
5. System Status Reports	X																							
6. Systems Documentation		X																						
7. Problem Resolution and Technical Assistance		X																						
8. User Training		X																						
9. OJT in Systems Analysis and Design		X																						

Figure 2–10.   Position task analysis forms.

LEGEND

A – ASSISTS
P – PERFORMS
L – LEADS
D – DIRECTS

DEPT./FUNCTION

DEPT./FUNCTION HEAD

POSITION TASK ANALYSIS FORM	Senior Systems Analyst			Systems Analyst			Senior Programmer Analyst			Programmer Analyst												
	A	P	L D	A	P	L D	A	P	L D	A	P	L D	A	P	L D	A	P	L D	A	P	L D
10. Cost-Benefit Estimates and Evaluation		X																			
11. User Recommendation Analysis		X																			
12. Systems Testing	X																				
13. Testing Acceptance Procedures	X																				
14. Project Analysis			X																		
15. Oversee Project Design, Development and Installation		X																			
16. Design Procedures for Control, Audit, Back-up, Recovery and Restart		X																			
17. Program Design through Implementation Coordination		X																			
18. Subordinate Performance Appraisal	X																				

Figure 2-10.   (continued)

LEGEND
A – ASSISTS
P – PERFORMS
L – LEADS
D – DIRECTS

DEPT./FUNCTION

DEPT./FUNCTION HEAD

POSITION TASK ANALYSIS FORM	Senior Systems Analyst			Systems Analyst			Senior Programmer Analyst			Programmer Analyst									Dept./Function Head		
	A	P	L D	A	P	L D	A	P	L D	A	P	L D	A	P	L D	A	P	L D	A	P	L D
19. Project Control Coordination		X																			
20. Conversion Techniques Design or Coordination		X																			
21. Manual Systems Modification to Computer System		X																			
22. Education Planning of Subordinates		X (May)																			
23. Develop Corporate Standards and Procedures for Systems and Programming		X (May)																			
24. Technical Consulting on Development Projects		X (May)																			
25. Project Life Cycle Audits		X (May)																			
26. Develop Data Base Design Procedures		X (May)																			
27. Coordinate Development Projects Throughout Life Cycle With All Interfaces		X (May)																			

Figure 2-10.   (continued)

TITLE: Senior Systems Analyst

REPORTING STRUCTURE: Associate Systems Officer/Systems Officer

GENERAL RESPONSIBILITIES:

Conducts or leads feasibility studies, systems design and system installations as assigned by responsible officer. Primary responsibilities involve analytical and technical duties relative to the analysis of business operations in the user areas and the design of computer systems to improve such operations within the corporation. In this position, corporate requirements can necessitate takeover or turnover of a vital project function within five weeks.

I. PREREQUISITES:

A. Education:

Bachelor's Degree in a science or business discipline, mathematics, statistics, computer science, economics, accounting or management preferred.

Equivalent business experience acceptable.

B. Experience:

In order to be considered for this position, a candidate should have the capabilities normally equated with six and one half to ten years of systems or programming experience with a minimum of two years in the design and implementation of complex computer systems utilizing state-of-the-art systems design techniques. Software experience should include Cobol or ALC in a multi-programming environment. He should have a good working knowledge of the techniques of systems analysis (e.g., feasibility reports, cost benefit evaluation, time studies, etc.). He should have a good working knowledge of file design and data base techniques, as well as systems parallel and acceptance-testing procedures. He should have a comprehensive knowledge of OS. He should be familiar with accounting and audit principles and know the scope of the entire project, as well as having education in project management and supervisory techniques. He should have the ability to communicate effectively with official and clerical staff in the user areas and be able to coordinate and manage systems analysts.

II. RESPONSIBILITIES:

A. Applications:

Conducts feasibility studies and makes final reports.

Conducts functional analysis and develops functional specifications.

Accomplishes or coordinates development of detailed design specifications.

Identifies problems or offers technical advice where appropriate.

Design specifications for or plans system test data.

Assists in or reports systems progress, efficiency and adherence to standards.

Accomplishes the maintenance and the updating of systems documentation.

Figure 2–11.

Maintains a level of technical expertise commensurate with present and planned future configuration of hardware and software.

Reforms training of user department personnel.

Provides on-the-job training in analysis and design.

Analyzes information flow in the user area.

Estimates and evaluates costs and benefits.

Analyzes user recommendations for validity and applicability.

Participates with programmers in systems testing procedures.

Coordinates or designs acceptance testing procedures.

Leads and directs analysis functions of a project segment.

Assists in the timing, coordination and execution of the design, development and installation of development projects.

Designs procedures for audit and control, backup and recovery and restart and recovery.

Coordinates programming functions from program design through implementation.

Supplies input to management regarding performance of subordinate personnel.

Coordinates project control activities for a project.

Designs or coordinates conversion techniques.

Increases his data processing knowledge by availing himself of self-education opportunities.

Modifies present manual systems to interface with computer systems.

May coordinate the design, scheduling and administration of educational courses.

May develop corporate standards and procedures for systems and programming including documentation, design techniques, coding techniques and implementation procedures.

May perform coordination of development projects to ensure that systems development, systems review, technical support and operations personnel contribute their expertise at all stages of the project life cycle.

May perform technical consulting assignments on development projects as directed by the technical or systems officer.

May perform audits of development projects at every stage of the project life cycle to ensure that corporate standards and procedures are followed.

May develop data base design procedures including the investigation of alternate systems and packages, the recommendation of the choice most suited to corporate objectives and the adoption and administration of the data base on all corporate development projects.

B. Projects:

Participates in the evaluation and/or plans for the use of package programs.

Figure 2-11.   (continued)

C. Policies and Methods:

Organizes programming efforts, depending on size and scope of projects.

Assists in or prepares documentation of systems being installed.

Makes suggestions on systems and programming standards and procedures.

Carries out administrative personnel duties as assigned.

D. Relationships:

The senior systems analyst normally interfaces with the associate systems officer/systems officer for performance and salary reviews, education and career path planning and personnel problems.

Normally the associate systems officer/systems officer assigns senior technical personnel to provide him with project-related on-the-job training and guidance.

Normally the associate systems officer/systems officer ensures that he attends the appropriate corporate management training classes.

Contributes to and makes reports to management. Interacts with systems programming, user department, systems review and operations personnel.

Works with outside consultants.

May contact or confer with outside representatives about available products and services specifically applicable to on-going or anticipated projects, as requested by supervisor.

He may attend classes or seminars given by vendors or equipment manufacturers and/or corporate management training classes.

E. Supervision:

1. <u>Given:</u>

None

2. <u>Received:</u>

Normally the associate systems officer/systems officer plans the senior systems analyst's formal education, develops his career path and administers his performance and salary reviews. He also reviews and approves his work or assigns the associate technical officer to review it.

III. <u>ACCOUNTABILITY—GAIN OR LOSS</u>:

Can cause a financial loss to the corporation as a result of poorly designed or audited systems.

Can cause substantial savings by the practical design and implementation of computer programs, as well, as the quality of technical direction or auditing provided.

Figure 2-11.   (continued)

the tasks involved in a job and the degree to which an employee will perform the task, by designating "A" for assisting in the task completion, "P" for performing the task by him/herself and "LD" for leading or directing the completion of the task.

From the task analysis form, personnel staffers then may easily draw up the input to the "responsibilities" section of the job description form. The staffers will still need to interview user management to obtain the additional information needed to complete the other portions; however, the task analysis form provides a head start in completing the most difficult portion of the job description form—identifying job tasks.

In some cases, user management may speed the process by developing the description right from an outline of the position description form, by filling in the blanks under each of the headings. Later, personnel can refine the form to enhance the information or can solicit further information if there are still existing gaps.

No matter which position description format is used, the end product will be the same. An example of a task analysis form can be found in Figure 2–10 and the resulting position description in the senior systems analyst job description in Figure 2–11.

WHY A SKILLS GLOSSARY IS NEEDED

The third component to the career development system—the composition of a skills glossary—is essential in the development of the human resources system.

Your organization will have to "speak with one voice" in the DP hiring, training and career ladder strategy. Your staffers—and all users, too—will have to understand the difference between a "task" and a "skill" when examining job description postings. For the career development system, a "task" is an action that is performed. A "skill" represents the required or acquired abilities needed to accomplish the job task.

A working example of defining a task is shown in the "writing a program" task. There are various skills needed to perform the generic task of writing a program. For example, what is the computer language to be used to write the program? Will it be in Cobol, Assembler or Fortran? Skills such as JCL (Job Control Language), utilities and dump reading are also necessary.

In relating tasks to skills, it is also essential that a manager understand the required skills needed to perform the job. He or she also needs to know the in-house skills the staff possesses to assign work to the properly qualified people. Second, in strengthening the hiring process, defining the required skills helps to determine whether or not the candidate will be able to perform the tasks required in the position he/she is being interviewed for. This also holds true for in-house mobility.

Skills definition is needed for proper career counseling/education planning. This can be appreciated in the following example, where a manager has determined that one of his/her employees requires additional programming background. The key here is to break the programming function down into the various skills that are needed to identify the specific skill deficiencies.

This is done to avoid sending an employee to a five-day Cobol programming class, for example, when all that is needed is a two-day class on JCL. It can also help in managing an education budget more effectively. As far as career counseling is concerned, defining skills for each of the positions assists a manager in communicating to his/her employees skills needed to improve in the current job and to prepare for the next step in the employee's career ladder.

A "skills glossary"—to be effective and speak with one voice—must identify all skills, technical and non-technical, associated with every position in a given job family. A typical detailed working example of this can be found in Figure 2–12 pertaining to the "systems and programming" job family.

All skills cited here fall into two classifications: core and peripheral. Core refers to skills that are designated as critical to the job. Peripheral refers to skills that are project-oriented or lacking in a wide range of applicability. In this example, the core skills in the "language" group are Cobol and IBM Assembler. There are, however, other kinds of hardware utilized by a smaller percentage of the staff which were placed in the peripheral language grouping.

Those skills are also broken down into four levels of proficiency, as follows:

- *Level one* represents training or exposure to a skill.
- *Level two* represents moderate use of a skill in practical application.
- *Level three* represents heavy use of a skill in practical application.
- *Level four* represents expertise in both knowledge and use of a skill.

Figure 2–12. Skills glossary: table of contents.

Figure 2–12.   (continued)

Figure 2–12.   (continued)

An example of the four levels of proficiency can be seen again in the languages skill grouping for Cobol shown in Figure 2–13.

THE SKILLS MATRIX: CROSSRELATING
JOBS AND SKILLS

The cross-relation of jobs and skills is illustrated in Figure 2–14. We have chosen the language family. You will note that there are two core skills in this group, namely Cobol and Assembler. The rest are

COBOL

Level 1: Knowledge of structure of COBOL program, the various divisions, syntax conventions, major verbs.

Level 2: From detailed programming specifications has coded and tested programs or modules adhering to shop standards. Experience in handling various COBOL options, such as variable length records, parm fields, simple I/O, internal tables, printer options, sequential data sets, compiler options and data representation.

Level 3: Has coded and tested programs or modules from general programming specifications. Experience in handling sophisticated COBOL options, such as random access techniques declaratives, complex I/O and error handling, sort verbs with I/O procedures, segmentations, multiple subscripting, indexing, BAL-COBOL interface techniques. Good knowledge of various trade-offs between logically equivalent coding schemes.

Level 4: Within a project environment, is capable of educating other programmers in efficient and complex COBOL options and developing COBOL programming standards. Has given direction to others in resolving complex problems and reviewing code. Abreast of "state-of-the-art" coding techniques.

Figure 2–13.   Skills definition.

LANGUAGES	Assoc. Prog.	Prog.	Sr. Prog.	Sys. Anal.	Sr. Sys. Anal.	ASO	Prog. Anal.	Sr. Prog. Anal.
Core								
Cobol	1	2	3	3	3	3	4	4
IBM Assembler	1	2	3	3	3	3	4	4

Peripheral
NEAT/3
Culprit
RPG II
Minicomputer Assembler Language (S/7 Assembler, Macro, PDP Assembler)
Structured Code
Fortran
PL1
Basic
QBAL
Burroughs Cobol
NCR Cobol
IRS
GRS

Figure 2–14.   Skill group/core skills matrix.

considered to be peripheral skills; they are noted in the system but not fully detailed with regards levels. You can see the hierarchical effect as an individual progresses through the career ladder.

This skills matrix created is actually the medium for the fifth component in the career development system—ths skills profiles report.

THE SKILLS PROFILE REPORT
AND THE INFORMATION IT PROVIDES

For the manager, the skills profile report produces an overall view of the skill proficiencies of the staff as well as serving as an efficient tool for education planning. For the employee, the profile report represents a picture of that person's current status in relation to current position and/or next position by pinpointing to the employee both strengths and individual weaknesses.

The skills profile report is then the output generated from a skills data base which has two types of information:

1. A comparison of the individual's skill level to the requirements of current and/or next position, as determined by the skills matrix.
2. A listing of available education courses which will assist the individual in attaining the recommended level of proficiency in the "deficient" skills for current position and/or next position.

Figure 2–15 serves as an example in conceptualizing this process. For example, when examining the entire skills profile on "Jane Doe's" current position, programmer analyst, it is clear that the profile includes all the core skills in a skill group and peripheral skills, if the individual has a skill level of 1 or greater.

By examining the "language" group, it becomes evident that in Jane Doe's current position as programmer analyst, her individual skill level for Cobol is 4 and for IBM Assembler, 2.

The recommended skill level is 0 for Cobol and 4 for IBM Assembler. As a result, her skill deficiency lies in Assembler langangue. Consequently, the recommended education depicts what courses she should take to increase her skill level from 2 to the recommended 4. It is also evident that she possesses more than what is required in terms of her Cobol skill.

SYSTEMS & PLANNING   RUN DATE :   PAGE 1

CAREER DEVELOPMENT SYSTEM
DOE, JANE
CURRENT POSITION SKILLS PROFILE REPORT

SOCIAL SECURITY NO	CURRENT POSITION TITLE	MANAGER'S NAME	6 MO COUNSELING DATE	LAST UPDATE DATE
	PROGRAMMER ANALYST			

GROUP NAME : HARDWARE

CORE SKILLS	INDV SKILL LEVEL	RECOMMENDED SKILL LEVEL	SKILL DEFICIENCY	RECOMMENDED EDUCATION
IBM HARDWARE & PERIPHERAL DEVS	3	3		

PERIPHERAL SKILLS

	INDV SKILL LEVEL	RECOMMENDED SKILL LEVEL	SKILL DEFICIENCY	RECOMMENDED EDUCATION
IV PHASE HARDWARE	2	.	.	
I/O SUBSYSTEMS	3	.	.	4-EXP

GROUP NAME : LANGUAGES

CORE SKILLS	INDV SKILL LEVEL	RECOMMENDED SKILL LEVEL	SKILL DEFICIENCY	RECOMMENDED EDUCATION
COBOL OR	4	0		
IBM ASSEMBLER	2	4	•	3-IBM0009
				3-IBM0010
				4-IBM0011

PERIPHERAL SKILLS

	INDV SKILL LEVEL	RECOMMENDED SKILL LEVEL	SKILL DEFICIENCY	RECOMMENDED EDUCATION
NEAT/3	2	.	.	4-EXP
STRUCTURED CODE	3	.	.	2-SEE EDUCATION ANALYST
FORTRAN	1	.	.	3-N/A
IRS	2	.	.	

GROUP NAME : SYSTEM SOFTWARE

CORE SKILLS	INDV SKILL LEVEL	RECOMMENDED SKILL LEVEL	SKILL DEFICIENCY	RECOMMENDED EDUCATION
OS CONCEPTS	3	4	•	1-N/A
OS/VS CONCEPTS	0	4	•	2-EDU2101-02
				2-EDU2108
JCL	4	4	•	4-EXP
UTILITIES	3	4	•	3-N/A
ISO	2	4	•	3-EDU1907-09
DUMP READING	2	4	•	4-EXP

Figure 2-15.

CAREER DEVELOPMENT SYSTEM RUN DATE : PAGE 2
DOE, JANE
CURRENT POSITION SKILLS PROFILE REPORT

GROUP NAME : SYSTEM SOFTWARE (CONTINUED)

PERIPHERAL SKILLS

	INDV SKILL LEVEL	RECOMMENDED SKILL LEVEL	SKILL DEFICIENCY	RECOMMENDED EDUCATION
ASP	2	.	.	3-N/A
SYNCSORT	2	.	.	3-N/A
FDR	2	.	.	3-N/A

GROUP NAME : ANALYSIS

CORE SKILLS

	INDV SKILL LEVEL	RECOMMENDED SKILL LEVEL	SKILL DEFICIENCY	RECOMMENDED EDUCATION
FEASIBILITY STUDIES	2	2	.	
FUNCTIONAL SPECIFICATIONS	2	2	.	
AUDITS & CONTROLS	2	2	.	
PERT/GANTT CHARTING	2	2	.	
PROJECT LIFE CYCLE	3	2	.	
COST/BENEFIT ANALYSIS	0	2	*	1-N/A 2-AS11100

PERIPHERAL SKILLS

	INDV SKILL LEVEL	RECOMMENDED SKILL LEVEL	SKILL DEFICIENCY	RECOMMENDED EDUCATION
PACKAGE EVALUATION	2	.	.	3-EXP

GROUP NAME : DESIGN

CORE SKILLS

	INDV SKILL LEVEL	RECOMMENDED SKILL LEVEL	SKILL DEFICIENCY	RECOMMENDED EDUCATION
DESIGN SPECIFICATIONS	2	3	*	3-EXP 3-DPN1003-09
FILE DESIGN	2	3	*	3-DIK1007 3-EDU1400
PROGRAM DESIGN	4	3		
CATALOGUED PROCEDURE DESIGN	3	3		
BACKUP & RECOVERY	0	2	*	1-N/A
TEST PLANS	2	3	*	3-EXP
SYSTEM CONVERSION TECHNIQUES	3	3		

PERIPHERAL SKILLS

	INDV SKILL LEVEL	RECOMMENDED SKILL LEVEL	SKILL DEFICIENCY	RECOMMENDED EDUCATION
STRUCTURED DESIGN	2	.	.	3-IBM0006 3-YDN0002

Figure 2-15. (continued)

CAREER DEVELOPMENT SYSTEM
DOE, JANE
CURRENT POSITION SKILLS PROFILE REPORT

GROUP NAME : IMPLEMENTATION

C O R E S K I L L S	INDV SKILL LEVEL	RECOMMENDED SKILL LEVEL	SKILL DEFICIENCY	RECOMMENDED EDUCATION
USER DOCUMENTATION	3	3		3-N/A
USER EDUCATION	3	3		4-DIK1015
APPLICATION ACCEPTANCE TESTING	2	4	•	4-YDN0003
				1-EXP
DDC PROCEDURES	0	3	•	2-EXP
				3-EXP

GROUP NAME : TELEPROCESSING

C O R E S K I L L S	INDV SKILL LEVEL	RECOMMENDED SKILL LEVEL	SKILL DEFICIENCY	RECOMMENDED EDUCATION
NO CORE SKILLS IDENTIFIED FOR THIS GROUP				

GROUP NAME : BUSINESS & INDUSTRY

C O R E S K I L L S	INDV SKILL LEVEL	RECOMMENDED SKILL LEVEL	SKILL DEFICIENCY	RECOMMENDED EDUCATION
ORAL COMMUNICATION	2	3	•	3-BOE0002
WRITTEN COMMUNICATION	3	3		
CORPORATION KNOWLEDGE	2	2		

P E R I P H E R A L   S K I L L S

	INDV SKILL LEVEL	RECOMMENDED SKILL LEVEL	SKILL DEFICIENCY	RECOMMENDED EDUCATION
TECHNICAL INTERVIEWING	2	-	-	3-EXP
DP INDUSTRY	2	-	-	3-EXP
CONTROLLERS	3	-	-	4-EXP
COMMERCIAL LOAN	3	-	-	4-EXP

GROUP NAME : MANAGEMENT

C O R E S K I L L S	INDV SKILL LEVEL	RECOMMENDED SKILL LEVEL	SKILL DEFICIENCY	RECOMMENDED EDUCATION
FUNCTIONAL MANAGEMENT	2	2		
MANAGEMENT TECHNIQUES	0	0		
PLAN, ESTIMATE & CONTROL	2	2		
BUDGET FORMULATION	0	0		
PERSONNEL SELECTION	0	0		
PERSONNEL EVALUATION	0	0		
HUMAN RESOURCE DEVELOPMENT	1	2	•	
PROJECT REPORTING	2	2		2-BOE0002
USER LIAISON				

Figure 2-15.   (continued)

EDUCATION COURSES MATRICES:
WHY THEY'RE IMPORTANT

The sixth and final component of the career development portion of the HR system is the education course matrices. The education course matrix is the output generated from the education courses' data base. It supports the career development system by providing the following information:

1. Skill groups listed for a given job family.
2. Sub-skills listed along with the four levels of proficiency.
3. Recommended education listed per level of proficiency and/or experience.

This education matrix is also shown in the skills profile report, which lists the recommended education for an individual, as previously mentioned.

Figure 2–16 depicts the education course matrix for the systems and programming family—language skills grouping. The recommended education can be found under each of the "level" headings. In some instances, the recommended education can be more than one course and/or other notations such as:

- EXP—for certain of the skill levels, the matrices indicate experience (EXP) rather than formal education. In these instances it is felt that experience alone will be required to achieve the level.
- N/A—a designation that signifies that no skill has been defined for that level, and, accordingly, no education is specified.
- SEE EDUCATION ANALYST—this indicates that education for that level is available, but it has not been evaluated.

The education course matrix was designed to assist the DPHR personnel (but could be utilized for non-DP education as well) to continually re-evaluate the marketplace in terms of the most effective education available to satisfy skill deficiencies to bridge the gap.

And now you've learned all about the intrinsic basics on how to organize and quantify your HR system. The next chapter becomes the next pivotal step in implementing a successful DPHR strategy for the DP achiever.

EDUCATION COURSE MATRIX FOR : SYSTEMS & PLANNING   RUN DATE :

NOTE: A BLANK APPEARS FOR THOSE SKILL LEVELS WHERE NEITHER FORMAL EDUCATION NOR EXPERIENCE HAS YET BEEN IDENTIFIED.

N/A INDICATES THIS LEVEL HAS NOT BEEN DEFINED IN THE SKILLS MATRIX.

GROUP   B00-LANGUAGES

SKILL B01-COBOL	LEVEL 1	LEVEL 2	LEVEL 3	LEVEL 4
	ISP1000	DTK1403-04	DTK1401-02 DTK1506-08	EXP

SKILL A02-IBM ASSEMBLER	LEVEL 1	LEVEL 2	LEVEL 3	LEVEL 4
	ISP1100	ISP1100	IBM0009 IBM0010	IBM0011

SKILL : B07-NEAT/3	LEVEL 1	LEVEL 2	LEVEL 3	LEVEL 4

SKILL : B08-CULPRIT	LEVEL 1	LEVEL 2	LEVEL 3	LEVEL 4
	N/A	CUL0001	N/A	SEE EDUCATION ANALYST

SKILL : B09-RPG II	LEVEL 1	LEVEL 2	LEVEL 3	LEVEL 4
	N/A	SEE EDUCATION ANALYST	N/A	SEE EDUCATION ANALYST,

Figure 2-16.

3
A View From Above

Both the short-term and long-range acquisition of human resources in the computer field of today and tomorrow perhaps represent the most limiting factor for the accelerated growth of technological advancement. For companies attempting to remain on an even keel or to aggressively push forward, there must be strategic and operational advantages in the way they conduct the acquisition game.

Simply put, there are certain key principles and procedures that will provide those advantages. Here's the step-by-step guidelines that will ensure human resources (HR) success in that crucial arena.

1. *Create a centralized function.* There must be a centralized function which has effective control over the acquiring of all HR. This control should reside in the HR area and should include the acquiring of resources from within via mobility and from outside through hiring or the use of consultants.
2. *Develop a strategic business plan.* There should be a strategic business plan reflecting the manpower needs of each area or department in detail for the coming year and in more general terms for at least two years hence.
3. *Provide a job requisition form.* The origin of any need for a human resource should be a job requisition form.
4. *Always promote from within.* Mobility of in-house deserving performers should always take precedence over hiring or the use of consultants.

WHY A SINGLE CONTROL STABILIZES
ACQUISITION CAPABILITIES

Our experience over the last nine years led to successful development of a centralized acquisition function as an essential part of the HR group. That development has been characterized by an ever-increasing demand for systems and programming resources—averaging 10 to 15 percent each year—and does not include the replacement of turnover.

Since we initially launched our HR strategy, the acquisition methods used have included mobility, hiring of both experienced and entry-level personnel and the use of both domestic and foreign consultants. The beginning years were characterized by control over a smaller and more manageable group. The middle and more recent years revealed an explosion of requirements which had to be handled by an inadequate number of acquisition personnel. The result was a loss of control. More recently, adequate resources have allowed us to stabilize all HR acquisition methods to a point where a balance of control and acquisition capability can be maintained with the line organization.

Figure 3–1 illustrates the organizational setup of the acquisitional area called "resource planning." The hiring arm consists of the recruiting of experienced data processing (DP) personnel by professional DP recruiters and the selection of entry-level programmer trainees for two classes of 20 each, which are run in February and July of each year. Consultant usage control is divided into the use of domestic consultants and that of foreign personnel. These categories will be discussed in detail in Chapters 4 and 5.

The single control of both methods allows for more unified and optimized approaches to providing maximum cost/performance acquisition solutions for the line organizations. At the same time, it also ensures the integrity of the importance of mobility and also pre-

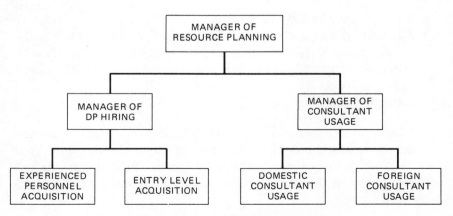

Figure 3-1. Organization of resource planning.

vents the misuse of consultants. It is most important to strive toward maintaining a strong in-house staff while utilizing consultants only when absolutely necessary. Projection of these goals to your own employees will, in itself, help to keep those staffers with the organization.

HOW TO ORGANIZE STRATEGIC BUSINESS PLANNING SECTIONS

Your organization's strategic business plan should minimally contain the following sections:

- *Executive Summary/Overview.* This is a narrative section describing the overall automation strategy in support of the user area served, and how the major deliverable projects fit into that strategy.
- *Deliverables Summary.* This section contains the scheduled completion of the milestones associated with each major deliverable.
- *Manpower Schedules.* This section details the work effort associated with each major project.
- *Project Narrative.* This section will contain a brief description of the major new projects initiated.

The business plan should be organized according to the following sequence:

- User area
- Business plan section (above)
- Business category (i.e., planning, on-going development, new development, enhancements, data base administration and support, minor maintenance and emergency maintenance)
- Major projects
- Calendar quarter.

In addition, for those departments where work effort is aligned to meet the needs of more than one user area, manpower summaries for the entire department should be developed. These documents will summarize the work effort for each area served and for the department as a whole.

For purposes of business planning, major deliverable projects are defined as any system or project having approved funds, or that is estimated to cost in excess of a specified amount (i.e., $250,000) or, in addition, any project that is defined by the user as being a major deliverable.

The sequence in which the major deliverables are ordered should be consistent throughout all sections of the business plan developed for each user area. The sections of the plan developed for each user area served should be assembled into a single document for each department. The business plans of the component departments of each group should also be further assembled into a single document for the group.

How to Prepare an Executive Summary/Overview

This section of the business plan should contain a narrative describing the overall automation plan in support of the user area served. It should also define how the major deliverable projects fit into that plan.

In those areas where the automation plan supports major strategic goals of a user area—and is part of the user's strategic plan—the relationship between the two should be described in this section and related to the major deliverable project outlined in the remainder of the business plan.

For non-systems and programming areas, this section should outline the major goals of the respective department during the planning horizon (i.e., one year), and should describe the relationship between those goals and the major deliverable projects outlined in the remainder of the business plan.

Also for non-systems and programming departments, this section should contain a narrative description of major efforts that will be undertaken in the department during the planning horizon covered by the business plan; for example,

- New hardware installations
- Implementation of upgraded systems software
- Support of additional user areas
- New standards development efforts
- Studies to define new services
- Description of expanded responsibilities.

Figure 3-2. Deliverables summary.

Department: _____
User: _____

Date: _____
Page: _____ of _____
Rev. No.: _____

	FIRST QUARTER	SECOND QUARTER	THIRD QUARTER	FOURTH QUARTER	FIRST QUARTER	SECOND QUARTER
Major Deliverable Name	Implementation (From 4Q .) Completed					
Approved Funds $1,475,000						
Cost to Date 225,000						
Est MM to completion N/A						
Major Deliverable Name	Implementation Cancelled					
Approved Funds						
Cost to Date						
Est MM to completion						
Major Deliverable Name	Implementation (From 4Q) (From 1Q)					
Approved Funds						
Cost to Date						
Est MM to completion						
* Major Deliverable Name			Proposal	Functional Analysis		
Approved Funds N/A						
Cost to Date						
Est MM to completion						

* Added to this Quarter

The description should include:

- Purpose of the efforts
- Start and completion dates of the effort.

How to Prepare a Deliverables Summary

This is a one-page summary of the major deliverables and the milestones to be completed in each quarter. Each major deliverable should be annotated with approved funds, cost-to-date and estimated man-months to completion of the effort.

Estimated man-months to completion should be taken from the manpower summary, if final implementation occurs within the planning horizon. They should be estimated, if final implementation will occur beyond the horizon. If movement of a milestone associated with a major deliverable occurs (e.g., if implementation is delayed from first quarter to second quarter), the milestone should be shown in its new quarter, with a notation showing from which quarter it was moved.

If a milestone is moved more than once, a history of its movement should be kept. Any new major deliverables added to the deliverable summary since the last business plan was prepared should be highlighted with an asterisk and footnoted. If a major deliverable has been cancelled or placed in hold, it should be noted on the summary (see Figure 3–2).

Manpower Schedules and Defining Each Major Deliverable Project

This section defines by quarter the work effort in man-months associated with each major deliverable. For each business plan category, the work effort associated with projects that are not considered major items should be summarized into an "other" category. If there are no major projects identified for a business plan category (e.g., emergency maintenance), all work effort estimated for that category may be summarized into a single set of totals.

For each major project in each quarter, the work effort estimates should be detailed as to full-time staff and consultants. Both foreign and domestic consultants should be included in the consultant category. For those work efforts that can be identified as being covered by a fixed-price contract, the man-month equivalent should be calculated by dividing the dollar amount of the contract by an average fixed-price contract rate (i.e., $40 per hour) to obtain an equivalent number of hours, and then dividing by 152 hours/months (consultants are normally assumed to be billed for 35 hours per week and 4.33 weeks per month; i.e., 152 hours/months) to obtain equivalent man-months. For those quarters in which fixed-price contracts are expected to be in effect, they should be noted in a footnote stating the effective dates and total cost of the fixed-price contracts. If a rate other than the average fixed-price contract rate is to be used, the rate used should be included in the footnote and the manpower summary, along with the effective dates of the contract, and the total estimated dollar value of the contract.

Quarterly totals and totals for the calendar year are to be developed for each business plan category and user area. Refer to Figure 3-3 for format and sequence. Estimated man-months to completion should be taken from the manpower summary, if final implementation occurs within the planning horizon. They should be estimated, if final implementation will occur beyond the planning horizon.

All staffing plans should be developed in conjunction with the area advisors from the HR department. Those plans should take into account user need, present staffing levels, any changes in current estimates of staff levels, department turnover, allocations of trainees and foreign consultants and achievable hiring levels. An example of a staffing plan is illustrated in Figure 3-4.

Project Narrative: What It Should Include

For on-going development or planning projects, the project narrative should include:

- A description of the current status of the project, including any problems or open items necessary for achievement of the remaining milestones. If a milestone has been delayed, specify the new completion date and discuss the impact on the remainder of the project. If a project has been cancelled or placed in hold, give the reasons.
- For any project in the system design or implementation phases, a description of any hardware or purchased software installa-

Department: Department Name and Number
Prepared by: Date: _____
Rev. No.:: _____ Page 1 of 4

USER DEPARTMENT NAME	SECOND QUARTER MM	THIRD QUARTER MM	FOURTH QUARTER MM	FIRST QUARTER MM	SECOND QUARTER MM	TOTAL MM
On-Going Development						
Major Deliverable 1						
Full-Time Staff	18	18	15	15	12	27
Consultant	6	6	0	0	0	0
Subtotal	24	24	15	15	12	27
Major Deliverable 2						
Full-Time Staff	25	25	27	24	24	48
Consultant	7	7	7	7	0	7
Sub-Total	32	32	34	31	24	55
Other						
Full-Time	6	6	6	16	6	12
Consultant	3	3	3	0	0	0
Sub-Total	9	9	9	6	6	12
Sub-Total On-Going Development						
Full-Time Staff	49	49	48	45	42	87
Consultant	16	16	10	7	0	7
Sub-Total	65	65	58	52	42	94

Figure 3-3. Business plan manpower summary.

Department: _____

Date: _____

Rev. No.: _____

	FOURTH QUARTER			FIRST QUARTER				SECOND QUARTER				THIRD QUARTER				FOURTH QUARTER			
	OCT	NOV	DEC	%	JAN	FEB	MAR	%	APR	MAY	JUN	%	JUL	AUG	SEP	%	OCT	NOV	DEC	%
NON-BILLABLE																				
Officers																				
Administrative																				
BILLABLE																				
Technical Staff																				
Foreign Consultants																				
Domestic Consultants																				
Fixed Price Contracts																				
Total by Month																				
Total by Quarter																				
Total Only																				

Figure 3-4. 1982 staffing plan.

tion requirements and production environment impact should be included.

- A definition of the remaining milestones to be completed for the major deliverable during the planning horizon. For business planning purposes, milestones are defined at the completion of the life cycle phases or other significant phases for each project. They should be accompanied by the estimated completion dates and completion costs of each milestone.

Department:_____   Date:_____

User:_____   Rev. No.____Page_____of_____

On-going Development

Major Deliverable Name

Description:

(Text)

Status:

(Text)

Production Environment Impact:

(Text)

Remaining Milestones: Name	Estimated Completion Date	Estimated Cost
Functional Analysis	Second Quarter '82	$121,200
Systems Design	First Quarter '83	$121,200
Implementation Phase I	Second Quarter '83	$ 66,000
Implementation Phase II	Fourth Quarter '83	$118,800

Appr. Funds:	$1,475,000	Planned First Quarter	$26,400	Planned YTD	$26,400
Cost to Date:	225,000	Actual First Quarter	25,500	Actual YTD	25,500
Bal. of Funds	$1,250,000	(Over)/Under Plan	$ 900	(Over)/Under Plan	$ 900

Figure 3-5. Project narratives.

For new projects added during the current quarter on which work has not yet begun, this section of the business plan should contain, for each user area, a description of the major systems or projects that are planned or in progress of the user area during the planning horizon. The description of the major projects should include:

- Purpose of the effort.
- Definition of milestones to be completed for the major projects during the planning horizon. For business planning purposes, milestones are defined as the completion of the life cycle phases or other significant phases for each project. They should be accompanied by estimated costs and completion dates of each milestone.

If a new project has been added since the last business plan was prepared, the project narrative should be submitted in the format of Figure 3–5.

THE REQUISITION ORIGIN STANDARDIZES HUMAN RESOURCE REQUIREMENTS

In order to standardize human resource requirements, the use of a job requisition form best serves the purpose. Figure 3–6 illustrates the DP hiring requisition form used by the line organization to transmit requirements for systems and programming personnel. In addition to the necessary information for general identification and approval, the skills system also allows for more specific information concerning the particular expertise needed and the corresponding levels of proficiency. This standardization aids the recruiting units in communicating exact needs to the employment marketplace. Chapter 5 will further elaborate on this process. The requirements form for consultant usage is nearly identical.

MOBILITY TAKES PRECEDENCE

At all times, the mobility of in-house deserving performers should always take precedence over hiring or the use of consultants. That is an important reality not to be ignored. The test of time has proven to us that the more and better career opportunities that an organi-

DEPARTMENT # _____

CORP. REQ. #   _____

Department:_____   Date Submitted: _____

Project Name:_____   Date Required: _____

Project Manager:_____   Position Title: _____

Area Manager:_____   Grade: _____
(Signatures required for all above)

Group Head:_____   Replacement of Consultant Yes_____ No_____
(If Applicable)

_____

Human Resource Advisor:_____
         Within Plan ☐
         Above Plan ☐
              (Explain) _____

_____

Skills List:
Identify the skills needed by assigning appropriate number (0–4) and either a D (desired) or R
(required) to the applicable skills.
         A) Level Explanations:
              LEVEL 0: HAS <u>NO KNOWLEDGE</u> OF SUBJECT MATTER
              LEVEL 1: HAS AN <u>AWARENESS</u> OF SUBJECT MATTER
              LEVEL 2: HAS HAD <u>MODERATE</u> USE OF SUBJECT MATTER
              LEVEL 3: HAS HAD <u>HEAVY</u> USE OF SUBJECT MATTER
              LEVEL 4: HAS <u>EXPERT</u> KNOWLEDGE OF SUBJECT MATTER

Operating systems (specify)	_____	Feasibility studies	_____
Programming language (specify)	_____	Functional Analysis	_____
JCL/PROCS	_____	Design specs	_____
Utilities	_____	Conversion/implementation	_____
Debugging	_____	Audits and controls	_____
On-line experience	_____	Documentation	_____
CICS	_____	User interface	_____
IMS	_____	Hardware (specify)	_____
Structured programming	_____	Other (specify)	_____

Figure 3-6.   DP hiring requisition form.

zation develops to demonstrate to its own staff that the system is
working for them, the better chance that employer will have to retain
them. Dr. Richard Nolan, of Nolan, Norton and Associates, estimates that the cost of losing a programmer analyst approximates

$25,000. The loss includes recruitment fees, the cost of training, lost productivity, etc.

The DP mobility process is perhaps one of the most elusive facts of life that an organization must confront and successfully do battle with. The competitive pulls of marketplace, the cultural and career path uncertainties of the employees in turbulent times and the required resources needed to make that process work are just a few of the roadblocks to a better organizational environment. Ours has been a process of continual testing and readjustment over the years. Our next chapter—"Obtaining Resources from Within"—will outline that evolution.

SUMMARY: COORDINATION OPTIMIZES PRICE/PERFORMANCE

The "view from above" must be a coordinated one. It should be a strategy that optimizes price/performance. It should be one that prevents misuse. It should demonstrate a rational management process to employees. It should be a strategy that freely provides additional skills-developing assignments to deserving performers for their unique efforts. That strategy should give to management meaningful information that definitively illustrates that the corporate personnel objectives are going the right way in terms of decreased turnover, increased hiring capability, increased mobility opportunities, decreased use of consultants and, finally, better cost/performance.

4

Obtaining Resources from Within

Providing a definitive employee skills inventory system paves the way for many creative opportunities for management to meaningfully reach out to its employees to motivate and reward them. No other method will provide a more subtle and yet positive effect to retaining deserving data processing (DP) performers than the successful implementation of a bonafide job mobility system. The job skills system provides a texture and fiber to an individual. It is also necessary for realistic job evaluation. Without that skills inventory update, management for the most part is operating in the dark. Using it, organizationwide mobility gains more credence and turnover drops dramatically.

During the last eight years, our human resources (HR) staffers have worked on methods of mobility. Enhancements are still added quarterly. It is our belief that no one can ever create the ideal HR system. That's because the changing needs of the organization itself dictate different strategies at different times.

When we were smaller and organized functionally—i.e., all systems and programming under one head—we created a "mobility draft system." Fashioned similarly to the NFL football draft, it was—and still is—designed to recognize outstanding performance. As we expanded and became more decentralized functionally, it became more difficult to execute the employee draft system. Thus, we switched to a freewheeling job posting system. This job mobility system has proven to have a wider-ranging impact because any deserving performer can utilize it.

The following sections describe each of these job mobility systems in detail. The procedures are reviewed, as are the pitfalls along the way. Experience dictates that an organization is better off with a job mobility system than without one. It helps to counteract the competitive forces from the marketplace which are continually snatching away good performers as the demand for computer specialists enlarges with each passing week.

HISTORY OF THE JOB MOBILITY SYSTEM

Providing DP employees a choice of alternate career opportunities within the organization began in 1974 after the system of skills inventory had been implemented. The HR strategy was to eliminate prior deficiencies in skills systems which resulted in nonuse or misuses of the systems. No longer would critically needed employees fail to see positive results because of their efforts and contributions.

A popular fallacy lay in management's feeble claims that the skill system would be used to select candidates for better jobs. It seldom was. Secondly, the systems were to be used for career planning. That never happened. The skills systems lay in disarray.

Our strategy was to create a living reality by selecting deserving candidates for challenging opportunities. We were offering them a reward—to choose or not—for their efforts. The mobility draft system was that vehicle. Conceptually, its origin was modeled after the National Football League annual college draft.

Its evolution from 1974 to 1980 was marked with experimentation and readjustment. In the mid-1970s, for example, we conducted draft meetings every two weeks, requiring all area managers to attend. At these meetings, the managers would have their requests processed and would also learn if one or more of their people had been drafted.

Managers were too embarrassed in public to refuse a draft request even though they had the option because of a critical project. So they no longer showed up. Understandably, we had to adjust the procedure to handle each job draft situation in private.

Thus, the mobility draft system would perfect itself over the years and serve well in providing challenging opportunities to deserving job performers. Managers would pay heightened attention to their good performers and make sure they were challenged and rewarded. Managers would also become reluctant to turn down an employee drafted because they realized the far-reaching implications of holding their staffers back.

In fact, toward the end of its formal use in 1980, more employees being drafted decided to remain with their present managers. At no time did a draft provide a promotion or money. It could not be given at the point of the draft. The offer served as a challenge. The new opportunity could lead to new career dimensions.

The next pages detail the job mobility draft system procedure in its refined form. The procedure is presented in an easily readable form and outlines all the necessary steps and considerations.

AN OVERVIEW OF THE MOBILITY DRAFT SYSTEM PROCEDURE

Objectives   The objectives of the mobility procedure are to:

- Ensure that open positions are filled with the most qualified staffers available in-house.
- Ensure that outside hiring is utilized only after all qualified in-house personnel are considered.
- Satisfy staffing needs as quickly as possible.
- Reduce employee turnover by offering good performers broadened career opportunities.
- Expand the opportunities for career development within the entire department.

Criteria   The following is a checklist to determine if a position can be filled through mobility:

- Does the required data processing or related expertise exist in-house?

Criteria
- Does the position offer a good opportunity for career development?
- If so, can the person selected become available within the timeframe required?

Documents   The mobility procedure uses the following documents:

- Job requisition form (see Figure 3–6)
- Employment synopsis (see Figure 4–1)
- Mobility release form (see Figure 4–2)

Name:_____   Project Manager:_____

Group Manager:_____

Area Manager:

Present Position:_____

Length of Time in Present Position:_____

Present Salary:_____

Last Salary Increase:_____

Last Performance Rating:_____

Last Potential Rating:_____

Date of Employment:_____

Years in DP:_____

Education:_____

Experience:_____

_____

_____

_____

_____

_____

_____

_____

_____

_____

_____

_____

Figure 4–1. Employment synopsis.

MOBILITY SUMMARY

Description The mobility procedure covers three types of mobility situations:

1) *Mobility draft procedure*, whereby resource planning selects, from all employees, deserving individuals who are qualified to fill a specific opening.

As of_____ ,_____ will be

transferred to Department _____ , to

the _____ Project.

List special circumstances, if any:

_____

_____

_____

_____

_____

_____

_____
Area Manager's Signature

Figure 4–2.   Mobility release form.

2) *Availability procedure*, whereby a deserving employee desires a move to a new position (individual request), or a manager feels his/her area cannot offer a deserving individual a challenging opportunity within a reasonable timeframe (area manager request). The individual's name is placed on resource planning's availability list.
3) *Availability due to budget adjustment*, whereby budget adjustments or reorganization require that an individual be moved to a new position. The individual's name is placed on resource planning's availability list.

The mobility draft procedure is the basis for all mobility. The availability procedure differs only in the method by which the employee enters the mobility system.

MOBILITY DRAFT PROCEDURE

Introduction   The following steps summarize the mobility draft procedure.

Procedures   *Step*   *Action*

1) Area manager submits job requisition to resource planning.

2) Resource planning and area manager discuss the position and determine that it can be filled through mobility.

3) Resource planning reviews its availability list and personnel files to select qualified individuals for the position and prepares an employment synopsis package on each. The requesting manager may also suggest individuals.

4) Resource planning presents employment synopsis package to requesting area manager for review. He/she may discuss them with the appropriate managers.

5) The requesting managers and resource planning mutually select the candidate to be interviewed.

6) Resource planning meets with candidate's area manager to discuss qualifications and availability.

7) Resource planning meets with candidate's group and project managers for up-to-date information about employee's performance to supply to the requesting manager.

Procedures	*Step*	*Action*

8) Candidate's current area manager, the requesting area manager and resource planning meet to complete the draft.

9) Project manager notifies candidate that he/she is being considered for a position.

10) Resource planning conducts initial interview with candidate to describe the mobility procedure and the open position.

11) Requesting project or group manager conducts management interview. Area manager may interview candidate.

12) Area manager decides whether or not to extend an offer. If not, return to Step 5.

13) If decision is to extend an offer, resource planning extends offer.

14) Candidate decides. If decision is *not* to accept offer, return to Step 5. If decision is to accept, resource planning discusses release date with candidate's current area manager and the requesting area manager. Current area manager signs mobility release form.

AVAILABILITY PROCEDURE: AREA MANAGER REQUEST

Introduction An area manager can place an individual in his/her area on the availability list when the area cannot offer a deserving individual a challenging career opportunity. Resource planning then investigates other areas within the department to determine if an appropriate opportunity exists for the individual.

Procedures	*Step*	*Action*

1) Area manager requests that resource planning investigate other areas within the department for an open position consistent with the goals of the individual.

2) Resource planning prepares an employment synopsis package on the individual.

3) Resource planning attempts to match the individual with an open position.

4) If none can be found, the individual remains in his/her present position. If one is found, resource planning presents the package to the requesting area manager for consideration.

5) If the individual is selected, the mobility draft procedure is followed, beginning with Step 9, notifying the candidate.

AVAILABILITY PROCEDURE: BUDGET ADJUSTMENT

Introduction   Shifts in manpower budgets within an area's budget plans may cause changes in project complements requiring an area manager to place individuals on the availability list.

Less frequently, budgets may be adjusted *after* budget plans are in place due to situations such as reorganization and postponement or cancellation of projects.

Such adjustments may also require that individuals be placed on the availability list.

Procedures   The steps taken in these instances are the same as discussed under "Availability Procedure: Area Manager Request."

Guidelines   Individuals placed in mobility for budgetary reasons are given *priority consideration* for openings in the department.
Individuals are *not* told that they are being considered for mobility until it is determined that suitable placement can occur.

AVAILABILITY PROCEDURE: INDIVIDUAL REQUEST

Introduction   An individual may want to initiate his/her own mobility.

Procedures   *Step*   *Action*

1) Individual discusses reasons for wanting to initiate mobility with project manager. This discussion *may* result in the individual deciding to remain in current position.

2) If the individual does not wish to remain in his/her current position, the project manager decides whether the individual is deserving of mobility. If the project manager feels the individual is *not* deserving, mobility is not allowed. If the employee does not agree with that decision, he/she may follow the standard grievance procedure described below.

Procedures	*Step*	*Action*

3) If the project manager feels the individual is deserving, the individual discusses his/her desires with the group manager, who may offer the person a more appropriate position in the group.

4) If a more appropriate position in the group is not available, the individual discusses his/her desires with the area manager, who can:
   - Offer the individual a better position within the area.
   - Place the individual's name on resource planning's availability list.

5) If the last action is taken, the individual is informed and resource planning meets with him/her to determine the employee's interest and goals. An employment synopsis package is prepared on that employee including a write-up of the information gathered at that meeting.

6) Resource planning attempts to match the individual with an open position. If none can be found, the individual remains in his/her current position.

7) If one is found, mobility draft procedure is followed, beginning with Step 11, the management interview.

Grievance Procedure

If an employee feels that his/her request for mobility was turned down unjustifiably by the project manager, that employee should discuss the situation with first the group manager and then the area manager. If the individual still does not agree with the decision, the problem may be discussed with the human resources department. In such cases, the human resources department investigates the situation, discussing the reasons for refusal with the managers. Human resources acts as a mediator to assist communication between the parties.

Company Mobility

If an employee desires mobility outside of data processing, he/she is sent to the personnel administrator of that employee's current department to discuss it. For more information on company mobility, contact with the personnel area of the human resources department is made.

DETAIL PAGES

Candidate Selection Procedure Criteria

Introduction

After it is determined that a position can be filled through employee mobility, resource planning reviews the job requisition to become thoroughly familiar with the job description and requirements before selecting candidates.

Sources

Resource planning selects candidates by reviewing the following:

- The availability list
- Summary of performance/potential ratings report
- Individual skills profiles
- Personnel files
- Suggestions from the requesting area manager.

Qualifications

To be considered for mobility leading into an open position, an employee must:

- Meet the skill requirements.
- Be at least a "fully adequate" performer who is deserving of the job opportunity.

Employment
Synopsis
Package

Resource planning prepares an employment synopsis package on each selected candidate. Significant documents such as resume, technical interview results, updated skills profile and performance reviews are included to create an inventory providing wide-ranging detailed information about the individual.

The employment synopsis form is a cover sheet which provides summary information on the employee's:

- Current position
- Current salary
- Performance and potential ratings
- Length of employment at the company
- Educational background
- Work history.

Candidate Review

Area Manager
Review

Resource planning presents selected employment synopsis packages to the requesting area manager for review. The qualifications of each candidate are discussed. Those found to be not qualified are eliminated.

Project/Group
Manager Review

If the area manager so desires, informational criteria about the selected candidates are then forwarded to the requesting project and group managers. The packages are again reviewed and qualifications are discussed.

Priority Choices

Resource planning and the requesting managers mutually agree upon priority choices—that is, the order in which the candidates are to be drafted.

Drafting the Candidate

Preparation   Resource planning meets with the candidate's area manager to verify that the candidate:

- Is qualified for the open position.
- Deserves the career opportunity.
- Can be made available within the required timeframe.

If Candidate is not Available   If the area manager feels he/she cannot release the individual within the required timeframe, the manager must explain why and inform resource planning when the employee can be considered for future mobility.

If Candidate is Available   If the area manager feels that the candidate can be released within the required timeframe, resource planning obtains the area manager's permission to speak to the current group and project managers about the candidate. Resource planning obtains a copy of the specific assignments outlined at the employee's last performance evaluation, and a summary of the individual's strengths and weaknesses and future assignments planned. This information is next included in the employment synopsis package.

Determining Interest   At this point, sufficient information has been compiled about the job candidate to enable the requesting manager to determine interest in drafting the individual.

It is critical that the requesting manager be strongly certain that he/she is interested in the candidate before actually speaking with him or her. The guideline to be followed here is that the manager be 90 percent certain of wanting the individual for the position. This keeps the number of interviews to a minimum and helps to eliminate undue disappointment on the part of the employee.

Initial Interview

Preparation The candidate is contacted by his/her project manager and informed of being considered for mobility. The candidate is next told to contact the resource planning manager to schedule an interview.

Objectives The objectives of the initial mobility interview are to:

- Inform the candidate about the mobility procedure.
- Briefly describe the open position.
- Provide the candidate the opportunity to decide whether or not to pursue it.

Next Step If the candidate decides to explore further discussions, resource planning arranges the management interview. If the candidate is not interested in the position, resource planning then begins processing the next candidate.

Management Interview

Introduction Because the requesting project/group manager has already reviewed significant information concerning the candidate, that executive can conduct a personal and in-depth interview. The area manager may attend this interview or conduct a separate one.

Objectives The objectives of the management interview are to:

- Obtain in-depth knowledge about the candidate's technical exposure, personal characteristics and professional attributes. That background will determine the employee's compatibility, dependability and potential contribution to the group and suitability for the position.
- Describe to the candidate the area, the project and the specific responsibilities of the position within the reporting structure and the career development opportunities the new position offers.

Area Manager's Interview   If the area manager did not attend the project/group manager interview, he/she may decide to interview the candidate at this time.

Completing the Mobility Procedure

Management Decision   The requesting area manager has the final responsibility to decide whether or not to extend an offer to the candidate. A decision not to extend an offer is rare in this procedure because the manager's interest in the candidate should have been firmly established before an interview takes place.

Notifying the Candidate   The area manager notifies resource planning of the decision. Resource planning then notifies the candidate.

Candidate Decision   If an offer has been made, the candidate is provided a maximum of one week (five business days) to consider the choice, and next notifies resource planning as soon as a decision has been reached.

Release Date   If the candidate accepts, resource planning provides a release date with the requesting area manager and the candidate's current area manager. The current area manager signs the mobility release form. That form lists the effective starting date and the new area and lists any special circumstances involved. If the candidate does not accept the offer, resource planning begins processing the next candidate.

Guidelines

Introduction   The following guidelines govern the mobility procedures described in this section.

Guideline 1   All communication with candidates regarding mobility must be through resource planning. Any manager or member of his/her team who speaks to a candidate before being authorized to do so, loses the right to make an offer to that individual.

Guideline 2   A candidate drafted by resource planning should be made available by the area manager if the position offers a better career opportunity. The decision as to whether the position offers a better opportunity must be arrived at mutually by resource planning and the area manager.

Guideline 3   If a challenging position opens up in the individual's area during the investigation process and *no* interviews have taken place, the area manager can withdraw the individual from mobility and offer him or her the new position. If a challenging position opens up in the area and an interview *has* taken place, the area manager cannot recall the individual. The new position is treated like any other position for which the individual is being considered (see Guideline 4).

Guideline 4　　A mobility candidate is presented with only one position at a time, regardless of the number of positions for which he/she is being considered. Resource planning determines the order of presentation depending on:

- The needs of the company
- The individual's qualifications
- The individual's desires.

Guideline 5　　Managers can interview only one candidate at a time for a particular position. A decision must be made on that candidate before another candidate may be seen for the position.

Guideline 6　　All decisions are final. A manager cannot reconsider a candidate he/she has turned down after seeing others. Once a candidate turns down an offer, he or she cannot reconsider after seeing what else is available.

RESOURCE PLANNING RESPONSIBILITIES

Description　　The responsibilities of resource planning in the mobility procedure are to:

- Determine which positions should be filled through mobility.
- Select appropriate candidates.
- Determine candidate's qualifications and availability.
- Prepare employment synopsis packages on selected individuals.
- Draft selected candidate.
- Conduct initial interview with candidate.
- Act as interface for all communication between requesting managers and candidate.
- Obtain release date for candidate.

- Maintain an availability list of employees who are eligible for mobility.

MANAGER'S RESPONSIBILITIES

Area Manager The requesting area manager's responsibilities in the mobility procedure are to:

- Evaluate staff needs and set priorities on open positions within the area.
- Submit job requisitions allowing sufficient lead time.
- Review employment synopsis packages to determine priority choices among candidates.
- Decide whether to draft the candidate.
- Optionally conduct interview with candidate.

The releasing (candidate's current) area manager's responsibilities are to:

- Discuss availability and qualifications with resource planning.
- Notify the individual that he/she has been drafted.
- Sign the mobility release form.

Project/Group Managers The requesting project/group managers' responsibilities in the mobility procedure are to:

- Notify area manager of staffing requirements.
- Complete job requisitions and present to area manager for approval.
- Review employment synopsis packages to supply priority choices to the area manager.
- Conduct management interview.

Project/Group Managers The releasing (candidate's current) project/group manager's responsibility is to:

- Discuss candidate's recent performance and personal attributes with resource planning.

DOCUMENT SUMMARY

Introduction   This page provides a checklist of the documents used in the mobility procedure.

Summary

DOCUMENT	PURPOSE	COMPLETED BY	AUTHORIZATION
Job requisition form	Inform resource planning of staffing requirement	Project manager	Area manager department head
Employment synopsis form	Summarize employee's • Work history • Performance • Appraisals • Qualifications to enable manager to determine interest in individual	Resource planning	N/A
Mobility release form	Inform personnel, both releasing and requesting area managers and, if move is interdepartmental, both department heads	Resource planning	Releasing area manager

HISTORY OF THE JOB POSTING SYSTEM

The job posting program made its career path debut as the direct result of a 1979 attitude survey that indicated the then current mobility system was somewhat limited and ineffective. The conclusion was understandable: Our organization had evolved from a basically functionally divided unit. This meant that systems and programming functioned as one group, computer operations as another, technical support as a third, etc. The separate functions created uncoordinated work flows and stoppages if any one of those functional areas experienced shutdowns or central computer unit difficulties. In order to better serve the data processing users for the 1980s, vertically integrated operation centers (VIOC) were formed. All profit centers and line departments would have their own contingent of systems and programming personnel, operations manpower and computer and technical support. Multiple VIOC centers were created. However, there would be only one central human resource group to service these new VIOC market segmented groups.

As a result of the VIOC reorganizations, the functioning of the draft system became more cumbersome when applied to separately organized groups. For example, dealing with five separate systems and programming groups—all reporting through different lines in the organization—became highly difficult to administer. It also did not reach enough people. A task force was then created to resolve the issues and concerns which had surfaced in the survey. This new mobility task force—consisting of project and group managers from all vertically integrated data centers—set objectives, discussed alternatives, presented strategies and mutually decided on a job posting program.

OVERVIEW

Objective: The objectives of the 1980s job posting procedure are to:

- Offer challenging jobs to all deserving staff members.
- Develop staff through job experiences and reward achievers with wider job opportunities.
- Allow staff members to openly explore other areas (as a viable alternative to leaving the company).
- Provide opportunities to eligible and qualified staff members before utilizing external labor marketplace sources.
- Improve employee morale by encouraging staff

	Senior Programmer Analyst-Grade 21
POSITION I.D.	POSITION TITLE — GRADE

HARDWARE ___4341___ LANGUAGE(S):___Cobol___ SYSTEM SOFTWARE:DOS/VSE

_____CICS_____

PREREQUISITE SKILLS

The candidate should have heavy Cobol programming in an on-line CICS

environment experience along with significant knowledge of JCL, utilities

and debugging techniques. The candidate should also have systems development

skills on large scale systems including feasibility studies, functional

specifications, design test and implementation specifications with user

interface.

JOB RESPONSIBILITIES

The candidate will be responsible for portions of the design and development

of the FEC (message switching) project phases. An understanding of all of

the FEC project and a contribution to the total design effort at all levels

is also part of this position.

CAREER OPPORTUNITIES

Career paths to officer can be achieved either up the technical ladder

or up the management ladder. The only limitation resides within the

candidate himself.

Figure 4-3.   Job posting description.

EMPLOYEE NAME   TITLE   DEPT NO.   TELEPHONE NO.

CURRENT PROJECT   POSTED POSITION I.D. NO.

CURRENT PROJECT RESPONSIBILITIES: LIST THE MAJOR TASKS THAT YOU
HAVE BEEN PERFORMING ON YOUR PROJECT FOR THE LAST 6 MONTHS.

_____

_____

_____

_____

_____

CURRENT SKILLS APPLICABLE TO POSTED POSITION: LIST THE SKILLS YOU
CURRENTLY POSSESS THAT ARE NECESSARY IN THE POSITION YOU ARE APPLYING FOR
AND BRIEFLY EXPLAIN THE TASKS YOU DO USING THIS SKILL.

_____

_____

_____

_____

_____

OTHER CURRENT SKILLS.   LIST ANY OTHER SKILLS YOU HAVE THAT SHOULD BE
CONSIDERED IN YOUR APPLICATION FOR THE POSITION.

_____

_____

_____

_____

EMPLOYEE'S SIGNATURE   H.R. ADVISOR'S SIGNATURE   DATE

Figure 4-4.   Work history sheet for job posting.

APPLICANT: _____

RELEASE DATE: _____

     <u>GUIDELINE</u>: MAXIMUM OF 6 WEEKS (NON - OFFICIAL) OR 8 WEEKS (OFFICIAL)
          FROM THE ACCEPTANCE DATE OF _____

TRANSFER FROM: _____ _____
               DEPARTMENT NUMBER   PROJECT

TRANSFER TO: _____ _____
              DEPARTMENT NUMBER   PROJECT

LIST SPECIAL CIRCUMSTANCES, IF ANY:

_____

_____

_____

_____

_____

_____

                               _____
                               DEPARTMENT HEAD SIGNATURE

CC:

Figure 4–4.   Continued

JOB POSTING SUMMARY CHART*

GRADE	TITLE	IMS	CICS	DOS/VSE	NEAT 3 VRX	PDP-11 PASCAL	DEC 20 PDP-11	DATA COMM.	VOICE SYSTEMS	TRUST & SECURITIES SYSTEMS	CORPORATE SYSTEMS	WHOLESALE SYSTEMS	RETAIL SYSTEMS	CORPORATE DATA CENTER
		TYPE OF PROJECT** (OTHER THAN IBM BATCH)								VIDC				
21	Senior Systems Analyst	5	9							1	1	9		1
21	Senior Programmer Analyst	4	7	2		1					4	8		
21	Senior Systems Engineer		3	3							1	1		4
18	Systems Analyst		2									2		
18	Programmer Analyst	2	2		1						2	1	1	
18	Systems Engineer													
16	Senior Programmer	4	4		1	1	1				2	5	1	1
14	Programmer	2	2								1	2		
23	Systems Specialist	2	2									2		
	Human Resource Advisor													
21	Telecommunications Project Manager								1		1			
21	Senior Telecommunications Specialist								3		3			
21	Senior Telecommunications Engineer							1			1			
16	Section Head						1				1			
14	Junior Telecommunications Analyst								1		1			
14	Associate Writer										1			
10	Computer Operator Level I						1				1			
10	Operator Technician Level I			1									1	
8	Operations Associate						1				1			
8	Tape Librarian												1	
8	Senior Key to Disk Operator										1			

*Please see reverse side for job posting package information.
**Some projects utilize more than one skill, e.g., A combination of IMS and CICS.

Figure 4–5.

APPLICANT: _____

RELEASE DATE: _____

GUIDELINE: MAXIMUM OF 6 WEEKS (NON - OFFICIAL) OR 8 WEEKS (OFFICIAL)
FROM THE ACCEPTANCE DATE OF _____

TRANSFER FROM: _____   _____
                DEPARTMENT NUMBER   PROJECT

TRANSFER TO: _____   _____
               DEPARTMENT NUMBER   PROJECT

LIST SPECIAL CIRCUMSTANCES. IF ANY:

_____

_____

_____

_____

_____

_____

_____
DEPARTMENT HEAD SIGNATURE

CC:

Figure 4–6.   Job posting release form.

members to become actively involved in their own career development.

Documents: The job posting procedure uses the following documents.

- Job posting description (see Figure 4–3)
- Work history sheet for job posting (see Figure 4–4)
- Job posting summary chart (see Figure 4–5)
- Job posting release form (see Figure 4–6)

JOB POSTING PROCEDURE

Introduction: The following steps summarize the job posting procedure.

Procedures   *Step*   *Action*

1) Area manager fills out the hiring job requisition form requesting job posting visibility.

2) Job listings are included with payroll statements.

3) Employees interested in applying for positions fill out a brief work history sheet; the document is obtained from their human resources advisor.

4) Applicants call their human resources advisor for an appointment to further discuss the position(s) in which they are interested.

5) Applicants, although encouraged to discuss their application with current managers, are not required to inform their managers at this time.

6) The advisor next reviews the work history sheet and compares the document's contents to the job requirement for the position(s) in which the applicant has expressed interest.

Procedures	*Step*	*Action*

7) The advisor coordinates the interview procedures and discusses results of the work history review with the applicant during the appointment.

8) If the applicant is not found qualified for the posted position, applicant and advisor review other positions for which the applicant is currently qualified. Next, the additional training alternatives are discussed so that the applicant may gain the necessary skills he or she is lacking so that the applicant may become qualified for similar future positions in the company.

9) If the applicant is determined qualified for the position, the advisor attaches the applicant's last two performance appraisals to the work history sheet and presents this job posting package to the requisitioning manager.

10) Although not required, an applicant may at this time wish to speak with his or her current manager to determine if the individual's career goals can be achieved on the applicant's current project.

11) Within three business days of receipt of the job posting package, the requisitioning manager must decide whether or not to interview an applicant presented by the advisor.

12) The requisitioning manager next contacts the advisor to schedule interview(s) or to discuss alternatives if the applicant is not to be interviewed.

Procedures	*Step*	*Action*

13) Applicants can apply for a maximum of three positions at one time and await those results.

14) The requisitioning manager must next inform his/her human resources advisor of what has been decided regarding each respective applicant within five business days after the interview.

15) If a manager rejects an applicant, exact reasons must be submitted to the advisor, enabling applicants to be advised of the results. Reasons for the rejection should reflect the manager's fair appraisal of the applicant's skills and qualifications for the vacant position.

16) The advisor contacts all rejected applicants and notifies them of the manager's decision. Job alternatives are also discussed.

17) The human resources advisor next contacts the accepted applicant and extends an offer.

18) If the respective applicant is seriously considering the new position acceptance, the staffer must inform his/her current manager of the offer before making a final decision. This step provides an additional opportunity for the employee to discuss the career opportunities of the present position (if this was not previously done).

19) The applicant has five business days to accept or reject the offered position—and to inform his/her manager and advisor of the decision that has been made.

Procedures   *Step*   *Action*

---

20) The advisor next notifies the requisitioning man-
    ager of the decision.

---

21) If the applicant accepts, the advisor contacts that
    applicant's current manager to arrange a trans-
    fer release date. The release date guideline is a
    maximum of six weeks from the date the advisor
    is informed of the applicant's acceptance of the
    offered position.

5

Obtaining Resources in the Competitive Marketplace

Even with a strong in-house human resources acquisition mechanism, not all manpower needs can be realistically met. Turnover itself dictates a shortfall. Increased user demands for additional skilled manpower and the outside world job-hopping pressures must come into play. It's not a crime to recruit externally. In a way, an organization strengthens itself by attracting people from the competitive marketplace. Those newcomers bring fresh ideas to the organization and can prevent their employees from becoming too ingrained.

There are critics who charge that bringing in people from the outside—with their accompanying wealth of fresh ideas and technological knowledge—disrupts the career ladder growth from within.

The critics charge that a newcomer's presence—regardless of technological skills inventory—may demoralize existing departmental staffers. Feeling that they've been effectively "passed over," these employees may jump ship to other organizations.

If the existing manpower/expertise does exist within the organization—but managers still go outside their company to bring in someone to fill the position that could have easily been advanced from within—there is validation to the critics charges. However, if outside recruiting is used to speed up and infuse new technologies into the respective organization—rather than starting the long and cumbersome process to re-invent the latest "state-of-the-art" wheel—the decision to bring in fresh resources becomes a good one.

Here's an example that took place recently in the face of repeated technological breakthroughs as they impacted one data processing

(DP)-based organization conducting business in a highly competitive field.

The organization had positioned its marketing strategy to use private companies to supply its communications needs. The private companies—realizing they were the organization's key communications suppliers—kept raising their prices each year. The increases—added on to the organization's already increased overhead—were now limiting its ability to remain competitive. The new management team in charge of implementing the new communications strategy had two choices. The first alternative was to start from scratch and sent its cadre off to school for a year or more to learn the latest state-of-the-art technologies. Later, that same cadre would then have to undergo additional and extensive "on-the-job" experience—probably coupled with many "hit and miss" results—that would still place that team at least 18 to 24 months behind schedule.

The second and fastest strategy—the recruiting of fresh talent and fresh ideas from the outside—would produce the fastest on-line results simply by coming aboard. In the case of the decision to go in-house with communications needs—rather than relying on outside vendors—this organization made the decision to hire fresh and tested talent. There were some minor disruptions caused by the appearance of the highly skilled outsiders but the resultant dividends—increased competitiveness, infusion of the latest "state-of-the-art" technologies and reduced operating costs—allowed that organization to push deeper into newer markets for new profit revenues.

The decision to recruit externally paid off handsomely for all concerned.

However many advantages result from competitive marketplace recruiting, it should be made clear that managers must attempt to fill higher level openings by promoting from within. DP management continuity is of vital importance. Always ensure that managers are promoted from within. Only when no alternative exists should a managerial position be filled from the outside competitive marketplace.

The following sections will detail many of the considerations in the worlds of hiring and consulting: First, in hiring experienced and entry-level personnel to fill permanent positions and, next, in contracting with consulting firms to fill temporary positions because of a temporary shortfall of permanent positions, maintenance duties and non-challenging tasks and, finally, hard-to-find, leading edge skills.

Understand that the principle enumerated in Chapter 3—namely, having both areas under a single control—is essential. Without a single control, the disjointed, independent dealing of separate groups will produce and result in undesirable cost/performance paybacks.

A HISTORY OF HIRING PROCEDURES
FOR DP MANPOWER

The hiring of both entry-level and experienced DP personnel has been accomplished in a coordinated manner since 1972. Previous to the start-up of the specialized recruiting team consisting of highly trained DP specialists to interview, screen and process all applicants with computer backgrounds, the assignment was formerly conducted by corporate personnel. DP hiring was then taking place in a non-co-ordinated manner.

Corporate personnel—already entrusted with the key mission of fulfilling the entire organization's manpower needs by providing a steady new supply of high-calibre job applicants—began realizing that DP recruiting was a more specialized assignment.

Observers point out that most recruiters—who do not have a DP background—are at a disadvantage because they are not able to grasp the intricate DP employment requirements.

Understanding the needs of the DP user community means knowing the difference between "hardware" and "software"—and then being able to understand the differences and advantages of the many different computer languages. Those languages are sometimes more difficult to learn than many foreign languages, it has been reported.

Thus, for corporate personnel to maintain 100 percent DP recruiting effectiveness to keep up with the mushrooming computer-based user area it was now servicing, this also meant that it had to train all of its employees in the respective computer languages and systems capabilities. But "one-shot" computer classroom instruction would not suffice, because it was also discovered that the company would have to keep sending its recruiters to additional DP classes every six months—or even more frequently—just to keep up with the constantly changing DP breakthroughs.

The subsequent decision to form a human resources recruiting area for the organization's growing DP needs meant that corporate personnel was now free to handle other specialized areas. At the same time, the in-house user community now expressed high admiration for the "direct action" results provided by the formation of the DP recruiting strategy.

The new human resources orientation meant that DP managers were now being serviced by computer/recruiting specialists who understood the needs of the DP community and spoke the specialized jargon of the highly technical computer languages.

The following provides a step-by-step guide explaining how the new DP hiring procedure was implemented. For experienced computer personnel, a dedicated group of professional DP recruiters works under the direction of the manager of resource planning as part of the Human Resource area that reports to the head of DP activities. For entry-level personnel, corporate recruiters screen applicants from within the company and from the competitive marketplace. The results-oriented DP recruiting staff has grown over the years from a single person function to a DP recruiting department of eight full-time people.

During this entire time, the recruiters have initiated and controlled the complete process from dealing with the managers in determining the candidate requirements through contacting the employment agencies and also processing the applicants.

OVERVIEW: HOW TO IMPLEMENT HIRING PROCEDURE OBJECTIVES

Objectives that Must be Adhered to at All Times

The objectives of the hiring procedure are to:

- Fill hiring requests as quickly as possible with the most qualified individual at the most reasonable cost.
- Provide effective screening of resumes and applicants.
- Provide in-depth technical evaluation of applicants.
- Supply managers with accurate and comprehensive documentation regarding an applicant's background.
- Provide management interviews that will determine growth potential, personality traits and value to the department.

- Assure that qualified applicants are considered for positions not just within a project, but throughout the entire department.
- Impress qualified applicants with organization's effective and thorough interviewing procedure, and department's strengths and company benefits.

Criteria
Requirements

The criteria for determining if the position should be filled through hiring are:

- Is employee mobility inappropriate or not feasible?
- Is the expertise required available in the market?

Documents

This procedure uses the following documents:

- Job requisition form (see Figure 5–1)
- Employment application (see Figure 5–2)
- Applicant resume (see Figure 5–3)
- Skills expertise evaluation (see Figure 5–4)
- Technical interview form (see Figure 5–5)
- Management interview form (see Figure 5–6)
- Salary offer form (see Figure 5–7)

A GUIDE TO HIRING PROCEDURES ACTIONS

Introduction   The following time-tested steps summarize the complete hiring procedure.

Procedures	*Step*	*Action*
	1)	Area manager submits job requisition to human resources advisor.

DEPARTMENT # _____

CORP. REQ. #   _____

Department:_____   Date Submitted: _____

Project Name:_____   Date Required: _____

Project Manager:_____   Position Title: _____

Area Manager:_____   Grade: _____
(Signatures required for all above)

Group Head:_____   Replacement of Consultant Yes_____ No_____
(If Applicable)

Human Resource Advisor:_____
        Within Plan ☐
        Above Plan ☐
           (Explain) _____

Skills List:
Identify the skills needed by assigning appropriate number (0-4) and either a D (desired) or R (required) to the applicable skills.
    A) Level Explanations:
        LEVEL 0: HAS <u>NO KNOWLEDGE</u> OF SUBJECT MATTER
        LEVEL 1: HAS AN <u>AWARENESS</u> OF SUBJECT MATTER
        LEVEL 2: HAS HAD <u>MODERATE</u> USE OF SUBJECT MATTER
        LEVEL 3: HAS HAD <u>HEAVY</u> USE OF SUBJECT MATTER
        LEVEL 4: HAS <u>EXPERT</u> KNOWLEDGE OF SUBJECT MATTER

Operating systems (specify)	_____	Feasibility studies	_____
Programming language (specify)	_____	Functional Analysis	_____
JCL/PROCS	_____	Design specs	_____
Utilities	_____	Conversion/implementation	_____
Debugging	_____	Audits and controls	_____
On-line experience	_____	Documentation	_____
CICS	_____	User interface	_____
IMS	_____	Hardware (specify)	_____
Structured programming	_____	Other (specify)	_____

Figure 5-1.   DP hiring requisition form.

PLEASE PRINT AND
COMPLETE THIS SIDE ONLY

EMPLOYMENT APPLICATION

LAST NAME		FIRST		MIDDLE		TELEPHONE NUMBER	
ADDRESS NUMBER AND STREET			CITY		STATE		ZIP CODE

| SOCIAL SECURITY NO. | DATE OF BIRTH | THE STATE LAW AND FEDERAL LAW PROHIBIT DISCRIMINATION BECAUSE OF AGE OR SEX. INQUIRIES AS TO AGE AND SEX ARE FOR RECORD PURPOSES ONLY | |

| ☐ MALE ☐ FEMALE | HEIGHT FT INS. | WEIGHT LBS. | HAVE YOU BEEN ILL FOR TWO WEEKS OR MORE IN THE LAST FIVE YEARS? ☐ YES ☐ NO | ARE YOU A U.S. CITIZEN? ☐ YES ☐ NO OR PERMANENT RESIDENT? ☐ YES ☐ NO ALIEN REGISTRATION CARD NUMBER DATE OF ENTF |

Have you ever been convicted of any of the following crimes: larceny, embezzlement, drawing or passing bad checks; forgery; or other similar crime involving a breach of trust or the unlawful taking or withholding of property belonging to another, or is there now pending against you any criminal proceeding for such a violation? (If you have, please answer 'Yes' regardless of the degree of the crime or its technical legal name.)
NO PERSON WILL BE REFUSED EMPLOYMENT OR DISCHARGED FROM EMPLOYMENT OR PENALIZED IN ANY OTHER WAY SOLELY BECAUSE OF AN ARREST DISCLOSED IN ANSWER TO THIS QUESTION.
Yes ☐   No ☐
If your answer to the preceding question was 'yes', please identify the crime and in your own words explain all the circumstances on a separate piece of paper.

HAVE YOU APPLIED FOR A POSITION WITH THIS COMPANY BEFORE?
☐ YES   ☐ NO   IF YES, WHEN MO _____ YR _____

POSITION OR TYPE OF WORK DESIRED	SALARY DESIRED	RELATIVES IN OUR EMPLOY: (If yes, give nar and relation)
LIST ALL BUSINESS MACHINES YOU CAN OPERATE		MANNER OF INTRODUCTION

EMPLOYMENT AND/OR U.S. MILITARY EXPERIENCE

DATE FROM	TO	NAME AND ADDRESS OF PREVIOUS EMPLOYERS AND/OR BRANCH OF U.S. MILITARY SERVICE				POSITION OR RANK	SALARY	REASON FOR LEAVING OI TYPE OF DISCHAR
		NAME						
		ADDRESS	CITY	STATE	ZIP			
		NAME						
		ADDRESS	CITY	STATE	ZIP			
		NAME						
		ADDRESS	CITY	STATE	ZIP			
		NAME						
		ADDRESS	CITY	STATE	ZIP			

EDUCATION

	FROM	TO	NAME OF SCHOOL	ADDRESS	DID YOU GRADUATE?	DEGREE OR COURSE OF STU
HIGH SCHOOL						
COLLEGE						
GRADUATE SCHOOL						
(OTHER INCLUDES SPEC. U.S. MILITARY TRAINING)						

IF EMPLOYED, REFERENCES WILL BE CHECKED CAREFULLY. GIVING FALSE INFORMATION ON THIS FORM WILL BE CONSIDERED GROUNDS FOR DISMISSAL.

DATE	SIGNATURE	INTERVIEWED BY

120

Figure 5-2.

John A. Plicant
835 E. 24th Street
New York, New York 10999

OBJECTIVE: To obtain a position in a progressive environment so that I could utilize and expand my technical skills, preferably including work with CICS on-line systems.

HARDWARE: IBM 3033, 370/158

SOFTWARE: OS/MVS, TSO/SPF, OS/Utilities, ISAM, VASAM
LANGUAGE: Cobol
EXPERIENCE: MAJOR INSURANCE COMPANY
Programmer/Analyst

8/79 to
Present   Designed, programmed, tested and implemented major enhancements to the Corporate Billing System. This IMS system supports billing by processing policy holder information, dates, etc. The system also interfaces with several statistical systems in the accounting department to further serve as a data base of financial information. My specific responsibilities were to design through implementation policy holders' flexible payment schedule. This included interfacing with both the Billing and Accounting Departments, modifications to, IMS Data Base (creating new segments, deletions), business and detail programming specifications and supervising two programmer/analysts.

Other duties included on-going maintenance to Billing System, design, coding, and implementing rates for homeowners' policies including new business.

EDUCATION: Brooklyn College, B.S.—Accounting
Grumman Data Systems—Certificate of Programming

REFERENCES: Furnished upon request.

Figure 5-3.   Applicant resume.

CANDIDATE'S NAME _____ DATE _____

SKILLS EXPERTISE

To better enable us to develop a comprehensive picture of "you" as a person, we would appreciate your assistance in determining your specific technical and analytical qualifications. The attached list contains certain skills which we consider necessary components of the data processing profession. Of course, not all skills listed apply to all job categories in this field.

Immediately below we have divided the full range of exposure to a subject matter into five general levels. Preceding each skill listed is a blank line on which to write the level number that best suits your experience.

LEVEL EXPLANATIONS:

Level 0:   Has <u>no</u> knowledge of subject matter
Level 1:   Has an <u>awareness</u> of subject matter
Level 2:   Has had <u>moderate</u> use of subject matter
Level 3:   Has had <u>heavy</u> use of subject matter
Level 4:   Has <u>expert</u> knowledge of subject matter

(Note: If a skill has not been utilized recently, indicate the highest level attained in the past and write a "P" after the level number.)

Figure 5–4.   Skills Expertise Evaluation.

SKILLS: TECHNICAL

_____ OS Concepts/Data Management

_____ Cobol

_____ BAL

_____ JCL/Procs

_____ Utilities

_____ Debugging

_____ On-line Experience

_____ CICS

_____ Structured Programming

_____ I/O Subsystems

    _____ COM

    _____ KODAK

    _____ MICR

    _____ Other   (Please indicate _____)

_____ Other Knowledge

    _____ TSO

    _____ CRJE

    _____ ASP

    _____ Non-IBM Hardware/Mini-computers

Figure 5–4.   (Part 2)

SKILLS: SYSTEMS

_____ Feasibility Studies

_____ Functional Analysis/Specifications

_____ Design Specifications

_____ On-line Design

_____ Conversion/Implementation

_____ Audits and Controls

_____ Written Communications/Documentation

_____ Oral Communications/User Interface

_____ CICS

_____ IMS

_____ Other Knowledge

    _____ Microfilm

    _____ Project Control

    _____ PERT

    _____ _____

    _____ _____

    _____ _____

    _____ _____

After reading the description of each of the five job categories explained in the following paragraphs, please indicate below the one which best corresponds with your personal experience.

_____   _____
     Job Category   Candidate's Signature

Figure 5-4.   (Part 3)

MANUFACTURERS HANOVER TRUST

JOB DESCRIPTIONS

SENIOR PROGRAMMER

A candidate should have the capabilities normally equated with three to five years of programming experience on new or current systems. This experience should include a good working knowledge of program design techniques (i.e., accomplishing the design through implementation of straightforward computer programs from general specifications and accomplishing the coding through implementation of complex programs from detailed specifications), standards and conventions of corporate systems and programming applications. Software experience should include Cobol or BAL and a good working knowledge of OS, JCL, and debugging techniques.

PROGRAMMER ANALYST

A candidate should have the capabilities normally equated with four and one half to seven years experience in programming with some systems design and maintenance. This experience should include the writing of both general and detailed program design specifications, coding, testing, documentation and implementation of complex computer programs. Other responsibilities include troubleshooting and debugging unusual problems and assisting in detailed systems design and feasibility studies. Software experience should include Cobol or BAL, and a good working knowledge of OS. The ability to communicate effectively both verbally and in writing is needed.

SYSTEMS ANALYST

A candidate should have the capabilities normally equated with four and one half to seven years experience in programming with some design and maintenance and a good working knowledge of OS. Software experience should include Cobol or BAL exposure in a multi-programming environment. A candidate should be familiar with the techniques of systems analysis, systems parallel, file design and data access techniques and with documentation standards and techniques. A candidate should be familiar with the scope of the entire project in order to coordinate the programming functions of writing, testing, debugging and documenting, to develop procedures for audits and controls, backup and recovery and restart and recovery, and to generally assist in the timing, coordination and execution of the design, development and installation of projects and the training of users. The ability to communicate effectively both verbally and in writing with all levels of personnel is necessary.

Figure 5–4.   (Part 4)

SENIOR PROGRAMMER ANALYST

A candidate should have the capabilities normally equated with six and one half to ten years of systems and programming experience with a minimum of two years in the design, implementation and maintenance of complex computer systems utilizing state-of-the-art design and programming techniques. Software experience should include Cobol or BAL, and comprehensive knowledge of OS. A senior programmer analyst is responsible for the technical support of programming personnel and projects. Therefore, a candidate should be able to accomplish or coordinate the program design, coding, testing, documentation and implementation of complex computer programs, to supply technical data as pertains to the total system design and to assist in the evaluation of new technical developments as they pertain to systems and programming activities. A candidate should also be able to assist in conducting feasibility and cost studies, in developing detailed system design, in preparing documentation of the system being installed, in generating specifications for program and systems test data and in on-the-job training of programming personnel and user department personnel. The ability to communicate effectively

SENIOR SYSTEMS ANALYST

A candidate should have the capabilities normally equated with six and one half to ten years of systems or programming experience with a minimum of two years in the design and implementation of complex computer systems utilizing state-of-the-art systems design techniques. Software experience should include Cobol or BAL in a multi-programming environment, and comprehensive knowledge of OS. A candidate should have a good working knowledge of the techniques of systems analysis (e.g., feasibility reports, cost benefit evaluations, time studies, etc.) in order to most effectively design, modify and analyze complex systems and develop detailed systems specifications. A candidate should have a good working knowledge of file design and data base techniques, as well as systems parallel and acceptance-testing procedures. Candidates should be familiar with principles of accounting and auditing to enable effective design of audit trails and controls, backup and recovery and restart and recovery procedures. A candidate must also learn the scope of the entire project, as well as having education in project management and supervisory techniques in order to assist in the timing, coordination and execution of the design, development and installation of projects, to coordinate programming functions from program design through implementation, to provide on-the-job training in analysis and design, to train user department personnel and to perform evaluations of the applicability of new technical developments as they pertain to systems and programming activities.The ability to interact and communicate effectively both verbally and in writing with all levels of personnel is necessary.

Figure 5–4.   (Part 5)

TECHNICAL INTERVIEW FORM

Applicant Name _____   Team Members _____

_____   _____

Date _____   _____

EXPLANATION OF LEVEL NUMBERS
    LEVEL 0: Has <u>no</u> knowledge of subject
    LEVEL 1: Has an <u>awareness</u> of subject
    LEVEL 2: Equivalent knowledge of someone with <u>moderate</u> use of subject matter
    LEVEL 3: Equivalent knowledge of someone with <u>heavy</u> use of subject matter
    LEVEL 4: <u>Expert</u> knowledge of subject matter

SUBJECT

O/S CONCEPTS/DATA MANAGEMENT   RATING
Knowledge of: LEVEL_____
    Insufficient knowledge of:

COBOL   LEVEL_____
Knowledge of: Insufficient knowledge of:

BAL   LEVEL_____
Knowledge of: Insufficient knowledge of:

JCL/PROCS   LEVEL_____
Knowledge of: Insufficient knowledge of:

Figure 5-5.   Technical Interview Form. (Part 1)

(2)

UTILITIES   LEVEL_____
Knowledge of: Insufficient knowledge of:

_____   _____
_____   _____
_____   _____
_____   _____

DEBUGGING   LEVEL_____
Knowledge of: Insufficient knowledge of:

_____   _____
_____   _____
_____   _____
_____   _____

ON–LINE EXPERIENCE   LEVEL_____
Knowledge of: Insufficient knowledge of:

_____   _____
_____   _____
_____   _____
_____   _____

CICS   LEVEL_____
Knowledge of: Insufficient knowledge of:

_____   _____
_____   _____
_____   _____
_____   _____

STRUCTURED PROGRAMMING
Indicate Depth of Experience

_____
_____
_____
_____

I/O SUBSYSTEM (i.e., COM, KODAK, MICR, etc.)
Indicate Depth of Experience

_____
_____
_____
_____

Figure 5-5.   (Part 2)

(3)

OTHER KNOWLEDGE: (i.e., TSO, CRJE, ASP, NON–IBM HARDWARE/MINI–
COMPUTERS, ETC.)
Indicate Depth of Experience

_____
_____
_____
_____

FEASIBILITY STUDIES   LEVEL_____
Knowledge of: Insufficient knowledge of:
_____   _____
_____   _____
_____   _____
_____   _____

FUNCTIONAL ANALYSIS/SPECIFICATIONS   LEVEL_____
Knowledge of: Insufficient knowledge of:
_____   _____
_____   _____
_____   _____
_____   _____

DESIGN SPECIFICATIONS   LEVEL_____
Knowledge of: Insufficient knowledge of:
_____   _____
_____   _____
_____   _____
_____   _____

ON–LINE DESIGN   LEVEL_____
Knowledge of: Insufficient knowledge of:
_____   _____
_____   _____
_____   _____
_____   _____

CONVERSION/IMPLEMENTATION   LEVEL_____
Knowledge of: Insufficient knowledge of:
_____   _____
_____   _____
_____   _____
_____   _____

Figure 5–5.   (Part 3)

(4)

AUDITS AND CONTROLS
Knowledge of:

_____

_____

_____

_____

LEVEL _____
Insufficient knowledge of:

_____

_____

_____

WRITTEN COMMUNICATIONS/
DOCUMENTATION
Knowledge of:

_____

_____

_____

_____

LEVEL _____
Insufficient knowledge of:

_____

_____

_____

ORAL COMMUNICATIONS/USER
INTERFACE
Knowledge of:

_____

_____

_____

_____

LEVEL _____
Insufficient knowledge of:

_____

_____

_____

CICS
Knowledge of:

_____

_____

_____

_____

LEVEL _____
Insufficient knowledge of:

_____

_____

_____

IMS
Indicate Depth of Experience

_____

_____

_____

_____

_____

_____

_____

OTHER KNOWLEDGE: (i.e., MICROFILM, PROJECT CONTROL, PERT, ETC.)
Indicate Depth of Experience

_____

_____

_____

_____

_____

_____

_____

_____

Figure 5-5.   (Part 4)

(5)

SUMMARY

RECOMMENDED ☐   NOT RECOMMENDED ☐

for position as:

☐ Programmer

☐ Senior Programmer

☐ Programmer/Analyst

☐ System Analyst

☐ Senior Programmer/Analyst

☐ Senior System Analyst

☐ Other_____

REMARKS: Briefly explain your decision (include both technical and personal impressions.)

_____
_____
_____
_____
_____
_____
_____
_____
_____
_____
_____
_____
_____
_____
_____

Figure 5-5.   (Part 5)

Applicant Name _____   Interviewed by: _____

Position _____   Project Manager _____

Project _____   Date _____

I.   How do the individual's technical and/or systems skills meet the requirements of your Job Requisition? _____
_____
_____
_____

II. How does the individual's experience (i.e., supervisory, applications, trouble shooting, etc.) meet the requirements of your Job Requisition? _____
_____
_____
_____

III. What personality traits (positive or negative) does the individual possess that will affect his career at the bank? _____
_____
_____
_____

IV. Results:

☐   Recommended for this position at a suggested salary of _____

☐   Recommended for a position with department

☐   Not recommended for a position within department

Please explain your decision.
_____
_____
_____

_____
Project Manager's Signature

V.   I have discussed with the project manager the evaluations detailed above and concur with the decision.
_____
Area Manager's Signature

Figure 5-6.   Management interview form.

Department # _____   Date _____

Corp. Req. # _____

DP Salary Offer Form

Area Manager _____ Project Manager _____
                     (Signature)   (Signature)

Candidate's Name _____

Present Employer _____

Current Salary (Detail separately
bonus or profit-sharing) _____

Years of related experience _____

Position Considerations

Grade Proposed _____   Title _____

For Offers Extended on Track Guidelines

Track Guideline: _____ _____   _____
(Use "B" Track)   Bi–Weekly   Annual

For Offers Extended on Salary Guidelines

Ranges   _____ _____ _____
(Bi-weekly)   Minimum   Mid   Maximum

For All Department's Use

Proposed Salary Offer   _____   _____
                                     (Bi-weekly)   (Annual)

Conditions Made with Job Offer _____

_____

_____

                                           Date Required _____

Department Manager's Approval (if applicable): _____

Figure 5–7.

Procedures	*Step*	*Action*
	2)	Human resources advisor reviews job requisition for compliance with plan and submits form to resource planning.
	3)	Resource planning notifies employment agencies about the opening. Newspaper ads are simultaneously placed for some jobs.
	4)	Resource planning receives resumes and telephone referrals from agencies, reviews incoming material for general acceptability and sets up screening interview when appropriate.
	5)	Selected candidate fills out skills expertise evaluation form.
	6)	Resource planning conducts screen interview.
	7)	Resource planning schedules technical interview with selected candidates.
	8)	Technical interview team conducts technical interview, completes technical interview form, and screens for qualified applicants.
	9)	Resource planning schedules management interview and applicants recommended by technical interview team.
	10)	Project manager conducts management interview and completes management interview form.

Procedures	*Step*	*Action*

11) Group and area manager interview applicant if appropriate.

12) If interested in hiring the candidate, project/group/area manager completes salary offer form.

13) If acceptable, personnel extends offer to applicant and arranges a start date.

HOW TO CONDUCT A DP SCREENING INTERVIEW TO DETERMINE LEVEL OF TECHNICAL EXPERTISE

Introduction   In most cases, resource planning cannot obtain enough information about an applicant simply from reviewing the resume. A telephone referral usually determines more than initial interest but is still highly lacking. However, only preliminary qualified applicants are asked to come in for an initial interview. Before the interview, the applicant completes the skills expertise evaluation form, most importantly stating his/her level of expertise/experience.

Objectives   The objectives of the screening interview are to:

- Enable resource planning to determine if the applicant should be given a subsequent technical interview.
- Obtain general information regarding the applicant's:
    - Employment history
    - Hardware and software knowledge
    - Experience in programming, analysis, design, management, etc.
- Next the applicant is informed about:
    - The internal DP structure

- Company benefits
- The hiring procedure.
- The staff then answers any questions the applicant may have.

After the Interview   If resource planning decides to pursue the applicant, the technical interview is conducted.

OBJECTIVES OF THE TECHNICAL INTERVIEW

Introduction   The technical interview is usually tentatively scheduled for the same day as the screening interview.

Objectives   The objectives of the technical interview are to:

- Evaluate the technical qualifications of the candidate for a position as:
  - Programmer
  - Senior programmer
  - Programmer/analyst
  - Senior programmer/analyst
  - Systems analyst
  - Senior systems analyst.
- Determine the candidate's skill level in technical and analytical areas as OS concepts, JCL, feasibility studies and system design.
- Present a positive image of the company to the candidate.

Other Positions   For positions other than those listed above, such as systems engineer, technical interviews can be arranged on request. In this case, systems project members may conduct the candidate's technical interview to determine the actual level of expertise before the regular management interview.

WHAT TO EXPECT FROM THE TECHNICAL INTERVIEW

Before the Interview After the screening interview, resource planning prepares a hiring booklet for selected applicants containing the skills expertise evaluation form completed by the applicant. The applicant's resume and salary information are excluded so as not to influence the team members' appraisal of the applicant.

At the Interview The interview begins with a general discussion of the candidate's background. Once team members feel they are familiar with his/her background, technical questioning begins. All of the candidate's skills that are pertinent to the environment are covered. At the close of the interview, the candidate is given the opportunity to question team members about organization, hardware, educational program, etc.

After the Interview Following the interview, team members next discuss each skill and jointly complete the technical interview form, indicating whether the candidate is technically qualified for a position at the company and, if so, what type of position. The information is forwarded to resource planning. Resource planning determines for which, if any, of the open positions the candidate is qualified.

TECHNICAL INTERVIEW TEAM

Function The technical interview team's main function is to evaluate the applicant's technical qualifications.

Responsibilities The specific responsibilities of the team are to:

- Determine and rate the applicant's technical skill level by conducting the technical interview.

- Determine whether the applicant is technically qualified for a company position and, if so, at what level.
- Present a positive image of the company.

Benefits   The team interview technique has three major benefits:

- Team members are the most qualified to judge an applicant's technical ability because they are among the most technically competent people in the department.
- The interview helps to weed out unqualified applicants before the management interview, thereby saving the manager considerable time.
- It indicates to applicants that the interviewing process is fair, quantitative and highly thorough.

Choosing Team Members   Team members must be technically competent, articulate, enthusiastic and able to present a positive image of the company and the environment.

Team Training Procedures   Resource planning conducts seminars to train the new team member in procedures and techniques for effective interviewing. Each team member receives guidelines for interviewing and a booklet containing sample technical questions. The team member sits in on two-person team interviews until he or she feels confident in the techniques of interviewing and comfortable with the procedure.

MANAGEMENT INTERVIEW OVERVIEW

Introduction   The management interview provides the project manager with a basis for deciding whether to hire the candidate. When resource planning feels that an applicant may be suitable for a particular position, the hiring booklet, including the request for management interview form, is sent to the requesting project manager. At this time, the hiring booklet already contains:

- Applicant's employment application
- Applicant's resume
- Skills expertise evaluation form
- Technical interview form.

If the project manager is interested in the applicant, resource planning arranges the management interview. If the project manager is not interested, he/she sends the hiring booklet to the area manager for concurrence and signature.

Objectives

The objectives of the management interview are to:

- Enable the manager to determine the applicant's suitability for the position in terms of compatibility, dependability and potential value to the department.
- Inform the candidate about the position, the department and the company benefits.
- Convey enthusiasm about the position and a positive image of the department and the company.
- Decide whether to offer the position to the applicant.

MANAGEMENT INTERVIEW DETAILS

Before the Interview

The project manager must be thoroughly familiar with the characteristics of the candidate before the interview takes place. This detailed information is supplied by comprehensive meetings between resource planning and the manager, and the hiring booklet, containing the comments and recommendations of the interviewing team.

At the Interview At the interview, the manager describes his/her position within the company and explains the format and purpose of the interview. The manager questions the applicant on his or her:

- Job history
- Past career development
- Past working relationships
- Management philosophy (if applicable)
- Professional goals
- Salary requirements.

The manager also informs the candidate about the:

- Specific responsibilities of the position
- Organization of the area and the department
- Benefits offered by the company.

After the Interview After the interview, the project manager completes the management interview form, indicating a decision regarding the applicant. The project manager may decide either to hire the candidate for the open position on the project, to recommend the candidate for hire by the department but not for the project, or to recommend that the candidate not be considered for any position in the department.

Group Manager Interview After the project manager completes the candidate interview, the manager introduces the candidate to the group manager, who briefly interviews the subject.

Area Manager
Interview

Area manager interviews are normally reserved for senior-level positions but may be arranged at the request of the area manager.

MANAGEMENT DECISION GUIDELINES

Introduction

After the interview, the project manager completes the management interview form, evaluating the candidate and making a recommendation which reflects his/her opinion and that of the group manager. There are three possible decisions.

Hire the
Candidate

The project and group managers decide that the individual is suitable for hire for the position on the project. An interview between the area manager and the candidate may be arranged. If the area manager concurs with the decision to hire, the salary offer form is completed and the hiring booklet is forwarded to resource planning.

Consider for
Other
Positions

The project and group managers decide that the candidate is suitable for hire within the department but not for the particular position. After this decision is verified by the area manager, the hiring booklet is returned to resource planning. Resource planning determines if the applicant is suitable for any other openings in the department. If the candidate is suitable, a management interview is arranged with the appropriate manager.

Do not
Hire the
Candidate

The project and group managers decide the applicant is unsuitable for any position in the department. After this decision is verified by the area manager, the hiring booklet is forwarded to resource planning for further processing.

RESOURCE PLANNING RESPONSIBILITIES

Description   Resource planning's responsibilities in the hiring procedure are to ensure:

- Selection of effective sources of DP personnel.
- Maintenance of a professional working relationship with selected sources.
- Effective screening of resumes, telephone referrals and applicants.
- Matching of qualified candidates to appropriate job requisitions.
- Technical expertise and professionalism of technical interview teams.
- Consideration of qualified applicants for all appropriate openings with department.
- Constant reappraisal of the overall effectiveness of the hiring procedure.

The resource planning group also has the responsibility to:

- Discuss each job requisition with the requesting manager to be fully informed about the opening.
- Decide, with the requesting manager, if the position is to be filled through hiring.
- Conduct screening interview.
- Select and train technical interview team members.
- Review completed hiring forms to ensure thorough documentation.

DOCUMENT SUMMARY

This chart provides a checklist of the documents used in the hiring procedures.

FORM	PURPOSE	COMPLETED BY	AUTHORIZATION
Job requisition form	Inform resource planning of staffing requirements	Project manager	Area manager, department head

FORM	PURPOSE	COMPLETED BY	AUTHORIZATION
Employment application	Obtain initial information on applicant	Applicant	N/A
Resume	Background information on applicant	Applicant or agency	N/A
Skills expertise evaluation	Applicant's appraisal of his/her own level of skill	Applicant	N/A
Technical interview form	Technical team evaluation of applicant	Team members	N/A
Management interview form	Project manager's evaluation and decision on hiring	Project manager	Area manager
Salary offer form	Propose salary and conclude hiring procedure	Project manager	Area manager (department head, in some cases)

MANAGERS' RESPONSIBILITIES IN THE HIRING PROCEDURE

Area Manager   The area manager's responsibilities in the hiring procedure are to:

- Evaluate staff needs and set priorities on open positions within the area.
- Submit job requisitions, allowing sufficient lead time.
- Evaluate candidates by reviewing hiring procedure documents.
- Make the final decision in the hiring of employees.

Group/Project Manager   The group or project manager's responsibilities in the hiring procedure are to:

- Complete the job requisition and present to area manager for approval.

- Familiarize him/herself with applicant's employment history before the management interview.
- Conduct the management interview.
- Describe the department, the area, the project, and the open position to the candidate and impress him/her with the department and the company.
- Evaluate the candidate in terms of potential contribution to the project, the department and corporate goals.

USE OF CONSULTANTS

History: Use of Consultants and How it Began

The use of domestic consultants is and has been an integral part of DP operations for many years. In fact, consultant usage is becoming a more prominent factor as the demand for computer talent continues to far outstrip the available manpower supply. There are analogies here between the current progress being made by sought-after athletes in terms of their bargaining power and that of system and programming personnel.

Consultants have been used by our company since the late 1960s. In the early 1970s, there was very little control over their use. Consultants were contracted for directly by users and largely created undesirable results. Starting in 1973, controls and procedures were instituted which strove toward proper usage and optimum cost performance. In the late 1970s, another market-driven explosion of requirements for users mushroomed the use of domestic consultants and rekindled control problems. Starting in 1981, adequate acquisition resources and new and tighter innovative procedures (which follow) have helped to put consultant usage under proper control.

The use of foreign consultants started in 1977 with a small experimental group of five DP specialists brought over from England. Over the last four years, this new human resource acquisition area has grown to the point where close to 100 British and Israeli highly trained computer experts are presently with our company through consulting firms. A number of these have become employees.

PROCEDURES FOR OBTAINING CONSULTANT MANPOWER USAGE

Objective The objective of the consultant procedure is to obtain specialized human resources (consultants) in an organized, timely manner and at reasonable cost from approved vendors.

Criteria The criteria used to determine whether a consultant should be used are:

- Is the expertise required available in-house?
- Is the expertise required not available through permanent hiring?
- Is the requirement short-term?

Documents The consultant procedure utilizes the following documents.

- Consultant requisition form (see Figure 5–8)
- Consultant technical interview form (see Figure 5–9)
- Consultant evaluation form (see Figure 5–10)
- Vendor average rate report (see Figure 5–11)

OBTAINING THE CONSULTANT: PROCEDURES TO FOLLOW

Introduction The following steps summarize the consultant procedure.

Procedure 1) Consultant requested completes consultant requisition form.

2) Specify the skill and grade level of consultant needed and enter this data in spaces provided on requisition.

Department: _____ Date Submitted: _____

Project Name: _____ Date Required: _____

Project Manager: _____ Position Title: _____

Area Manager: _____ Grade: _____

Group Head: _____ Skill Level: _____

Human Resource Advisor: _____ Average Rate: _____

(Signatures required for all above)

Brief description of duties to be performed: _____

_____

_____

_____

_____

I. Skills List:

Identify the skills needed by assigning appropriate number (0-4) to the applicable skills.

    A)   Level Explanations:

        Level 0: Has no knowledge of subject matter
        Level 1: Has an awareness of subject matter
        Level 2: Has had moderate use of subject matter
        Level 3: Has had heavy use of subject matter
        Level 4: Has expert knowledge of subject matter

Operating systems (specify)	_____	Feasibility studies	_____
Programming language (specify)	_____	Functional analysis	_____
JCL/PROCS	_____	Design specs	_____
Utilities	_____	Conversion/implementation	_____
Debugging	_____	Audits and controls	_____
On-line experience	_____	Documentation	_____
CICS	_____	User interface	_____
IMS	_____	Hardware (specify)	_____
Structured programming	_____	Other (specify)	_____
I/O sub-systems	_____		

Figure 5-8.   Two-part document: Consultant requisition form. (Part 1)

II. <u>Vendor Selection:</u>

- Do you require assistance from Consultant Usage Group in identifying vendors?

  Yes _____   No _____

- If no, which vendors are you planning to contact?

Vendor Name	Vendor Average Rate	If higher than average rate, why are you considering this vendor?
_____	_____	_____
_____	_____	_____
_____	_____	_____
_____	_____	_____
_____	_____	_____
_____	_____	_____
_____	_____	_____
_____	_____	_____
_____	_____	_____

Note: This form must be submitted to HR Advisor prior to interviewing process.

Figure 5-8.   (Part 2)

3) Access the consultant vendor rate report. Next determine average rate for consultants at the same skill/grade level as the consultant required. Enter this data in the space provided on the requisition.

4) Consultant user selects vendors that he/she wishes to contact, always utilizing approved vendors list and consultant vendor rate report. Vendors selected should offer rates competitive with average rate. If assistance is required, consultant usage group will participate at this point.

5) Complete all additional data requested on form, obtain needed approval/signatures and submit requisition.

Applicant Name: _____   Date: _____

Vendor: _____   Interviewer: _____

Department: _____   Interviewer: _____

Project Name: _____

Based on your interview, rate the consultant on the following skills based on the rating system below. Place the appropriate number rating in the space provided next to each skill.

Explanation of Level Numbers:

Level 0: Has no knowledge of subject
Level 1: Has an awareness of subject
Level 2: Equivalent knowledge of someone with moderate use of subject matter
Level 3: Equivalent knowledge of someone with heavy use of subject matter
Level 4: Expert knowledge of subject matter

Operating systems (specify)	_____	Feasibility studies	_____
Programming language (specify)	_____	Functional analysis	_____
JCL/PROCS	_____	Design specs	_____
Utilities	_____	Conversion/implementation	_____
Debugging	_____	Audits and controls	_____
On-line experience	_____	Documentation	_____
CICS	_____	User interface	_____
IMS	_____	Hardware (specify)	_____
Structured programming	_____		
I/O Sub-systems	_____		
Other Knowledge (specify)	_____		

Figure 5–9.   Two-part document: Consultant technical interview form. (Part 1)

EQUIVALENT GRADE LEVEL

☐ Programmer   ☐ Senior Systems Analyst

☐ Senior Programmer   ☐ Senior Programmer Analyst

☐ Programmer Analyst   ☐ Project Manager

☐ Systems Analyst   ☐ Technical Specialist

☐ (Other, please specify) _____

Briefly describe the nature of the work to be performed in the project by the consultant and the applicability of the consultant's skills to your project requirements: _____

_____

_____

Average Rate _____ (From Consultant Vendor Rate Report)

Vendor Requested Rate _____

    Is Requested Rate equal to or lower than Average Rate?   Yes ☐   No ☐

Has Consultant Requisition been previously submitted?   Yes ☐   No ☐

Requested Start Date _____

```
┌──────────────────────────────────────────────────────────────┐
│  Sign-off Section                                              │
│                                                                │
│  Project Manager _____     │
│                                                                │
│  Group Manager _____      │
│                                                                │
│  Area Manager _____      │
│                                                                │
│  If answer to either of the above two questions is No, Group   │
│  Head signature is required.                                   │
│                                                                │
│                              _____      │
│                                    Group Head                  │
└──────────────────────────────────────────────────────────────┘
```

For Consultant Usage Group Only

Final Rate _____

Authorized Signature _____

Figure 5-9.   (Part 2)

Consultant Name _____   Company _____

Project _____   Contract Dates _____

Project Manager _____   Area Manager _____

Please evaluate those skills listed below being utilized by the above-named consultant.

Rating: Level 0 = <u>No</u> knowledge of subject matter
Level 1 = <u>Awareness</u> of subject matter
Level 2 = <u>Moderate</u> use of subject matter
Level 3 = <u>Heavy</u> use of subject matter
Level 4 = <u>Expert</u> knowledge of subject matter

Technical Skills	Rating	Systems Skills	Rating
Cobol coding	_____	Feasibility study	_____
BAL coding	_____	Functional analysis	_____
Other coding: _____	_____	Design	_____
_____	_____	Conversion/implementation	_____
JCL	_____	Documentation	_____
Procs	_____	User interface	_____
Utilities	_____	PERT charts	_____
Debugging	_____	GANTT charts	_____
On-line programming	_____	Project control procedures	_____
CICS	_____	Supervision	_____
TSO	_____	Other (please specify:)	
OS	_____	_____	_____
DOS	_____	_____	_____
Other operating system	_____	_____	_____
IMS	_____		

Figure 5-10.   Three-part document: Consultant Evaluation Form (Part 1)

II.   Technical Accountabilities (Rating: NA = Not Adequate; F = Fair; FA = Fully Adequate; AE = Above Expectancy; EX = Exceptional):

● Demonstrates a thorough and current knowledge of the techniques required in this field.   _____

● Works effectively with minimum supervision.   _____

● Meets work schedules with determination, providing advance notice and alternate plans when necessary.   _____

● Represents the unit competently and tactfully in obtaining information and devising solutions.   _____

● Communicates articulately in written work and in conversation.   _____

III. Personal Accountabilities (use ratings defined in II):

Attitude towards job   _____   Initiative   _____

Ability to take supervision   _____   Adaptability   _____

Ability to work under pressure   _____   Perseverance   _____

IV. Summary of Performance: □ Fully Adequate
     □ Not Adequate   □ Above Expectancy
     □ Fair   □ Exceptional

V.   Position Best Qualified for at the Bank:

     □ Programmer   □ Sr. Programmer Analyst

     □ Sr. Programmer   □ Sr. System Analyst

     □ Programmer Analyst   □ Other _____

     □ System Analyst

Figure 5-10.   (Part 2)

VI. Based on the above evaluations, would you recommend this person for a permanent position at the bank? Please explain your decision, elaborating on both positive and negative technical/personal traits.

_____

_____

_____

_____

_____

_____

_____

_____

_____

_____

VII. Do you wish to hire this consultant after his 90-day period is over?

☐ Yes   ☐ No

If no, please explain. _____

_____

_____

_____

_____

_____

_____

Evaluated by: _____   Area Manager: _____

Date: _____   Date: _____

Figure 5–10.   (Part 3)

VENDOR CO.	15	20	30	40	43	50	53	55	60	65	70	75	78	80	85
SKILLS LEVEL															
Company Average Rate	$350*	$355	$306	$316	$331	$371	$406	$391	$368	$287	$446	$426	$442	$399	$468
Firm 1	350*													402	
Firm 2														460	
Firm 3							425	390						425	
Firm 4						385	410								
Firm 5											475	415			
Firm 6			307			389	425	381	368*			408		396	
Firm 7				364										350*	
Firm 8				300*											
Firm 9															
Firm 10		355*													
Firm 11						360		325*						350*	
Firm 12				300*										400	
Firm 13										260*					468
Firm 14											425				
Firm 15								285						420	
Firm 16					294*			340					475	425	
Firm 17											400	400			
Firm 18												475		415	
Firm 19												425		410	
Firm 20														380	
Firm 21								420							
Firm 22								520							
Firm 23															
Firm 24											375*				
Firm 25															
Firm 26															
Firm 27			300*										425*	400	
Firm 28						285*				300				440	
Firm 29						425									
Firm 30			310							375*		400			
Firm 31											463				
Firm 32					343	350									
Firm 33							385*						425*	350*	
Firm 34														400	
Firm 35										300	640				

*Best rate in skill class   Total senior consultants = 82

SKILL =	DESCRIPTION
10	COBOL/BAL Programming
15	NCR Programming
17	RPG/SYS III
20	CICS Programming
23	Technical Writing/Documentation
30	IMS Programming
40	IMS/CICS Programming

SKILL #	DESCRIPTION
43	Data Base Design
50	CICS Design
53	IMS Design
55	CICS/IMS Design
60	DEC
63	Office Automation
65	Minicomputers (Datapoint, SYS)

SKILL #	DESCRIPTION
70	Telecommunications
75	Systems Programming
78	Systems Performance Evaluation
80	Analysis/Analytical Skills
85	NCR Systems Design
90	Project Manager
95	Operations Manager

Figure 5-11.   Vendor Average Rate Report: Senior consultants category.

6) Upon authorized receipt, consultant usage group will check selected vendors for:

- Current price performance
- Existing negative performance reports in vendor files
- Over-dependency on a particular vendor in a particular department.

7) Consultant usage group contacts consultant user to offer assistance and to discuss any legal and work-related concerns that arise from the above-mentioned checking process.

8) Consultant user contact vendors, communicates requirements and sets up technical interviews with prospective candidates.

9) Technical interviews are conducted, using consultant technical interview form.

10) Qualified consultant is identified. Criteria used should include skill/grade competency plus rate competitiveness with average rate.

11) On consultant technical interview form, enter average rate (based on grade and skill-level competency). If vendor requested rate is higher than average rate *or* if consultant requisition form was not submitted previously, you must obtain the signature of your group head. Note: In the latter case, consultant requisition must still be submitted along with consultant technical interview form.

12) Upon receipt, consultant usage group will negotiate final billing rate and inform consultant user.

THE APPROVED VENDOR LIST: WHY IT IS IMPORTANT
FOR PROPER SERVICE

Objective   The purpose of the approved vendor list is to identify those consulting vendors who are viewed as desirable and reputable and to control the number of vendor firms with approved authorization status to provide service to the company.

Procedure   **Steps**   **Action**

1) The approved vendor list will be updated and reissued quarterly in order to ensure that existing vendors are providing quality services. Questionnaires are sent to consultant users to solicit data on vendor performance.

2) In the event a consultant user cannot secure a qualified consultant from the approved vendor list, the user should contact the consultant usage group.

3) The Consultant Usage Group will provide assistance to locate a vendor:
   - From the approved vendor list
   - If a vendor cannot be obtained from the approved vendor list, then, by working with the consultant user, a new vendor will be found from the prospective vendor file.

4) A consultant user wishing to recommend a vendor for consideration to the approved vendor list should contact the consultant usage group.

EVALUATING THE CONSULTANT: HOW THE
PROCEDURE WORKS

Objective   The objectives of the consultant evaluation procedure are:

- To enable human resources to ensure a uniform standard of consultant performance.
- To determine if the company may later want to extend an offer to hire the consultant as an employee.

Procedures After Six Weeks

The project manager receives the consultant evaluation form six weeks after the consultant begins work. The primary purpose of this evaluation is to ensure that the consultant's technical skills, work habits, and personal attributes are at the level required by the assignment. This form is to be used for the three-month evaluation.

Procedures After Three Months

After three months (twelve weeks), the company can extend an offer to hire the consultant (provided for in the standard agreement with firms). At this time, the project manager completes the consultant evaluation form, indicating whether the manager would like to hire the consultant. The form is signed by the area manager and returned to the consultant usage group. If a consultant appears to be a viable candidate for permanent job offer, the consultant usage group will call the consultant user.

The consultant's performance sometimes begins to deteriorate after a few months. The manager should indicate this if and when it begins to occur by contacting the consultant usage group. In these situations, consultant usage will provide assistance to rectify the problem. This may necessitate interface with the vendor to correct the situation or location of a suitable replacement.

CONSULTANT USAGE RESPONSIBILITIES: GUIDELINES FOR THE PROJECT MANAGER

Objective	To detail the responsibilities of the consultant usage group in the domestic consultant procedure.

Responsibilities	Consultant usage responsibilities in the consultant procedure are to:

- provide guidance, information and clarification to any manager with questions or problems pertaining to consultant usage, procurement, etc. Also ensure adherence to procedures pertaining to consultant usage, procurement, etc.
- Negotiate and design bulk discount arrangements with vendors to offer cost savings to consultant users.
- Maintain data on consultants on assignment and historical data on vendor activities.
- Produce monthly consultant reports for management use, (e.g., average vendor rate report), to ensure competitive bidding.
- Upon receipt of consultant requisition, next check the selected vendors on the following points.
- Price performance
- Good standing (lack of any negative performance reports in vendor files)
- Over-dependency on a particular vendor in a particular department.
- Provide assistance to obtain qualified consultants in a timely manner at competitive billing rates.
- Ensure the existence of ethical business practices between the company and consultant vendors. Provide a central point of control for all DP consulting activities.

- Negotiate final billing rate with vendors when consultant technical interview form is received from consultant user.
- Review and approve all vendors under consideration for addition to the approved vendor list.
- Handle all inquiries from prospective vendors who wish to do business with the company.
- Administer procedures for evaluating consultant performance.
- Coordinate all negotiations with vendor when attempting to hire a consultant as a permanent employee.
- Handle all rate increases by negotiation with the vendor.

AREA MANAGER RESPONSIBILITIES IN THE CONSULTANT PROCEDURE

Objective

To list the responsibilities of the area manager and project/group manager in the consultant procedure.

Area Manager Responsibilities

The area manager responsibilities in the consultant procedure are:

- To approve consultant requisition. A 30-day minimum lead time period is required prior to consultant start.
- To approve all consultant evaluation forms.
- To approve variances as stated on the consultant technical interview form

Project/Group Manager Responsibilities

The project/group manager's responsibilities in the consultant procedure are:

- To submit consultant requisition—with approval signature—one month before consultant start date.

- To provide staff members from the project to perform technical interview.
- To conduct management interview.
- To select candidate based on technical ability and rates to fill position.
- To submit consultant technical interview form with appropriate approvals/signatures as required.
- To evaluate consultant performance.
- To contact the consultant usage group to inform area of any problems encountered with an approved vendor.
- To refer any solicitations and inquiries from non-approved vendors to the consultant usage group.

DOCUMENT SUMMARY

This page provides a checklist of the documents used in the consultant usage procedures.

FORM	PURPOSE	COMPLETED BY	AUTHORIZATION
Consultant requisition form	Inform resource planning of staffing requirements	Project manager	Area manager, department head
Consultant technical interview form	Evaluate consultant technical skills and ensure that the best possible has been obtained	Project manager	Project manager, group manager, area manager
Vendor average rate report	Provide monthly analysis of average vendor rates by skill and determine average company rates	Resource planning	Resource planning
Consultant evaluation form	Evaluate consultant's performance, attitude and capabilities	Project manager	Area manager

OVERSEAS CONNECTION

Since 1977, we have been involved with utilizing overseas consultants. Human resources recruiters now fly regularly to Europe to personally interview and recruit highly skilled overseas DP specialists for assignments in the United States. The human resources dividends have been extraordinary and have produced an amazing "results-oriented" solution for our organization.

The motivation to venture abroad was based on supply and demand in the tight New York marketplace. The available DP resources were increasingly difficult to obtain because of the rapid growth of the DP industry. The alternate solution to hiring permanent employees was to use more locally available consultants. However, that meant a steep and correspondingly high cost factor. After some brainstorming, the in-house decision was made to consider the overseas DP manpower market.

It would be called the "overseas connection" and would address the immediate problem of manpower requirements through the procurement of overseas DP consultants—but at a considerably lower cost factor than domestic consultant rates. Furthermore, it also complemented the permanent hiring requirement when the overseas consultant subsequently obtained his or her immigration certificate, called the "green card," and MHT offered the consultant permanent employment. Highly skilled and trained DP persons—not available in the U.S.—now would also become American citizens.

The primary source of overseas DP consultants has been Great Britain, but other nations providing DP consultants were Israel and Canada. Other sources being explored include Australia, Hong Kong, New Zealand, South Africa/Rhodesia and India. The three basic requirements for an overseas DP resource to be considered are as follows:

1. The overseas DP resource must be English speaking.
2. The resource must be highly-skilled in the latest DP technology.
3. The resource must be attracted to the U.S. DP pay scale, usually higher than the prevailing overseas salary rate.

Meanwhile, the original intention of the "overseas connection" was to deliver highly skilled DP workers—not available in the U.S.—

who would eventually become permanent employees. Here's how that was done: First, they were flown to New York as employees of the overseas consulting firm and then assigned to projects. After a three-month evaluation period, a follow-up decision was made by management whether or not to retain their services. If the decision was "yes," then the consultant was asked whether he or she wished to become a permanent U.S. resident and could subsequently receive an offer of permanent DP employment after receiving the Immigration Service's green card (permanent residency). The next step was to process the application for permanent residency.

The overall overseas recruiting program has been an unqualified success because urgently needed skilled resources have been provided at a cost-effective expense filling a critical manpower shortage.

However, there are several problems that bear addressing. These problems relate to the status of the overseas person employed as consultants for long periods of time. First is that the U.S. Immigration Department regulations require a "sponsor" to bring a newcomer into the U.S. and provide guarantee of work for those newcomers— regardless of their education expertise. There are other considerations to keep in mind.

The overseas DP consultant will probably have distinct problems that fall into both organizational and psychological categories:

1. The consultants cannot readily obtain financial or credit facilities because they do not have a credit history in this country.
2. They are told they will be treated as permanent employees but they are not eligible for tuition refunds or employee loans or credit cards.
3. Mentally, the process of obtaining a green card is a grueling one. After an application is submitted, no status is received to let the applicants know how they're doing for long periods of time. This has the effect of "mentally harassing" the people. This is carried into work with them and in some cases it is translated into a feeling of "I can't wait to get out of here."

An additional human resources consideration is the dilemma of handling the problem of these consultants when many of these problems originate from the overseas consulting firm. Thus, the consulting firm becomes an intermediary, which must usually be included in the problem-solving process and diminishes human resource's ability to effect solutions in an orderly and expedient manner.

An inherent risk with the present situation is the danger of an overseas consultant leaving the employer before receiving the green card. Since the consulting firm handles the attainment of green cards, the overseas consultant may leave the bank due to problems encountered with the consulting firm.

At the inception of the program, the overseas DP consultants were few in number and handled in such a way that a considerable amount of attention was given to each one. As their number increased rapidly, this same level of attention was no longer available and, as a result, comprehensive follow-up coordination did not take place. Here's the best way to eliminate the latter condition:

The major consideration is to treat the overseas consultants—whenever possible—the same way as permanent employees. Utilize the tools already in place for permanent employees but also develop new ones relevant to the overseas consultant's unique situation.

In mid-1982, we began to sponsor for temporary and permanent visas. Basically, this step was taken in light of the accumulated experience we had gained from being involved with overseas professionals. It was felt that our needs were such that the demand for overseas talent would continue for some time and, this being the case, we could solve many of the aforementioned problems as well as realize a cost savings.

This involved creating a facility in London capable of finding potential candidates, organizing recruiting trips and providing follow-up with candidates who have been made offers. This has been accomplished by hiring an experienced DP recruiter and locating her in our already existing London facility.

In addition to the London location, we are also involved with relocation considerations here in New York, such as temporary and permanent housing accommodations as well as visa processing and help to acclimate foreign consultants to a new environment.

6

Evaluating Performance

The underlying premise for managing the human resource is to approach the assignment in a similar fashion as for managing other resources. Industrywide, it is generally accepted that a manager is accountable to utilize all resources effectively and develop those resources to their maximum potential. It naturally follows that industry should hold a manager just as accountable for the people factor as is expected of machine, project completion or productivity yield goals.

If managing the human resource sounds easy enough, why has it been so difficult to actually implement? There are three major difficulties constantly cited:

1. *How to determine human resource capability and potential.* Everything surrounding this arena is dynamic: human nature, recession, the environment, unexpected company plans, etc. Some say it's like grabbing a tiger by its tail. Others disagree.
2. *How to develop a viable internal system*—one which truly aids managers in identifying strengths and weaknesses and offers direction in correcting deficiencies.
3. *How to change reward systems (and attitudes)* to reward managers who develop their human resources (see Chapter 9).

We have been working and enhancing our performance appraisal process system for nearly eight years, and today can note of the following human resources achievements:

1. For the period 1973 to 1978, we did not have to hire managers from outside the organization. All managers were developed

from within. Since that time, due primarily to rapid growth and expansion, only five percent have been hired from the outside.

2. Considerable increases in productivity have surfaced in some areas as a direct consequence of dramatically reducing turnover. The resultant continuity of management made that achievement possible.

3. Expanded computer systems have emerged. Managers are implementing "management by objectives" programs which integrate the basic process they are familiar with in managing people and implementing business planning efforts.

We are firmly convinced that, like brand new technology, extended periods of time will be required to experiment and fine-hone the new management systems before peers can fully appreciate the benefits and assimilate the new techniques into universal applied management behavior.

Before detailing the integral components, it is important to set a backdrop—specifically citing what was sought to accomplish in the appraisal system development and subsequent implementation project.

The primary objectives of the performance appraisal were to:

1. Provide management with a standardized vehicle to evaluate employee performance.

2. Evaluate the employee's specific work assignments in terms of quality and timeliness.

3. Evaluate the employee in overall professional accountabilities such as technical, supervisory and personal objectives.

4. Set specific and tangible objectives for the coming review period.

Stated simply, the evaluation process was one of constructively communicating objective feedback to an employee so that both the individual and the organization would be enhanced by identifying and working toward realizing the potential of the individual.

Beyond the primary objectives, evaluation systems would also serve the sponsoring organization as a basis for salary administration, career succession planning, EEO compliance, etc. The organization's goals could not dominate the evaluation process. For any evaluation system to be successful, the "ownership" would be at the manager/employee level (see "Implementing a Performance Appraisal System").

A GUIDELINE FOR PERFORMANCE APPRAISAL
SYSTEM COMPONENTS

"If you don't know where you're going, you'll probably end up somewhere else." This statement also serves as the basis of the foundation directly applicable for the concrete basis of job understanding. If job project/postings have been carefully defined—whatever their format—that action will ensure that the basis for all performance comparison consists of valid job expectations, and that subsequent goals and objectives are appropriate.

Meanwhile, within a large organization—where many individuals perform in the same job function, such as programmers, for example—the need for consistent work output and performance comparison is even greater. There will always be on-the-scene managers who are more or less critical/demanding concerning appraisal mechanisms. But if human resources staffers provide equalizers—such as in job definition—they are at least providing integrity of job understanding. It's to the entire organization's advantage to do so.

The benefit of using job descriptions, meanwhile, is to guard against three typical traps corporate managers fall into:

- Comparing one individual to another. This is dangerous, even for the most experienced manager.
- Evaluating only a few aspects of performance. Even where job specialization dominates, (e.g., a high tech specialist), there are almost always other dimensions which are critically important, such as the following areas: project control, communication skills, ability to work with peers, etc. It is to the organization's benefit to examine more than just a candidate's technical expertise. Keep in mind that if for no other reason, the other considerations are equally as important because today's technicians may become tomorrow's managers.
- Relying on what you "think" the job to be.

Fully detailed job position descriptions provide managers with a solid framework. Excerpt specification listings from two programmer position descriptions follow. The posting on the right is for a senior programmer and illustrates an increased level of responsibility over the programmer posting found on the left. Good job descriptions take the guesswork out of job understanding. They also eliminate future performance disappointments if conducted accordingly.

Programmer

May perform the following functions while assigned to a programming project:

- Using detailed specifications, codes straightforward computer programs.

- Using detailed specifications, maintains and updates current programs and their documentation.

- With assistance from senior technical personnel, tests, debugs and documents straightforward new programs.

- Generates computer test data under the control of senior technical personnel.

- Becomes familiar with the applications for which he/she codes.

- Increases his/her DP knowledge by taking advantage of self-education opportunities.

Senior Programmer

May perform the following functions while assigned to a programming project:

- Accomplishes the design through implementation of straightforward computer programs from general specifications.

- Accomplishes the coding through implementation of complex programs from detailed specifications.

- Reviews the design of computer programs with senior technical personnel.

- Generates computer test data under the control of senior technical personnel.

- Increases his/her DP knowledge by taking advantage of self-education opportunities.

- Refines current programs to efficiently utilize software and hardware capabilities.

- Becomes increasingly familiar with thecorporation's computer applications.

- Maintains and and updates current programs and documentations.

A recent enhancement is the use of a job content form introduced at the beginning of each review period. This job-related aid allows the manager and employee to jointly agree on current job aspects, and their subsequent relative weight, which will be the basis for the evaluation period. This advantage provides an accommodation of variations which is usually found even with two programmers at the same grade level performing on the same project. Using the job content format, specific objectives can be set and weights agreed upon prior to the start of the review period (see Figure 6–1 for an example of the job content form).

Rating System Scoring Guidelines

The only good rating system is one which leaves an invisible yet clearly impressionable mark. (Only a supreme being can possibly achieve a 100 percent rating.)

Below is the system we have used. It is intended to reinforce measurement against what is expected of a "fully adequate" performer who is satisfactorily performing all the functions of a given position.

Description	The performance ratings that follow are used in Part I of the performance appraisal form and for the summary rating. Ratings should be measured against what is expected of a "fully adequate" performer who is performing all the functions of the position.
Exceptional (EX)	Performance has been consistently outstanding and far exceeds what is expected of an employee in this position.
Above Expenctancy (AE)	Performance has measured above what is expected of an employee in this position.

NAME		JOB TITLE	GRADE	DEPT. NO.

INSTRUCTIONS

Below are a list of items divided into two sections: performance items and work habits. Staff members and supervisors are asked to follow the procedure outlined below to agree upon the performance items that are relevant to the appraisal of performance in the staff member's job.

TO THE STAFF MEMBER:

1. Read over all performance items and work habit items; make a mental note of which performance items represent important behavior in your job—**DO NOT CHECK ANY ITEMS AT THIS POINT.**
2. Go back through the performance items; place a check (✓) in Column I next to any item that represents an aspect of your job sufficiently important to serve as the basis for evaluating performance. No more than 8 performance items should be chosen. Options are available to combine performance items and/or elaborate on the job within one performance item so that the limit of 8 is more workable (see below). The use of options may be discussed with your supervisor at the job content meeting. All work habit items will be used by all staff members so that only weighting need be discussed.
3. Do not consider column IV, weight, until meeting with your supervisor.
4. Once completed, hand this form in to your supervisor.

TO THE SUPERVISOR:

1. Please identify those performance items which represent a significant aspect of the staff member's job by a check next to that item in column II. No more than 8 performance items should be chosen, options are available so that the job may be adequately represented with 8 items (see below).
2. Obtain and review the staff member's copy of this Job Content Form; transfer all checkmarks from column I of the staff member's form to your copy of the form.
3. Where checks appear in columns I and II place a check in column III.
4. Where there is disagreement between columns I and II, carefully consider this job aspect before meeting with the staff member. Disagreement may result from different interpretations of the items or the checking of items that do not warrant independent evaluation.
5. Schedule the job content meeting with the staff member; at this time return to the staff member his/her copy of the form. Discuss the use of performance items to represent the job including the need for the options described below. The use of options should be outlined in the space available on page 7 of this form. Options are not used for work habit items.
6. When an understanding is reached as to how the job is to be represented by the items, each item should be weighted for relative importance to the overall job. Weighting is done using the scale on page 6 of this form.

OPTIONS (To be used only for performance items)

Two options are available to portray the job as best as possible. How innovative you are in using this form will determine how effective the form is; one or both options may be used.

Option One: Allows the supervisor and staff member to specify objectives or goals within the general performance items. For example: Item 11 (Plans and designs research projects) may be broken down as follows:
> 11-1: Plans and designs job analysis projects
> 11-2: Conducts test validations

At the time of review the staff member may be evaluated only on the general performance item (e.g., Item 11) or on each specific objective (e.g., 11-1, 11-2). This should be decided at the time of weight determination; weighting should reflect the evaluation plan.

Option Two: Allows supervisor and staff member to combine performance items that are seen as overlapping and discuss them (and eventually evaluate them) as one. For example: It may be that Items 30 and 32, concerning delegation of work and interaction with staff, are most easily evaluated and discussed together for this employee. When evaluating the staff member on these performance items, the supervisor should write down the two items and bracket them on page 5 of this form. Only one weight and one evaluation is given for bracketed items.

$$\left.\begin{matrix} 30 \\ 32 \end{matrix}\right] \begin{matrix} \text{wt.} \\ 4 \end{matrix}$$

7. The agreement process outlined above should be followed for performance reviews as well as for new hires, any change in supervision or in job assignment (transfer, promotion).

Figure 6-1.   Job Content Form. (Page 1) (Copyright and property of Manufacturers Hanover).

	I Staff member	II Supervisor	III Agreement	IV Weight

SECTION I—PERFORMANCE ITEMS

1. Accurately balances items, securities, money amounts, or other entries periodically (daily, weekly, etc.) in order to "prove out."
2. Accepts and/or disperses large accounts (money, securities, food stamps, lottery tickets, etc.) efficiently and accurately.
3. Knows and applies appropriate debiting and crediting procedures in order to maintain up-to-date account records.
4. Identifies errors in accounts or signed documents and follows through until problems are resolved.
5. Diligently follows bank policy and security procedures to prevent possible loss, e.g., check encashment, stop payment, etc.
6. Keeps records and/or files of important memos, documents, or other material to provide the area or individuals that he/she supports with easy access to information.
7. Ensures that inventory (forms, money, supplies, records, etc.) is efficiently managed and available when needed for the everyday operation of business.
8. Receives and processes incoming or outgoing correspondence (mail, coupons, etc.) and routes or delivers to appropriate personnel or location quickly and efficiently.
9. Analyzes or reviews content of various in-house jobs and makes classification or salary recommendations in a clear, concise form.
10. Devotes considerable attention to accuracy and completeness in gathering and reviewing information for financial or statistical research work.
11. Plans and designs research or computer systems projects carefully, consulting all involved, anticipating potential problems, and setting realistic time frames.
12. Provides clear, concise, and complete documentation that supports computer systems installation or research findings.
13. Reviews and/or verifies research project or computer systems work prepared by other company personnel for procedural quality, accuracy, and adequacy in meeting requirements and resolves problems that are identified.
14. Gives considerable attention to accuracy, detail, and style in the preparation of reports, memoranda, etc.
15. Reviews credit proposals to ensure their completeness and adequacy in light of current credit policy and relevant financial conditions.
16. Reviews credit agreements for adequacy in light of current credit policy and follows up on problems that may arise with regard to that agreement.
17. Uses good judgment in credit recommendations; ably identifies possible risks and rewards.
18. Prepares complete, concise, and accurate customer or industry profiles to support credit decisions.
19. Researches and/or follows up on inquiries, problems, or complaints from customers or users (other departments, outside agencies, etc.), and resolves the matter in a competent, timely fashion.
20. In telephone contact with the public (customers, outside agencies, etc.), represents the Corporation personably, efficiently, and tactfully.
21. In face to face contact with the public (customers, outside agencies, etc.), represents the Corporation personably, efficiently, and tactfully.
22. Effectively counsels customers or potential customers as to the use of existing branch, retail, or credit services.
23. Aggressively sells or promotes branch, retail, or credit services to potential clients.
24. Deals effectively and tactfully with the staff of other departments, units, or their management in accomplishing joint ventures.

Figure 6-1.   (Page 2)

	I Staff member	II Super- visor	III Agree- ment	IV Weight

SECTION I—PERFORMANCE ITEMS (Continued)

25. Proposes new projects or changes in operations to a user area, effectively sells the proposals to senior management or to the staff affected, and follows through to implementation.

26. Makes accurate and well-founded staffing decisions based on effective interview techniques.

27. Makes clear, concise, and effective presentations with or without the use of audio-visual aids.

28. Knows the functions and responsibilities of all jobs, units or sections within his/her area and successfully integrates them to solve problems or complete projects in the most efficient manner possible. Where required, adequately represents area progress or status to management and ensures the accuracy of any work passed on.

29. Provides sound coaching, training, and cross-training of staff members and individuals new to the job or task to ensure the competency and flexibility of the unit.

30. Effectively manages the workflow for his/her area of responsibility. Delegates work to the appropriate level and prioritizes any new work taken on. Shows a good sense of the strengths and capacities of staff to get the most from the unit and to keep staff interested and challenged.

31. Effectively conducts developmental performance appraisals, both formally at time of review and informally throughout the year. Provides effective feedback and direction. Motivates and assists subordinates in their personal development and gives appropriate credit and praise. Ties monetary reward to performance. Criticizes privately and constructively.

32. Interacts with staff in a manner which shows tact, stability, and concern for staff welfare; commands respect from employees and in turn demonstrates a respect for them through the establishment of upward and downward communication channels.

33. Receives visitors, answers questions, and refers them to appropriate personnel or locations.

34. Provides vigilant security and armed protection and calmly handles potential problems.

35. Notifies designated individuals of meetings and telephone messages, makes luncheon or travel arrangements, or performs similar administrative functions. (Functions may be further specified on page 5).

36. Types accurately from stenographic notes in a grammatically correct manner.

37. Types accurately from straight copy, rough draft or dictation; clears up any confusion before typing final copy so as to avoid wasted time and effort.

38. Types accurate tables, graphs or charts based on data supplied from others.

39. Translates bilingual business correspondence accurately and efficiently.

40. Operates keyboard machinery (typewriter, word processor, keypunch machine, computer terminal) at an acceptable pace with a minimum of errors.

41. Efficiently processes bank, cut-off, or credit statements in order to maintain up-to-date records.

42. Prepares data for entry into the computer system accurately and efficiently; demonstrates knowledge of program correction and similar routines.

43. Identifies and corrects breakdowns, shortcomings, or errors in data processing systems.

Figure 6-1.   (Page 3)

	I Staff member	II Supervisor	III Agreement	IV Weight

SECTION I—PERFORMANCE ITEMS (Continued)

44. Operates job-related machinery (other than keyboard) in a prescribed manner at an acceptable pace with a minimum amount of errors, e.g., unit inscriber, proof machine, tabulating machine, microfilm machine, microfich machine, duplicating machine, multilith.

44. ___ ___ ___ ___

45. Competently provides service functions to the company, e.g., maintenance, cleaning, repair tasks, moving furniture and equipment. (Functions may be further specified on page 5.)

45. ___ ___ ___ ___

46. Possesses a knowledge of vehicle routes and pick-up points and makes prompt and efficient deliveries of mail, supplies, personnel, etc.

46. ___ ___ ___ ___

47. Possess a thorough understanding of credit practices, relevant foreign or domestic markets, and other pertinent economic or financial information and applies it in analysis and report preparation.

47. ___ ___ ___ ___

48. Applies knowledge in a high-level technical or professional field relevant to the job (e.g., computer science, behavioral science, economics, law, accounting, etc.) and keeps abreast of new developments in that field. Specify field:

_____

_____

48. ___ ___ ___ ___

49. Applies the secretarial skills of spelling and grammar in the preparation and/or editing of correspondence and reports.

49. ___ ___ ___ ___

SECTION II—WORK HABITS

The work habit items listed below do not require the agreement used for performance items in as much as all staff members, regardless of their jobs, should be evaluated on them as a matter of course. Supervisors and incumbents should discuss the weight applied to each work habit; use the weighting scale described on page 6.

Weight

1. Organizes time and work efficiently to meet deadlines, recognizes work flow priorities and carefully plans short-term and long-term projects.   _____

2. Exhibits a high energy level, approaches work enthusiastically, takes on work without being told, sets high goals and is willing to work toward them, strives to learn more about the job, willing to work on a problem until completion, persevering, not easily distracted.   _____

3. Works well with others, supportive, concerned about the needs of others as well as job goals, offers help and assistance when it is needed to the benefit of the functioning of the unit or area.   _____

4. Is supportive of management decisions; readily adjusts to changing work priorities, new worker relationships, or changes in operational procedures; can accept criticism and direction.   _____

5. Works effectively with minimum supervision; follows instructions or established procedures with little problem; performs in an efficient, professional manner in unusual or difficult situations and ably identifies problems which require the assistance of supervisors.   _____

6. Adheres to personnel policies regarding absenteeism, punctuality, and personal use of the phone.   _____

Figure 6–1.   (Page 4)

Space is provided below to combine and/or specify within selected performance items. Please copy down the number of the items that you wish to combine or further elaborate on. For each specific objective or goal dealing with a general performance or work habit item designate a numberical character; e.g., 40-1, 40-2, etc. Under option one the supervisor may weight and evaluate the incumbent on each objective specified or give only one weight and evaluate the more general item. Under option two only one weight is assigned to each set of bracketed items.

Item Number	Objective	Weight

Figure 6-1.   (Page 5)

WEIGHTING: To be completed when the staff member and the supervisor meet—Once performance items have been agreed upon, all performance items checked in column III and all work habit items must be assigned weights mutually agreed upon by supervisor and staff member using the scale provided below. Agreed-upon weight are recorded in Column IV.

WEIGHTING SCALE

WEIGHT	DEFINITION
5	This aspect is extremely important and highly relevant to the successful performance of the job.
4	This aspect is important to the job and should be given considerable weight in determining performance.
3	This aspect is relevant to the successful performance of the job and should be given weight in evaluating over-all performance.
2	This aspect, while relevant, has somewhat limited importance relative to other aspects in describing overall performance in this job.
1	Relatively infrequent or unimportant when compared to major job duties. Still, this aspect should be given some weight in determining performance.

OVERALL WEIGHTING

To be completed when the supervisor and the staff member meet—Each job requires both good performance and good work habits. However, jobs differ as to which of these aspects is more important (in some jobs they may be equally important). The staff member and supervisor should now agree upon the relative weight assigned to the Performance Item Section and the Work Habits Section in determining the overall performance rating. Use the five point weighting scale (above) to evaluate the importance of both the performance aspect and the work habit aspect of this job; record these weights in the spaces provided below.

Weight

Performance _____

Work Habits _____

This completed form represents final agreement between the staff member and supervisor on all relevant aspects of the job. This information will be the basis for the performance appraisal. The supervisor and staff member should each retain a copy of the form.

Acknowledgement

_____
Staff Member

_____
Supervisor

_____
Date

To the supervisor: The relevant performance item and all work habit item numbers and weights should be transferred to the PR-3802 form so that performance evaluation can begin. Both the supervisor and incumbent should have the Job Content Form before them throughout the evaluation interview.

7650 12/80

24447F

Figure 6-1.   (Page 6)

Fully Adequate (FA)	Performance has measured satisfactorily to what is expected of an employee in this position.
Fair (F)	Performance has not fully measured up to what is expected of an employee in this position; needs improvement.
Not Adequate (NA)	Performance has been consistently below what is expected of an employee within this position; probation should be considered.
Unable to Evaluate (UE)	Unable to evaluate employee's performance; this rating may be given because the employee has not yet had an opportunity to demonstrate performance in a particular area.

The challenge with any rating system is to stay away from the common comparison which most human resources professionals originally experienced in school; i.e., a C rating is "average." Even if ratings are numerical, the time-tested experience has been to use a different scale other than 0–100.

Sample of Numerical Scale

EVALUATION SCALE

PERFORMANCE POINTS

80

(EX)*	PERFORMANCE IS UNUSUAL AND CLEARLY OF DISTINGUISHED QUALITY. CONTRIBUTION IS NOTICEABLY OUTSTANDING FOR THIS GRADE AND JOB.

---

*Relation to rating system described on previous page. The advantages of using numerical scores is the facility of "weighting" specific objectives or accountabilities. Perhaps the only disadvantage is that it is harder to achieve a separation of substance versus mechanics in the actual review process.

70

PERFORMANCE IN MOST CASES EXCEEDS STANDARDS FOR THIS
GRADE AND JOB.
(AE) CONTRIBUTION IS ABOVE EXPECTANCY OVERALL.

65

(FA) PERFORMANCE MEASURES SATISFACTORILY TO ALL STANDARDS.

56

PERFORMANCE COMES CLOSE TO MEETING STANDARDS BUT THE
NEED FOR FURTHER DEVELOPMENT IS RECOGNIZABLE IN ONE OR
(F) MORE ASPECTS.

50

PERFORMANCE IS CLEARLY BELOW THE LEVEL OF ACCEPTABIL-
ITY. DEVELOPMENT OR OTHER JOB ACTION IS REQUIRED IN A
(NA) RELATIVELY SHORT PERIOD.

20

Evaluation of Results

Serving as a reinforcement to the evaluation process and being a re-
flection of the individual to the job expectations, these two sections
serve to look at specific assignments, within the context of overall
performance.

Statement of Results

Description

This section is used to evaluate the major assignment given to the employee during the last year.
See Figure 6–2, Section A.

---

*Major
Assignments*

Major assignments listed should reflect the objectives set for the employee at the last review.
The manager refers to the objectives sections of
the employee's last performance appraisal and

COMPUTER PROCESSING AND RESEARCH

PERFORMANCE APPRAISAL FORM

NAME: _____

DATE: _____

PART I: PERFORMANCE APPRAISAL

STATEMENT OF RESULTS

MAJOR ASSIGNMENTS: LIST THE MAJOR PROJECT ASSIGNMENTS FOR THE REVIEW PERIOD JUST PAST. INDICATE THE RESULT IN TERMS OF QUALITY AND TIMELINESS.

ASSIGNMENT	QUALITY (RATING)	TIME- LINESS*	SUPERVISOR'S COMMENTS (OPTIONAL)

*INDICATE AHEAD OF SCHEDULE (AS), ON SCHEDULE (OS), OR BEHIND SCHEDULE (BS).

STATEMENT OF ACCOUNTABILITIES

RATING

A. TECHNICAL ASSIGNMENTS: ADD OTHERS, IF NECESSARY.

1. DEMONSTRATES A THOROUGH AND CURRENT KNOWLEDGE OF THE TECHNIQUES REQUIRED IN THE FIELD OF SPECIALIZATION AND IMAGINATIVELY APPLIES THEM IN AN ACCURATE AND THOROUGH EXECUTION OF WORK ASSIGNMENTS. _____

2. WORKS EFFECTIVELY WITH MINIMUM SUPERVISION, NOT REQUIRING UNDUE GUIDANCE BUT ONLY IDENTIFYING THE PROBLEMS WHICH REQUIRE THE ASSISTANCE OF SUPERVISORS. _____

3. MEETS WORK SCHEDULE WITH DETERMINATION PROVIDING ADVANCED NOTICE AND ALTERNATE PLANS WHEN CHANGING CIRCUMSTANCES MAY AFFECT THE DEADLINE. _____

4. REPRESENTS THE UNIT COMPETENTLY AND TACTFULLY IN OBTAINING INFORMATION AND DEVISING SOLUTIONS WITH ASSOCIATES, MEMBERS OF OTHER DEPARTMENTS, ACCOUNT OFFICERS, OR CUSTOMERS. _____

5. FORMULATES PROPOSALS, PROBLEMS AND RESULTS ARTICULATELY IN WRITTEN WORK AND IN CONVERSATION. _____

RATING

B. SUPERVISORY ASSIGNMENTS: ADD OTHERS, IF NECESSARY.

1. SUPERVISES THE WORK OF THE UNIT, MEETING WORK SCHEDULES AND CUSTOMER REQUIREMENTS IN ACCORDANCE WITH OPERATING PROCEDURES, CONTROLS AND STANDARDS. _____

2. TRAINS AND DEVELOPS STAFF MEMBERS TO PROVIDE THE QUALITY AND CUSTOMER SERVICE REQUIRED, AND DEVELOPS INDIVIDUAL ABILITIES TO TAKE ADVANTAGE OF THE POTENTIAL OF EACH PERSON, AS WELL AS PROVIDE THE FLEXIBILITY NEEDED BY ABSENCES AND PEAK PERIODS. _____

3. MOTIVATES THE STAFF TO MAXIMUM PERFORMANCE AND COOPERATION BY PERSONAL EXAMPLES OF LEADERSHIP, PROPER COMMUNICATIONS AND RECOMMENDATION OF APPROPRIATE PERSONNEL ACTION (e.g. SALARY INCREASES, PROMOTIONS, JOB ASSIGNMENTS AND IF NECESSARY, DISCIPLINARY ACTION). _____

4. KNOWS THOROUGHLY ALL OF THE WORK, CONTROLS AND AUTHORITIES OF THE UNIT, ENABLING HIM TO EFFECTIVELY SUPERVISE, TO PROVIDE ASSISTANCE AS REQUIRED BY ABSENCES AND WORKLOAD, AND TO RECOMMEND IMPROVEMENTS. _____

5. DEMONSTRATES A CONSTANT AWARENESS OF BUSINESS DEVELOPMENT THROUGH QUALITY CUSTOMER SERVICE BY PERSONALLY INCREASING PRESENT RELATIONSHIPS. _____

M-5590 8/75

Figure 6-2.   Performance appraisal form. (Part 1)

STATEMENT OF ACCOUNTABILITIES – CONTINUED

C. PERSONAL ACCOUNTABILITIES: RATE THOSE ACCOUNTABILITIES APPLICABLE TO THE EMPLOYEE IN HIS CURRENT POSITION. ADD OTHER PERSONAL ACCOUNT-ABILITIES, IF NECESSARY.

	RATING		RATING
ATTITUDE TOWARDS JOB		INITIATIVE	
ABILITY TO TAKE SUPERVISION		ADAPTABILITY	
ABILITY TO WORK UNDER PRESSURE		PERSEVERANCE	

D. ADDITIONAL ACCOUNTABILITIES: OPTIONAL – FOR ACCOUNTABILITIES NOT COVERED IN A, B, or C (e.g. APPLICATIONS KNOWLEDGE)

RATING _____

ATTENDANCE AND PUNCTUALITY

OCCURRENCES:

FROM: / / TO: / / NUMBER OF DAYS ABSENT _____

NUMBER OF DAYS LATE _____ NUMBER OF OCCASIONS ABSENT _____

REASON FOR EXCESSIVE ABSENCE:

SUPERVISOR'S COMMENTS

FIRST LINE MANAGER'S COMMENTS:

ADDITIONAL COMMENTS OF SECOND LINE MANAGER:

SUMMARY RATING

SUMMARY OF PERFORMANCE:

☐ EXCEPTIONAL ☐ ABOVE EXPECTANCY ☐ FULLY ADEQUATE

☐ FAIR ☐ NOT ADEQUATE

Figure 6-2. (Part 2)

PART II: OBJECTIVES

A. **OBJECTIVES FOR DEFICIENT ACCOUNTABILITIES:** USE IN AREAS WHERE THERE ARE ACCOUNTABILITY IMPROVEMENTS NECESSARY BECAUSE OF A FAIR (F) OR NOT ADEQUATE (NA) RATING IN ANY OF THE STATEMENT OF ACCOUNTABILITIES.

B. **JOB RELATED OBJECTIVES/ASSIGNMENTS:** LIST THE EMPLOYEE'S MAJOR PROJECT ASSIGNMENTS TO BE ACCOMPLISHED OVER THE NEXT REVIEW PERIOD.

C. **ACCOUNTABILITY OBJECTIVES:** LIST THOSE OBJECTIVES REQUIRED FOR THE SUCCESSFUL ACCOMPLISHMENT OF THE EMPLOYEE'S WORK ASSIGNMENTS AND NECESSARY FOR HIS FUTURE GROWTH.

1. **TECHNICAL ACCOUNTABILITIES:**

2. **SUPERVISORY ACCOUNTABILITIES:**

3. **PERSONAL ACCOUNTABILITIES:**

Figure 6-2. (Part 3)

PART III: SIGNATURES

OFFICER SIGNATURES:

FIRST LINE MANAGER: _____ TITLE: _____ DATE: _____

SECOND LINE MANAGER: _____ TITLE: _____ DATE: _____

THIRD LINE MANAGER _____ TITLE: _____ DATE: _____

DEPARTMENT HEAD: _____ TITLE: _____ DATE: _____

PERSONNEL: _____ TITLE: _____ DATE: _____

EMPLOYEE COMMENTS & ACKNOWLEDGEMENT: IF YOU HAVE ANY COMMENTS REGARDING THIS REVIEW, STATE THEM BELOW. IF NO COMMENT, SO INDICATE.

EMPLOYEE'S ACKNOWLEDGEMENT: _____ DATE: _____

**MANUFACTURERS HANOVER TRUST
COMPUTER PROCESSING AND RESEARCH
PERFORMANCE APPRAISAL FORM**

Figure 6–2.   (Part 4)

six-month counseling forms. Other major assignments not previously specified as objectives must also be included.

Example

If the employee is assigned to perform the design and implementation of a large, complex program, one assignment entry might mention the design, another the coding and implementation and a third the system and program documentation.

Statement of Accountabilities

Description

These sections evaluate the employee in terms of technical assignments (B in Figure 6–2), supervisory assignments (C), personnel accountabilities (D) and additional accountabilities (E). These are the aspects of the employee's performance that account for the quality and timeliness ratings given in the statement of results section. The ratings for these sections are also based on the "explanation of performance ratings"; i.e., EX, AE, FA, F, NA or UE. Non-applicable accountabilities are left blank.

*Technical
Assignments*

This section (B) is used to evaluate the employee's technical skills pertinent to his or her present position. The manager may want to add and evaluate technical assignments not covered in Items 1 through 5, based on the technical objectives set at previous reviews.

*Supervisory
Assignments*

This section (C) is used to evaluate the employee's supervisory skills pertinent to his or her present position. This section is used only for employees who have been given some degree of supervisory responsibility. The manager may want to add and evaluate supervisory assignments not covered in Items 1 through 5, based on supervisory objectives set at previous reviews.

Personal
Accountabilities

This section (D) is used to evaluate the employee's personal attributes that affect his or her performance. The manager may want to add and evaluate the personal accountabilities not listed and based on personal objectives set at previous reviews. Because of the subjective nature of these accountabilities, they are further defined below.

Attitude
Toward Job

Demonstrates a professional approach to one's work and its quality; is concerned about the success of the overall department; maintains a positive and constructive attitude to one's job.

Ability to Take
Supervision

Willingly accepts assignments, direction and constructive suggestions from one's supervisor.

Ability to Work
Under Pressure

Maintains a consistent level of productivity during periods when reasonable circumstances may require a "more than normal" effort.

Initiative

Approaches assignments aggressively; uses ingenuity in their completion; seeks additional responsibility within one's capacity.

Adaptability

Is able to adjust oneself to changes affecting assignments.

Perseverance   Shows consistent determination in tackling one's assignments; persists in overcoming obstacles.

Additional   This section (E) is used to evaluate any ac-
Accountabilities   countability not covered by Sections B through D. Accountabilities may be listed here and evaluated using the same ratings as in previous sections.

A recent and dramatic improvement over the personal accountabilities checklist has been the substitution of an updated section called "work habits." These inputs may be weighted, based on the importance to the job.

WORK HABITS

The work habit items listed below do not require the agreement used for performance items inasmuch as all staff members—regardless of their jobs—should be evaluated on them as a matter of course. Supervisors and incumbents should discuss the weight applied to each work habit.

WORK HABITS EVALUATION CRITERIA*

1. Organize time and work efficiently to meet deadlines, recognizes work flow priorities and carefully plans short-term and long-term projects.   _____

2. Exhibits a high energy level, approaches work enthusiastically, takes on work without being told, sets high goals and is willing to work toward them, strives to learn more about the job and is willing to work on a problem until completion, persevering and not being easily distracted.   _____

3. Works well with others, is supportive, is concerned about the needs of others as well as job goals and

---

*Copyright MHT. (see Figure 6-1 for complete form).

offers help and assistance when it is needed to the
benefit of the functioning of the unit or areas. _____

4. Is supportive of management decisions, readily adjusts to changing work priorities, new worker relationships or changes in operational procedures and
can accept criticism and direction. _____

5. Works effectively with minimum supervision, follows instructions or established procedures with little
problem, performs in an efficient, professional manner in unusual or difficult situations and ably identifies problems which require the assistance of
supervisors. _____

6. Adheres to personnel policies regarding absenteeism,
punctuality and personal use of the phone. _____

THE EVALUATION PROCESS USING
CHECKS AND BALANCES

Too often, a corporate manager approaches a pending appraisal with
the foregone conclusion syndrome.

"I know this employee is an exceptional performer," notes the
manager. "What rating will justify a certain salary increase?" is a
question that may be raised. Or, worse, a response such as: "Infla-
tion is 15 percent, and I need to keep employee John Jones, even
though John Jones is just OK."

The foregone conclusion syndrome, if pervasive, is dangerous.
And if the system allows that self-destructive syndrome to prevail,
something is critically wrong. The syndrome wastes actual dollars,
and it does not accomplish anything much in the way of communicating to and developing the human resource.

Inherent in a two-dimensional human resources review is a system
of checks and balances. A manager searches for tangible results, and
the reasons behind those results. For example, it would be incon-
sistent to view ratings of above expectancy (AE) for the quality of
assignments for a project supervisor, and subsequently see fully adequate (FA) under relevant supervisory accountabilities.

A project leader's responsibility is to manage the productivity of
all team members to complete a goal. Reading through the account-

ability descriptions should aid a manager in finding strengths/weaknesses to truly isolate specific areas for praise or reform.

Objectives

Whether a manager chooses to separate the evaluation process into two separate sessions—close enough, one would hope, so there is logical continuity—the evaluation is only complete with setting objectives and goals for the coming year.

Ideally, discussions about performance, development, career choices, etc., should take place whenever appropriate, but it's routinely assumed that many managers have difficulty finding the time.

Our experience has been to complete the entire evaluation process. However, the objectives portion should be one of collaboration, not a *fait d'accompli*. For that key reason, it may be more productive to hold this discussion within a day or two of the formal review, so that both the manager and the employee have time to construct realistic objectives relative to job improvement/advancement.

Objectives Section

Deficient Accountabilities, Job-Related	The objectives section is used to set into action three types of objectives: objectives for deficient accountabilities (I), job-related objectives/assignments (J) and accountability objectives (K). Sections I and J are discussed here; Section K is discussed on the next page.
Objectives for Deficient Accountabilities,	This section (I) is used to define objectives which address those accountabilities of rated fair or not adequate in Part I. If there are no fair or not adequate ratings, this area is left blank. "Deficiency" objectives must be stated in specific terms to provide a clear understanding between manager and employee concerning the nature of the deficiency, the recommended methods of improvement over

the coming year, and the criteria that will be used to evaluate the improvement.

Job-Related Objectives/ Assignments

This section (J) is used by the manager to state the specific assignments the employee is expected to accomplish over the next year. These assignments will be evaluated 12 months later at the employee's next performance appraisal in terms of quality and timeliness, i.e., under the statement of results section in Part I. However, because assignments often change over the course of a year, the manager has the option of modifying these objectives at the employee's six-month counseling session. These assignments should be specific enough to include all various aspects of an assignment to be evaluated rather than the assignment as a whole. Whenever possible, target dates should be indicated.

Technical Supervisory, Personal

This section (K) is used to identify objectives relating to the accountabilities associated with the employee's present and/or next position. The objectives should include areas of improvement and growth that the manager expects of the employee through working on the assignments listed in Section J (job-related objectives/assignments). Accountabilities objectives are divided into three categories— technical, supervisory and personal (the same as in the statement of accountabilities, Part I). Most of these objectives should be specific in nature and pertain directly to one or more of the assignments listed. Whenever possible, the accountability objective and the corresponding assignment should be stated. Some objectives may be of a more general nature (i.e., an improvement expected through work on all the assignments or responsibilities).

Technical Accountabilities

This section (K) is required for personnel at all grade levels. It includes objectives relating to technical abilities, such as development of programming skills, systems skills and communication skills.

Example

Following are two examples of technical accountability objectives, one specific and one general.

- *Specific:* Increase knowledge of coding techniques through work on the Phase 3 Control Program.
- *General:* Improve the logical structure and organization of code through better allotment of time spent in the initial stages of flowcharting and planning.

Supervisory Accountabilities

This section (L) is required only for individuals who are to be given functional supervisory responsibility during the next year. These include objectives such as the planning of work assignments, distribution of work assignments, development and utilization of personnel.

Personal Accountabilities

This section (M) is required for personnel at all grade levels. These objectives tend to be more general than the others; e.g., improving one's attitude toward the job, working more independently and with more initiative.

How Do You Get Managers to Write Good Objectives?

Objectives should satisfy the requirements of who, what and when will be measured, with an accompanying statement of quality.

Objective Example

"Construct user specifications on the ABC project, approved by John Jones VP and your project leader by August 15, 1983. Tolerance for variance to specifications cannot exceed 15 percent."

Writing good objectives is difficult. It is the responsibility of both the manager and the staff member because that action is the crux of future evaluation.

Comments Section

Section G calls for comments for both the first and second line manager. There is a subtle but strong reason why the organization asks the second line manager to participate. A good first line manager should be accountable for the visibility of all subordinates. Second line managers should take an interest. The employee should reap the benefit. It is hoped that this will not be used as a battleground of disagreement between the opinions of the first and second manager.

Summary Rating

"If this was filled in first, we're back at square one," is not the best approach to begin the process. The following outlines the correct avenues for implementing the summary rating action.

Summary Rating	The summary rating (H) is an evaluation of the employer's overall performance. The manager reviews all the ratings on the form, carefully weighting them to arrive at the summary rating. Assignments are weighted by their relative importance to each other. Factors that determine the importance of an assignment are:

- The criticality of the project to the user.
- The size of the project; the length of time spent on it in the review period.
- The complexity of the project.

Accountabilities are weighted by their criticality to the responsibilities described in the position description. For example, technical accountability, Number 5 (communicates proposals, problems and results articulately in written work and in conversation), is weighted more heavily for a systems analyst than for a systems engineer since it is more critical to the successful performance of the system analyst position.

As mentioned earlier, use of a numerical system greatly facilitates weighting and coming up with an overall weighted average.

IMPLEMENTING A PERFORMANCE APPRAISAL SYSTEM

Mentioned earlier was the aspect of "ownership." It is paramount that managers and staff (your future managers)—feel that the system belongs to them. For example, they feel it makes sense, it reflects their needs, they can identify with the specific system's aspects: job descriptions, accountabilities and the process as a whole. Simply, it must speak their language and be broadly applied.

The system described in this book—and, in fact, all the processes—was developed by DP professionals who had joined the human resources (HR) ranks because they believed there were better and more creative solutions to managing DP staffers—their own kind. And together with line managers, these systems took firm roots.

It is not surprising that, when corporate personnel required that all departments conform to a new companywide appraisal system, the DPHR pioneers felt invaded. However, in the aftermath, when all the dust settled, a better system emerged—one that allowed us to retain the aspects of our system and take advantage of some new ideas in the companywide version. The new ideas incorporated were:

- A standard job content form which allowed for selection from a wide range of accountabilities, those which will be used for the coming review period. Objectives—specific project-related or professional—are still set and tied into the appropriate accountability.
- Numerical ratings. Same definitions but the added flexibility to weight (on a scale of 1 to 5, 5 being most important) each accountability. Specific projects may also receive individual weights.
- Vastly improved personal accountabilities.

TIPS ON BEGINNING THE PROCESS

Whether you are starting from scratch, revising, or cooperating with corporate personnel—regardless of whether you are responsible to a specific department or in corporate personnel—the key to success is to establish and reinforce corporatewide "ownership" throughout the project development and implementation.

Set up a management task force which reviews and participates every step of the way. Conduct sessions with groups of first and second line managers. Most important, obtain senior management support at project onset and during the development. We rarely made any project changes without the involvement of managers, and that cross-involvement strategy really paid off.

Tip

It requires a great deal of time and effort to enlist and involve user management, ranging from line managers up through senior management. Those are the players who will either make or break a system. Don't ever implement or consider a project plan for developing and launching a new or different appraisal process without directly involving user management. Meanwhile, if another analogy is required, consider the implementation of a universal DP project. Those projects with the highest success marks were those in which the user has had active, continual involvement.

THE PROCESS: A COMPLETED APPRAISAL FORM

Previous sections went through the components of a performance appraisal system, the product of many hours of discussion between DP managers and the DPHR staff. Readers examined a form, and rather detailed explanations of each section. The next section details how to arrive at the final product—a completed appraisal form—also known as the process.

Briefly cited, there is more to a good appraisal system than a form. Training managers in the process in an integral part of an evaluation system. The following explains why.

The Law of Thirds

However ambitious the goals of a newly planned HR system are, consider this:

- One-third of your managers will probably have good skills and the kind of attitude that invites new ideas.
- One-third of your existing managerial ranks probably will never have good skills, because they originally should never have been promoted to manager.
- One-third of your managerial ranks* could have good skills.

Objective

To repeat what was previously mentioned, "the evaluation process is one of constructively communicating feedback to an employee so that both the individual and the organization is enhanced by realizing the potential of the individual."

Delivering a fair evaluation is hard work and "no-nonsense" decision making. Better preparation yields greater satisfaction for both manager and employee—and the corporation also becomes a happy winner/participant.

Providing a good evaluation requires experience on top of hard work. Subsequent lower turnover rates and vastly improved employee morale show that "the proof is in the pudding."

---

*These are the managers you can teach to do fair performance appraisals, and some will go on to become exceptional managers. With a good system, you should get "two-thirds," a very acceptable majority. (What you do with the other third will not be addressed in this chapter.)

HOW TO PREPARE THE REVIEW

Prepare Yourself for the Assignment

What are you going to rate? What project-related and job-related objectives are relevant to the previous employee review period?

It's a good idea to review the criteria with the employee before you begin. Documentation need not be current. If that is the case, it may be appropriate to adjust the weight of certain items. Make it a priority to review all pertinent documentation in the employee's file, particularly if the review involves a new or transferred employee. When rating a formerly transferred employee, the previous manager should be consulted. A joint review is highly feasible, should circumstances permit.

Tip

Before starting the process, it is also a good idea to review the employee's current job description. This "anchors" expectations, and provides useful reference both during preparation and actually conducting the review.

How to Prepare the Employee for the Review Process

Go over what is going to happen at the review. Review the appraisal form and request that the employee arrive prepared to discuss the past year's accomplishments and also give input to objectives for the coming year.

Rate Assignments for Quality and Timeliness

Construct carefully prepared notes explaining what criteria led you to produce a particular rating. The notes are important. After all, you will have to substantiate your rating to the employee, and those same notes will further help you in identifying future specific objectives.

If you are using a numerical scale—as appears on page 174—be consistent in applying scores when there is a point spread between categories. It's best to use the midway point if you feel the performance is somewhere "in between" one of the categories. Many a review discussion has been lost to the mechanics of numbers.

Rate Accountabilities

Technical, personal and supervisory (if appropriate) rate accountabilities constitute the crucial "check and balances" phase. There should be a logical relationship of project/assignments ratings and the accountability ratings. Again, construct concrete notes to support the subsequent explanation to the employee during the review.

How to Prepare the Summary Rating

If you are using a numerical system, this then becomes purely mathematical. If the numerical system is not used, be very thorough in reviewing each rating and its contribution to the overall performance. Asterisk those projects or assignments carrying the most weight so you can easily refer to them during the review.

Write comments in the area provided for the first line supervisor. Most important, don't short-change this opportunity—or yourself—to offer gems of praise, noteworthy contribution, etc. This key document will also probably be read by several other key players, notably, your manager, in addition to becoming part of the employee's permanent file.

Review the Appraisal With Your Manager

It is highly recommended to review Part I with your manager—at least until you are both comfortable with the rating process before going on to tackle the objectives section. Chances are favorable that you will both benefit greatly from the discussion. There will be subsequent constructive ideas and suggestions to incorporate in Part II just ahead. Have your manager add his/her comments either now or after Part II is complete.

Tip

If disagreements take place between first and second line managers, here's the game plan. In this process, the second line manger is a coach, a sounding board and a resource for ideas. If wide disagreements exist—where neither side is willing to budge—there's a serious problem. It points to a problem originating outside preparing the performance appraisal. As a general rule—when unresolved performance rating differences linger without resolution, second line managers should support their subordinate managers in ratings, and take up the issue at the subordinate manager's review.

How to Prepare Objectives for the Coming Year

This should be a collaborative effort. Avoid filling in the objectives in pen and don't monopolize the entire space! Leave sufficient room for the collaborator. Make all entries on a separate page, and, by all means, don't let the form size of the box constrain the content. Keep in mind that the objectives will be difficult to construct. Plan them in advance carefully, and always aim for satisfying the crucial who, what and when criteria.

Signatures

Review the entire appraisal with your manager and obtain the necessary signatures. Space has been included for third managers and department heads. The line for personnel and the section for the employee will be filled in after the review.

What About Salary Increase?

If you plan to discuss a salary increase, make sure you have received the necessary approvals. Have a firm grasp of company and department policy on salary administration before entering that area—you'll be stepping on a mine-field. Make sure you're absolutely certain of the individual's salary history, department budget guidelines, the next employee salary review date and the augmenting policy on promotional raises, etc. Most important, make sure the employee understands the link between increases/promotions and performance. You'll be missing a golden opportunity for motivation if you don't, or don't use it.

Rehearse your Plan of Action

It's one of the best techniques employed to help you culminate the process and support your explanations. Rehearse what you plan to say—with your manager or someone in a human resource capacity. If that is not possible, just go over the tough parts. You'll gain confidence, and subsequently find that you'll be more relaxed when meeting "face-to-face" with the respective employee.

Guidelines for Conducting the Review

If all advance preparation, "homework," has been accomplished, conducting the review will be easy. Here's how to next set the interview into action.

- Set the interview time in advance, and allow at least an hour.
- At all costs, avoid interruptions.
- Review the "agenda" with the staff member.
- Be sure to have copies of all pertinent documents.
- Don't assume the employee knows as much about the process, definitions, etc., as you do. Take time to discuss each sections.
- Encourage feedback and questions.
- This meeting is not a social affair—or the time to be weak and uncertain. You must be in control. If there is a particular item which becomes deadlocked, return to it later. If necessary, take the opportunity to think about the matter overnight to help you make the correct decision.

Remember: Providing a fair evaluation is hard work. It's not uncommon to require three or four hours of advance preparation, and another one or two hours to implement. Better preparation produces the joint likelihood of satisfaction for both manager and employee. Experience is the best teacher!

WHAT WAS LEARNED

What we have learned throughout the entire evolutionary process would fall into three areas: 1) general issues, 2) specific enhancements and 3) on-going challenges.

THE GENERAL ISSUES

1. We have learned that senior management needs to reinforce the process by placing emphasis on its quality and provide appropriate rewards. As a result, this system today enjoys far more success in areas where middle and senior management origi-

nally invested quarterly periods of time to conduct informal reviews.

2. We have learned that no system is perfect and that no one system works for all areas. We have discovered that considerable adaptation was required when we undertook to implement a similar system in the data operations center. The adaptation was required primarily because the environment was a "task-oriented" one—not a project orientation, which we had operational in the systems and programming area. The basic concepts worked well, but required being supplemented with even far greater structure.

3. We also have learned that first-hand interaction with the user group needs to be frequent and constructive. This frontline task is the primary role of the HR advisors who have the responsibility of reviewing all performance appraisals for quality and completeness. Previous to implementing the advisor role, we sensed that we had lost "hands-on" touch with the system and the subsequent dynamics of environment had truly taken over. We also discovered that new managers were not using the appraisal process properly—and for good reasons. It was out of date. We knew what would bring the process up-to-date: Job descriptions needed review, regular training needed to be scheduled and changes in company procedures needed to be accommodated, etc. We also created a "monitor" strategy to ensure updated feedback at all times.

SPECIFIC ENHANCEMENTS

These key modifications—vital to the mushrooming success of the process—have been included in the text on the pages indicated:

1. Job content form (p. 168)
2. Rating scale (p. 174)
3. Work habits (p. 182)

ON-GOING CHALLENGES: A CONSTANT DYNAMIC

Every organization struggles daily with the dynamics of human nature, its own corporate culture and bold pressures inflicted by external forces. These shouldn't come as a surprise and they can be dealt with accordingly. In the meantime, the key internal challenges must be continued to be met and accepted by the new HR leaders. Those frontline responsibilities include the around-the-clock priorities of:

1. Identifying and training individuals with management potential in the contemporary techniques of managing people.
2. Linking performance appraisal with salary administration programs.
3. Understanding and responding to the continuing changes in EEO regulations to keep appraisal systems "honest" and yet meaningful.

It should be noted that the above-mentioned appraisal process—and most all the processes discussed in this book—were designed by DP people who joined the HR ranks because they believed there was a better way to manage their contemporaries in an expanding Computer Age. Our experience over the past years can best by typified by the comment from one key HR player; "The greatest satisfaction has been in being a part of the cultivation process which has produced new and better applications, not to mention some superb managers."

7

Career Counseling

Data processing (DP) people are professionals and require professional management, development and utilization. In these labor-short times, they'll need "above and beyond" career counseling treatment if your organization plans to retain them for any expanded period of time in this decade. And like the rest of America's 100 million workers, they are also known to complain about their daily function in life. Why all this dissatisfaction among the nation's workforce—and sometimes in DP? With some, of course, the correct career has not been found, under-utilizing their talents. Others feel unappreciated, unmotivated, lost in the crowd. Each person must be made to feel that he or she is important. Without that employee, we would have no business, no industry, no economy.

How do we reverse this pattern of dissatisfaction in the DP field? Our career counseling process assists in this effort. We provide a means for people to grow in their jobs through education. We show a clear path ahead, and assure them that their work is leading to advancement, to a desired goal: a feeling of choice, of guiding their own futures. And because of the realities of the tight DP labor market, this concept has an even more specialized application—and can produce significant productivity yields for those organizations who follow it.

The following pages show how that process works. Formal career counseling sessions should occur once a year between the first line manager and the employee. The sessions will provide an opportunity to discuss the individual's career growth and objectives.

These are true counseling sessions and focus in clearly on career path, skills expertise, skills deficiencies, skills development and career development. The subsequent sections define the process in more detail.

CAREER COUNSELING AS AN APPRAISAL/DEVELOPMENT TOOL

Six-Month Counseling The six-month counseling process is both an appraisal and a development tool. It includes an interim performance appraisal and the facility to revise the work objectives established at the performance appraisal. The employee's short- and long-term career goals are discussed and career development objectives are set.

Objectives The objectives of the six-month counseling session are to:

- Conduct an informal evaluation of the employee's performance.
- Discuss the employee's short- and long-term career goals.
- Establish career development objectives for the employee and complete a skills enhancement and education plan.
- Allow the manager to reset the job-related objectives that were established at the last review.

Documents The documents used at this session are as follows.

- Skills update turnaround report (see Figure 7-1)
- Skills profile report (see Figure 7-2)
- Employee education turnaround report (see Figure 7-3)
- Current and next position description (see Figure 7-4)
- Six-month counseling form (see Figure 7-5)
- Previous performance appraisals form (information only)

```
                    CAREER DEVELOPMENT SYSTEM                              REPORT  HRA3300A
                  SKILLS UPDATE TURN-AROUND REPORT                        PAGE NUMBER   1
                                                                          RUN DATE

EMPLOYEE NAME
PRESENT POSITION    SYSTEMS ANALYST                     PAYROLL NUMBER   000 000 -0000
PROJECTED POSITION  SENIOR SYSTEMS ANALYST              SOC.SEC.NUMBER   000 000 -0000
DEPARTMENT          85600
LAST SKILL DATE              NEXT COUNSELING DATE
```

GROUP NAME	SKILL NUMBER	SKILL NAME	SKILL INDV	LEVEL RECM'D	NEW SKILL LEVEL
HARDWARE					
CORE SKILLS					
	AA001	IBM HARDWARE & PERIPHERAL DEVICES	0	2	—
PERIPHIAL SKILLS					
	AA018	COMMUNICATIONS HARDWARE	3		—
	AA020	INSTALLATION PLANNING & LAYOUT	2		—
LANGUAGES					
CORE SKILLS					
	AB001	COBOL	1	3	—
	AB002	IBM ASSEMBLER	0	3	—
	AB014	CICS COMMAND		3	—
	AB015	DL/1 PROGRAMMING		3	—
PERIPHIAL SKILLS					
	AB016	STRUCTURED CODE	2		—
	AB017	FORTRAN	2		—
SYSTEM SOFTWARE					
CORE SKILLS					
	AC001	OS CONCEPTS	0	3	—
	AC002	OS/VS CONCEPTS	0	3	—
	AC003	JOB CONTROL LANGUAGE	1	3	—
	AC004	UTILITIES	0	4	—
	AC005	TIME SHARING OPTION (TSO)	0	3	—
	AC006	DUMP READING	0		—
ANALYSIS					
CORE SKILLS					
	AD001	FEASIBILITY STUDIES	1	2	—
	AD002	FUNCTIONAL SPECIFICATIONS	2	2	—
	AD003	AUDITS & CONTROLS	0	2	—
	AD004	PERT/GANTT CHARTING	0	2	—
	AD005	PROJECT LIFE CYCLE	0		—
	AD006	COST/BENEFIT ANALYSIS	0	2	—

Figure 7-1.   Skills update turnaround report. (Part 1)

```
                                    CAREER DEVELOPMENT SYSTEM                    REPORT   HRA3300A
                                  SKILLS UPDATE TURN-AROUND REPORT               PAGE NUMBER   2
                                                                                RUN DATE

                                                          PAYROLL NUMBER
                                                          SOC.SEC.NUMBER

EMPLOYEE NAME
PRESENT POSITION      SYSTEMS ANALYST
PROJECTED POSITION    SENIOR SYSTEMS ANALYST
DEPARTMENT            88600
LAST SKILL DATE          NEXT COUNSELING DATE
```

GROUP NAME	SKILL NUMBER	SKILL NAME	SKILL LEVEL INDV	RECM'D	NEW SKILL LEVEL
PERIPHIAL SKILLS					
	AD007	HIPO		2	—
	AD010	USER LIAISON/DATA GATHERING		2	—
	AD015	SIMULATION AND MODELING	2		—
DESIGN					
CORE SKILLS					
	AE001	DESIGN SPECIFICATIONS	2	3	—
	AE002	FILE DESIGN	2	3	—
	AE003	PROGRAM DESIGN	2	3	—
	AE004	CATALOGUED PROCEDURE DESIGN	0	2	—
	AE005	BACKUP & RECOVERY	2	2	—
	AE006	TEST PLAN	2	3	—
	AE007	SYSTEM CONVERSION TECHNIQUES		3	—
	AE009	SYSTEMS DESIGN		3	—
	AE011	FORMS DESIGN		3	—
	AE012	DATA BASE DESIGN		3	—
IMPLEMENTATION					
CORE SKILLS					
	AF001	USER DOCUMENTATION	3	3	—
	AF002	USER EDUCATION	2	3	—
	AF003	APPLICATION ACCEPTANCE TESTING	2	2	—
	AF005	PROGRAM DOCUMENTATION		3	—
	AF006	UNIT TESTING		3	—
	AF007	INTERGRATION TESTING		3	—
	AF008	PARALLEL TESTING			—
BUSINESS & INDUSTRY					
CORE SKILLS					
	AI001	ORAL COMMUNICATION	2	3	—
	AI002	WRITTEN COMMUNICATION	3	3	—
	AI003	CORPORATION KNOWLEDGE	2	2	—
PERIPHIAL SKILLS					
	AI009	DATA PROCESSING INDUSTRY	2	3	—
	AI024	COMMERCIAL LOAN	1	2	—

Figure 7-1. (Part 2)

```
                              CAREER DEVELOPMENT SYSTEM                                    REPORT  HRA3300A
                            SKILLS UPDATE TURN-AROUND REPORT                               PAGE NUMBER  3
                                                                                          RUN DATE

EMPLOYEE NAME       SYSTEMS ANALYST                              PAYROLL NUMBER
PRESENT POSITION    SENIOR SYSTEMS ANALYST                       SOC.SEC.NUMBER
PROJECTED POSITION
DEPARTMENT          8Z600
LAST SKILL DATE          NEXT COUNSELING DATE


GROUP NAME          SKILL      SKILL NAME                        SKILL LEVEL   SKILL LEVEL   NEW SKILL
                    NUMBER                                       INDV          RECM'D        LEVEL

                    AI025      PERSONNEL/PAYROLL                     1            _____

MANAGEMENT

     CORE SKILLS
                    AJ001      FUNCTIONAL MANAGEMENT                 1            2
                    AJ003      PLAN, ESTIMATE & CONTROL             2            2          _____
                    AJ008      PROJECT REPORTING                    2            2          _____
                    AJ009      USER LIAISON                                      2          _____
                    AJ010      PROJECT LIFE CYCLE                                2          _____
                    AJ011      PROJECT CONTROL                                   2          _____

     PERIPHIAL SKILLS
                    AJ005      PERSONNEL SELECTION                  2            2          _____
```

Figure 7-1. (Part 3)

CAREER DEVELOPMENT SYSTEM
SKILLS UPDATE TURN-AROUND REPORT

REPORT HRA3300A
PAGE NUMBER 4
RUN DATE

GROUP NAME

SKILL NUMBER	SKILL NAME	SKILL LEVEL INDV RECM'D	SKILL LEVEL RECM'D	NEW SKILL LEVEL

ENTER THE PROJECTED POSITION IF OTHER THAN ABOVE _____

SIGNATURES:

EMPLOYEE'S SIGNATURE _____

MANAGER'S SIGNATURES _____

UPDATED SKILLS DATE _____

TO OBTAIN THE "PRESENT VERSUS PROJECTED POSITION SKILLS REPORT" INDICATE SO BELOW.

PROJECTED POSITION PROFILE _____ .

Figure 7-1. (Part 4)

```
                              CAREER DEVELOPMENT SYSTEM                              REPORT     HRA2700
                           SKILLS IDENTIFIED FOR IMPROVEMENT                         PAGE NUMBER        1
                                                                                     RUN DATE

EMPLOYEE NAME                                                          PAYROLL NUMBER  000 000 -0000
PRESENT POSITION   SENIOR PROGRAMMER ANALYST                           SOC.SEC.NUMBER  000 000 -0000
DEPARTMENT         88600
LAST SKILL DATE
                   ****************************************************
                   *                                                  *
                   *           SKILL LEVEL SELECTION CRITERIA         *
                   *                                                  *
                   *      1 - LESS THAN RECOMMENDED BY 1              *
                   *      2 - LESS THAN RECOMMENDED BY 2              *
                   *      3 - LESS THAN RECOMMENDED BY 3 OR MORE      *
                   *                                                  *
                   ****************************************************
```

GROUP NAME	SKILL NUMBER	SKILL NAME	SKILL LEVEL INDV	RECM'D	CRITERIA 1	2	3
HARDWARE							
	AA001	IBM HARDWARE & PERIPHERAL DEVICES	2	4	X	X	
LANGUAGES							
	AB002	IBM ASSEMBLER		4	X	X	X
	AB014	CICS COMMAND		4	X	X	X
	AB015	DL/1 PROGRAMMING		4	X	X	X
SYSTEM SOFTWARE							
	AC001	OS CONCEPTS	2	4	X	X	X
	AC002	OS/VS CONCEPTS	2	4	X	X	X
	AC003	JOB CONTROL LANGUAGE	2	4	X	X	X
	AC004	UTILITIES	2	4	X	X	
	AC005	TIME SHARING OPTION (TSO)		4	X	X	X
	AC006	DUMP READING		4	X	X	
ANALYSIS							
	AD004	PERT/GANTT CHARTING	2	3	X	X	X
	AD005	PROJECT LIFE CYCLE	1	3	X	X	X
	AD006	COST/BENEFIT ANALYSIS		2	X	X	
	AD007	HIPO		3	X	X	X
	AD010	USER LIAISON/DATA GATHERING		3	X	X	X
DESIGN							
	AE001	DESIGN SPECIFICATIONS	3	4	X	X	
	AE002	FILE DESIGN	2	4	X	X	X
	AE003	PROGRAM DESIGN	3	4	X	X	
	AE004	CATALOGUED PROCEDURE DESIGN	3	4	X		

Figure 7-2. Skills profile report. (Part 1)

```
                              CAREER DEVELOPMENT SYSTEM                          REPORT      HRA2700
                            SKILLS IDENTIFIED FOR IMPROVEMENT                    PAGE NUMBER  2
                                                                                RUN DATE

EMPLOYEE NAME                                                    PAYROLL NUMBER
PRESENT POSITION     SENIOR PROGRAMMER ANALYST                   SOC.SEC.NUMBER
DEPARTMENT           88600
LAST SKILL DATE
```

GROUP NAME	SKILL NUMBER	SKILL NAME	SKILL LEVEL INDV	RECM'D	CRITERIA 1	2	3
DESIGN							
	AE005	BACKUP & RECOVERY	2	4	X	X	X
	AE006	TEST PLAN		4	X	X	
	AE007	SYSTEM CONVERSION TECHNIQUES	3	4	X	X	X
	AE009	SYSTEMS DESIGN		4	X	X	X
	AE011	FORMS DESIGN		4	X	X	
	AE012	DATA BASE DESIGN					
IMPLEMENTATION							
	AF002	USER EDUCATION	2	3	X	X	
	AF003	APPLICATION ACCEPTANCE TESTING		4	X	X	X
	AF005	PROGRAM DOCUMENTATION	2	4	X	X	X
	AF006	UNIT TESTING		4	X	X	X
	AF007	INTERGRATION TESTING		4	X	X	X
	AF008	PARALLEL TESTING					
BUSINESS & INDUSTRY							
	AI003	CORPORATION KNOWLEDGE	2	3	X	X	X
MANAGEMENT							
	AJ001	FUNCTIONAL MANAGEMENT	2	3	X	X	
	AJ002	MANAGEMENT TECHNIQUES		3	X	X	
	AJ004	BUDGET FORMULATION		2	X	X	
	AJ005	PERSONNEL SELECTION		2	X	X	
	AJ006	PERSONNEL EVALUATION		2	X	X	
	AJ007	HUMAN RESOURCE DEVELOPMENT	1	2	X	X	
	AJ008	PROJECT REPORTING		3	X	X	
	AJ010	PROJECT LIFE CYCLE		3	X	X	X
	AJ011	PROJECT CONTROL		3	X	X	X

Figure 7-2. (Part 2)

CAREER DEVELOPMENT SYSTEM
EMPLOYEE EDUCATION TURN-AROUND REPORT – PROJECTED JOB

REPORT HRA3530A
PAGE NUMBER 1
RUN DATE

EMPLOYEE NAME
PROJECTED POSITION SYSTEMS ANALYST
DEPARTMENT 88600

PAYROLL NUMBER
SOC.SEC. NUMBER

SKILL NUMBER	COURSE DATES	MHT STATUS	COURSE CODE	COURSE NAME	MEDIA TYPE	HRS	DAYS	TUITION COST	SKILL LEVEL INDV	COURSE LEVEL RECM'D	EDUC LEVEL
AA001				IBM HARDWARE & PERIPHERAL DEVICES					1	2	
	/__/__/		ASI1401	MANAGING TIME	V	3.5					1
	/__/__/		ASI1402	WHAT CAN I CONTRIBUTE	V	3.5					1
	/__/__/		ASI1403	FOCUS ON TOMORROW	V	3.5					1
	/__/__/		DTKI201	DP CONCEPTS FOR MANAGERS – PART I 7-010	V	3.0					1
	/__/__/		DTKI202	DP CONCEPTS FOR MANAGERS – PART II 7-020	V	3.0					1
	/__/__/		DTKI203	SYSTEMS PROCESS 7-030	V	3.0					1
	/__/__/		DTKI204	THE SYSTEMS STUDY	V	3.0					1
	/__/__/		DTKI205	THE SYSTEM SPECIFICATIONS	V	3.0					1
	/__/__/		EDU1600	360/370 I/O DEVICES	V	16.0					1
	/__/__/		SRA1000	COMPUTING SYSTEMS FUNDAMENTALS	M	4.0					2
AB001				COBOL					1	3	
	/__/__/		IBM7000	ANS COBOL	V	80.0					1
	/__/__/		IBM9020	STRUCTURED ANS COBOL I	M	30.0					1
	/__/__/		IBM9030	STRUCTURED ANS COBOL II	M	30.0					1
AB002				IBM ASSEMBLER					1	3	
	/__/__/		AGS0002	OS ADVANCED ASSEMBLER	I		12.0	1130			2
	/__/__/		IBM0010	OS/VS ASSEMBLER INTERFACE SAM/BDAM H3783	P		5.0				3
	/__/__/		IBM0048	ASSEMBLER LANGUAGE CODING WORKSHOP K3603	P		5.0	760			2
	/__/__/		IBM5050	ASSEMBLER LANGUAGE CODING TECHNIQUES		4.5					1
	/__/__/		IBM7025	ASSEMBLER CODING	V	90.0					1
AB014				CICS COMMAND						3	
	/__/__/		IBM5575	COMMAND LEVEL CODING FOR CICS/VS	M	40.0					2
	/__/__/		MCC1000	CICS-COMPONENTS, STRENGTHS, & PITFALLS	M		5.0				1
	/__/__/		TCT0003	CICS/VS STRUCTURE & PROGRAMMING	I		5.0	225			2
AB015				DL/1 PROGRAMMING						3	
	/__/__/		IBM8007	DL/1 BASIC PROGRAMMING	T	11.0					2
	/__/__/		IBM8008	DL/1 ADVANCED PROGRAMMING	T	6.0					3
	/__/__/		TCT0004	CICS DL/1 INTERFACE	I		2.0	90			2
AC001				OS CONCEPTS						3	
	/__/__/		IBM8002	BASIC OS JCL TRAINING	T	7.0					2

Figure 7-3. Employee education turnaround report. (Part 1)

```
                    CAREER DEVELOPMENT SYSTEM                         REPORT    HRA3500A
        EMPLOYEE EDUCATION TURN-AROUND REPORT - PROJECTED JOB         PAGE NUMBER  2
                                                                      RUN DATE

EMPLOYEE NAME
PROJECTED POSITION   SYSTEMS ANALYST                    PAYROLL  NUMBER
DEPARTMENT           88600                              SOC.SEC. NUMBER
```

SKILL NUMBER / COURSE DATES	COURSE STATUS	MHT	COURSE CODE	COURSE NAME	MEDIA TYPE	HRS	DAYS	TUITION COST	SKILL LEVEL INDV	SKILL LEVEL RECM'D	COURSE EDUC LEVEL
AC002				OS/VS CONCEPTS						3	
__/__/__			GUI1000	VIRTUAL CONCEPTS	M	1.0					1
__/__/__			IBM0076	OS/VS FACILITIES INTRODUCTION H3780	P		2.0				1
AC003				JOB CONTROL LANGUAGE					1	3	
__/__/__			IBM8002	BASIC OS JCL TRAINING	T	7.0					2
__/__/__			IBM9080	OS/JCL FOR PROGRAMMERS	M	25.0					2
AC004				UTILITIES					1	3	
AC005				TIME SHARING OPTION (TSO)						4	
__/__/__			IBM8006	USING TSO EFFECTIVELY	T	11.0					2
__/__/__			MHT1000	BASIC TSO	T	9.0					2
AC006				DUMP READING						3	
__/__/__			AGS0001	MVS ESSENTIALS OF DEBUGGING	I		2.0	60			2
AD001				FEASIBILITY STUDIES						2	
__/__/__			BEN0001	BASIC SYSTEMS ANALYSIS	V		5.0	22			1
__/__/__			DTK1001	DATA GATHERING,ANALYSIS,INTERVIEWING	V	3.0					1
__/__/__			DTK1008	SYSTEM DESIGN AND TECHNICAL FEASIBILITY	V	3.0					1
__/__/__			DTK1010	OPERATIONAL AND ECONOMIC FEASIBILITY	V	3.0					1
__/__/__			DTK1017	MANPOWER PLANNING	V	3.0					2
__/__/__			IBM0077	SYSTEM DESIGN AND ANALYSIS PRINCIPLES E3167	P		5.0	350			1
__/__/__			MHT0008	PROJECT LIFE CYCLE	I		5.0				1
AD002				FUNCTIONAL SPECIFICATIONS						2	
__/__/__			ASI1001	QUASI CORP. STUDY - PROJECT CONCEPTS	V		5.0				1
__/__/__			ASI1002	THE PHASES APPROACH - MANPOWER PLANNING	V		5.0				1
__/__/__			BEN0001	BASIC SYSTEMS ANALYSIS	I		5.0	22			1
__/__/__			EDU1001	INTRODUCTION AND INTERVIEW	V	2.0					1
__/__/__			EDU1002	SYSTEM DEVELOPMENT PROCESS	V	2.0					1
__/__/__			MHT0008	PROJECT LIFE CYCLE	I		5.0				1
AD003				AUDITS & CONTROLS						2	

Figure 7-3. (Part 2)

```
                    CAREER DEVELOPMENT SYSTEM
     EMPLOYEE EDUCATION TURN-AROUND REPORT - PROJECTED JOB
```

EMPLOYEE NAME
PROJECTED POSITION   SYSTEMS ANALYST
DEPARTMENT   88600

PAYROLL NUMBER
SOC.SEC. NUMBER

SKILL NAME

SKILL NUMBER / COURSE DATES	COURSE STATUS	MHT COURSE CODE	COURSE NAME	MEDIA TYPE	HRS DAYS	TUITION COST	SKILL LEVEL INDV	SKILL LEVEL RECM'D	COURSE EDUC LEVEL
/ /		DTK1009	CONTROLS: ASSURING SYSTEM ACCURACY	V	3.0				2
/ /		MOY0001	BANK ACCOUNTING FOR EDP ANALYSIS	I	6.5				4
AD004	PERT/GANTT CHARTING								
/ /		BEN0001	BASIC SYSTEMS ANALYSIS	I	3.0		1	2	1
/ /		DTK1018	WORK PLAN AND DESIGN REVIEW	V	5.0	22			1
AD005	PROJECT LIFE CYCLE								
/ /		MHT0008	PROJECT LIFE CYCLE	I	5.0		1		1
AD006	COST/BENEFIT ANALYSIS								
/ /		ASI1100	COST BENEFIT ANALYSIS	V	24.0			2	2
AD007	HIPO								
/ /		IBM5400	HIPO-DESIGN AID	M	4.0			2	2
AD010	USER LIAISON/DATA GATHERING								
/ /		MHT0008	PROJECT LIFE CYCLE	I	5.0			2	1
AE001	DESIGN SPECIFICATIONS								
/ /		DTK1003	SYSTEM REQUIREMENTS SPECIFICATIONS	V	3.0				2
/ /		DTK1004	DECISION TABLES	V	3.0				2
/ /		DTK1005	FORMS AND RECORD DESIGN	V	3.0				2
/ /		DTK1008	SYSTEM DESIGN AND TECHNICAL FEASIBILITY	V	3.0				1
/ /		IBM0077	SYSTEM DESIGN AND ANALYSIS PRINCIPLES E3167	P	5.0	350	1	3	
AE002	FILE DESIGN								
/ /		DPN1003	FILE CONTROL AND DATA COLLECTION	V	.5				3
/ /		DPN1004	TRANSACTIONS AND OPERATION MODES	V	1.0				3
/ /		DPN1005	FILE STRUCTURE AND DESIGN	V	1.0				3
/ /		DPN1006	STORAGE ALLOCATION AND THE FILE	V	3.0				3
/ /		DPN1007	DESCRPT RECORDS/ISAM STRUCTURE & DESIGN	V	1.5				3
/ /		DPN1008	RANDOM FILE ORG & RANDOMIZING TECHNIQUES	V	1.0				3
/ /		DPN1009	MULTIPLE FILE ORGANIZATION	V	2.0				3

Figure 7-3. (Part 3)

```
                          CAREER DEVELOPMENT SYSTEM                              REPORT   HRA3500A
              EMPLOYEE EDUCATION TURN-AROUND REPORT - PROJECTED JOB              PAGE NUMBER 4
                                                                                RUN DATE

                                                      PAYROLL  NUMBER
                                                      SOC.SEC. NUMBER
EMPLOYEE NAME
PROJECTED POSITION  SYSTEMS ANALYST
DEPARTMENT          88600

         SKILL NAME
```

SKILL NUMBER	COURSE DATES	COURSE STATUS	MHT COURSE CODE	COURSE NAME	MEDIA TYPE	HRS	DAYS	TUITION COST	SKILL LEVEL INDV	LEVEL RECM'D	COURSE EDUC LEVEL
	/_/_/		DTK1007	SYSTEM 360/370 FILE DESIGN TECHNIQUES	V	3.0					3
AE003				PROGRAM DESIGN					1	3	
AE004				CATALOGUED PROCEDURE DESIGN						2	
AE005				BACKUP & RECOVERY						2	
AE006				TEST PLAN						3	
	/_/_/		DTK1014	DEVELOPING A TEST PLAN	V	3.0			1		1
AE007				SYSTEM CONVERSION TECHNIQUES						3	
	/_/_/		DTK1015	CONVERSION,EVALUATION,MAINTENANCE PLAN	V	3.0					2
	/_/_/		IBM6000	MANAGING APPLICATION CONVERSION PROJECTS	M	8.5					3
AE009				SYSTEMS DESIGN						3	
	/_/_/		DTK1003	SYSTEM REQUIREMENTS SPECIFICATIONS	V	3.0					1
	/_/_/		DTK1006	SYSTEM DESIGN FUNDAMENTALS	V	3.0					1
	/_/_/		DTK1007	SYSTEM 360/370 FILE DESIGN TECHNIQUES	V	3.0					1
AE011				FORMS DESIGN						3	
	/_/_/		DTK1005	FORMS AND RECORD DESIGN	V	3.0					1
AE012				DATA BASE DESIGN						3	
AF001				USER DOCUMENTATION					2	3	
	/_/_/		DTK1013	PREPARING A USER MANUAL	V	3.0					2
	/_/_/		MHT0008	PROJECT LIFE CYCLE	I		5.0				2
AF002				USER EDUCATION					2	3	
	/_/_/		DTK1019	EFFECTIVE PRESENTATION TECHNIQUES	V	3.0					2
AF003				APPLICATION ACCEPTANCE TESTING						2	
	/_/_/		DTK1014	DEVELOPING A TEST PLAN	V	3.0					2

Figure 7-3. (Part 4)

CAREER DEVELOPMENT SYSTEM
EMPLOYEE EDUCATION TURN-AROUND REPORT - PROJECTED JOB

EMPLOYEE NAME
PROJECTED POSITION   SYSTEMS ANALYST
DEPARTMENT   88600

PAYROLL NUMBER
SOC.SEC. NUMBER

SKILL NAME

SKILL NUMBER / COURSE DATES	COURSE STATUS	MHT COURSE CODE	COURSE NAME	MEDIA TYPE	HRS DAYS	TUITION COST	SKILL LEVEL INDV	LEVEL RECM'D	COURSE EDUC LEVEL
/_/_/		DTK1015	CONVERSION,EVALUATION,MAINTENANCE PLAN	V	3.0				4
AF005			PROGRAM DOCUMENTATION					3	
AF006			UNIT TESTING					3	
/_/_/		ASI1003	CONTINGENCY PLANNING - MONITORING SCHED.	V	5.0				1
AF007			INTERGRATION TESTING					3	
/_/_/		ASI1003	CONTINGENCY PLANNING - MONITORING SCHED.	V	5.0				1
AF008			PARALLEL TESTING					3	
/_/_/		ASI1003	CONTINGENCY PLANNING - MONITORING SCHED.	V	5.0				1
AI001			ORAL COMMUNICATION				2	3	
/_/_/		DTK1019	EFFECTIVE PRESENTATION TECHNIQUES	V	3.0				2
AI002			WRITTEN COMMUNICATION				2	3	
/_/_/		DTK1013	PREPARING A USER MANUAL	V	3.0				2
/_/_/		MHT014A	EFFECTIVE WRITING	I	25.0				2
/_/_/		MHT014B	EFFECTIVE WRITING FOLLOW-UP	I	2.5				2
AI003			CORPORATION KNOWLEDGE					2	
/_/_/		MHT0005	BANK MANAGEMENT SEMINAR	I	9.0				2
/_/_/		MHT0015	INTRODUCTION TO COMMERCIAL BANKING	I	10.5				2
/_/_/		MOY0001	BANK ACCOUNTING FOR EDP ANALYSTS	I	6.5				1
/_/_/		MOY0002	EDP MANAGERS VIEW OF BANK ACCOUNTING	I	3.5				2
AJ001			FUNCTIONAL MANAGEMENT				2	2	
/_/_/		MHT002A	BASIC SUPERVISION - PART I	I	5.0				3
/_/_/		MHT002B	BASIC SUPERVISION - PART II		2.0				3
/_/_/		MHT002C	BASIC SUPERVISION - FOLLOW-UP		2.0				3
AJ003			PLAN, ESTIMATE & CONTROL				2	2	
/_/_/		CPT0001	PROJECT IMPLEMENTATION	I	5.0				2

Figure 7-3. (Part 5)

```
                              CAREER DEVELOPMENT SYSTEM                        REPORT  HRA3500A
                    EMPLOYEE EDUCATION TURN-AROUND REPORT - PROJECTED JOB      PAGE NUMBER  6
                                                                              RUN DATE

        EMPLOYEE NAME
        PROJECTED POSITION  SYSTEMS ANALYST                    PAYROLL NUMBER
        DEPARTMENT          8.JU                                SOC.SEC. NUMBER

                      SKILL NAME                                          SKILL LEVEL  COURSE EDUC
                                                                         INDV RECM'D  LEVEL
        COURSE  COURSE MHT COURSE      COURSE NAME          MEDIA HRS DAYS TUITION
        DATES   STATUS CODE                                 TYPE          COST
SKILL
NUMBER

AJ008  PROJECT REPORTING                                                              2    2        2

  /_/         BEN0001 BASIC SYSTEMS ANALYSIS                I     5.0
  /_/         CPT0001 PROJECT IMPLEMENTATION                I     5.0    22                2        2

AJ009  USER LIAISON                                                                   2    2

AJ010  PROJECT LIFE CYCLE

  /_/         CPT0001 PROJECT IMPLEMENTATION                I     5.0                               3
  /_/         IBM6050 MANAGING THE APPL. DEV. PROCESS:PROJECT REVIEW  M  7.5                        3

AJ011  PROJECT CONTROL                                                                2

  /_/         CPT0001 PROJECT IMPLEMENTATION                I     5.0                               3
  /_/         IBM6050 MANAGING THE APPL. DEV. PROCESS:PROJECT REVIEW  M  7.5                        3
```

Figure 7-3. (Part 6)

REPORT   HRA3500A
PAGE NUMBER   7
RUN DATE

CAREER DEVELOPMENT SYSTEM
EMPLOYEE EDUCATION TURN-AROUND REPORT - PROJECTED JOB

NEXT CAREER COUNSELING DATE_____(MM/YY)

SIGNATURES:

EMPLOYEE'S SIGNATURE_____

MANAGER'S SIGNATURE_____

DATE_____

Figure 7-3.   (Part 7)

CAREER DEVELOPMENT SYSTEM
PRESENT VERSUS PROJECTED POSITION SKILLS REPORT

REPORT HRA2800
PAGE NUMBER 1
RUN DATE

		PAYROLL NUMBER	
EMPLOYEE NAME		SOC.SEC. NUMBER	
PRESENT POSITION	PROGRAMMER		
PROJECTED POSITION	SENIOR PROGRAMMER		
DEPARTMENT	88600		
LAST SKILL DATE			

GROUP NAME / SKILL NUMBER	SKILL NAME	PRESENT POSITION SKILL LEVEL INDV	PRESENT POSITION SKILL LEVEL RECM'D	PROJECTED POSITION SKILL LEVEL RECM'D
HARDWARE				
AA001	IBM HARDWARE & PERIPHERAL DEVICES	1	1	2
LANGUAGES				
AB001	COBOL	3	2	3
AB002	IBM ASSEMBLER	0	2	3
AB014	CICS COMMAND			3
AB015	DL/1 PROGRAMMING			
SYSTEM SOFTWARE				
AC001	OS CONCEPTS	2	2	3
AC002	OS/VS CONCEPTS	2	2	3
AC003	JOB CONTROL LANGUAGE	2	2	3
AC004	UTILITIES	2	4	4
AC005	TIME SHARING OPTION (TSO)		2	3
AC006	DUMP READING	3		
ANALYSIS				
AD001	FEASIBILITY STUDIES	1	1	1
AD002	FUNCTIONAL SPECIFICATIONS	0	1	1
AD004	PERT/GANTT CHARTING	2	1	1
AD005	PROJECT LIFE CYCLE	2	1	1
AD007	HIPO			1
AD010	USER LIAISON/DATA GATHERING			
DESIGN				
AE001	DESIGN SPECIFICATIONS	0		2
AE002	FILE DESIGN	2		2
AE003	PROGRAM DESIGN	2		2
AE004	CATALOGUED PROCEDURE DESIGN	3		2
AE006	TEST PLAN	N		2
AE007	SYSTEM CONVERSION TECHNIQUES	0	1	
AE009	SYSTEMS DESIGN		1	

Figure 7-4. (Part 1)

```
                                                                          REPORT    HRA2800
                  CAREER DEVELOPMENT SYSTEM                                PAGE NUMBER   2
          PRESENT VERSUS PROJECTED POSITION SKILLS REPORT                  RUN DATE
```

```
EMPLOYEE NAME                                        PAYROLL  NUMBER
PRESENT POSITION      PROGRAMMER                      SOC.SEC. NUMBER
PROJECTED POSITION    SENIOR PROGRAMMER
DEPARTMENT            88600
LAST SKILL DATE
```

GROUP NAME	SKILL NUMBER	SKILL NAME	PRESENT POSITION SKILL LEVEL INDV	PRESENT POSITION SKILL LEVEL RECM'D	PROJECTED POSITION SKILL LEVEL RECM'D
IMPLEMENTATION					
	AE011	FORMS DESIGN		1	2
	AE012	DATA BASE DESIGN		1	2
	AF001	USER DOCUMENTATION	2	2	2
	AF002	USER EDUCATION	2	2	2
	AF003	APPLICATION ACCEPTANCE TESTING		2	2
	AF005	PROGRAM DOCUMENTATION		2	2
	AF006	UNIT TESTING		2	2
	AF007	INTERGRATION TESTING			
	AF008	PARALLEL TESTING			
BUSINESS & INDUSTRY					
	AI001	ORAL COMMUNICATION	0	2	2
	AI002	WRITTEN COMMUNICATION	3	2	2
MANAGEMENT					
	AJ001	FUNCTIONAL MANAGEMENT	1	1	1
	AJ003	PLAN, ESTIMATE & CONTROL	1	1	1
	AJ008	PROJECT REPORTING	1	1	1
	AJ010	PROJECT LIFECYCLE			1
	AJ011	PROJECT CONTROL			1

Figure 7-4. (Part 2)

COMPUTER PROCESSING AND RESEARCH

SIX MONTH COUNSELING FORM

EFFECTIVE DATE: _____

NAME: _____

PART I: PERFORMANCE COUNSELING

INTERIM PERFORMANCE APPRAISAL: COMMENT ON THE EMPLOYEE'S PERFORMANCE OVER THE LAST SIX MONTHS BASED UPON THE ASSIGNMENTS ACCOMPLISHED AND THE OBJECTIVES SET AT HIS ANNUAL PERFORMANCE APPRAISAL.

PART II: CAREER COUNSELING

A. EMPLOYEE'S OBJECTIVES: LIST THE SHORT TERM (UP TO ONE YEAR) AND LONG TERM CAREER OBJECTIVES DESIRED BY THE EMPLOYEE.

B. CAREER DEVELOPMENT OBJECTIVES:

1. **SKILLS ENHANCEMENTS:** UTILIZING THE INDIVIDUAL'S UPDATED SKILLS PROFILE, DEVELOP A SKILLS ENHANCEMENT PLAN.
   (SEE INSTRUCTIONS ATTACHED.)

NAME: _____ DATE: _____

SKILL		INDV.	DIFF.	COURSE #/ EXP.	PRI.	DATE DES.	REMARKS
CODE	DESCRIPTION						

M-5590-1 8/75

Figure 7-5. (Part 1)

CAREER COUNSELING – CONTINUED

B. CAREER DEVELOPMENT OBJECTIVES – CONTINUED:

2. **POSITION RESPONSIBILITIES:** UTILIZING THE RESPONSIBILITIES LISTED IN THE EMPLOYEE'S CURRENT POSITION DESCRIPTION AND/OR NEXT POSITION DESCRIPTION, SET APPROPRIATE OBJECTIVES NECESSARY FOR HIS FUTURE GROWTH.

C. **REVISED JOB RELATED OBJECTIVES/ASSIGNMENTS:** IF NECESSARY, DUE TO A CHANGE IN THE PROJECT REQUIREMENTS, THE QUALITY OF THE EMPLOYEE'S WORK PERFORMANCE, OR THE CAREER DEVELOPMENT OBJECTIVES SET, MODIFY THE JOB RELATED OBJECTIVES/ASSIGNMENTS GIVEN AT THE ANNUAL PERFORMANCE APPRAISAL.

PART III: SIGNATURES

EMPLOYEE COMMENTS: IF YOU HAVE ANY COMMENTS REGARDING THIS COUNSELING SESSION, STATE THEM BELOW. IF NO COMMENT, SO INDICATE.

SIGNATURES:

FIRST LINE MANAGER: _____ DATE: _____

EMPLOYEE: _____

MANUFACTURERS HANOVER TRUST
COMPUTER PROCESSING AND RESEARCH
SIX MONTH COUNSELING FORM

M5590-1 (BACK)

Figure 7-5. (Part 2)

HIGHLIGHTS OF THE SIX–MONTH
COUNSELING PROCEDURE

Introduction   The following steps summarize the six-month counseling procedure.

Procedures	*Step*	*Action*
	1.	The skills update turnaround report, a blank six-month counseling form and a copy of the objectives section of the last performance appraisal form are sent to the manager.
	2.	Manager meets with employee to complete the skills update turnaround report.
	3.	An updated skill profile is run off from the computer system and given to manager, who reviews it and then gives a copy to the employee.
	4.	Manager completes the six-month counseling form and the employee education turnaround report.
	5.	Manager conducts the six-month counseling session.
	6.	Personnel sends a copy of the employee education turnaround report to the education department for scheduling.

HOW TO COMPLETE THE SKILLS UPDATE
TURNAROUND REPORT

Purpose   The purposes of the skills update turnaround report are to:

- Enable the manager and the employee to decide upon appropriate skills to be upgraded.
- Serve as input to the automated career development system to generate a current skills profile report.

Description   The automated career development system produces a skills update turnaround report for each employee. The form lists the employee's current skill level for each skill within nine skill groups. There is space to indicate a new skill level for each. In addition, new skills (levels) can be added. The employee completes the form, and the manager reviews and validates it.

Skill Groups   The nine skill groups are:

- Hardware
- Languages
- System software
- Analysis
- Design
- Implementation
- Teleprocessing
- Business and industry
- Management.

READING THE SKILLS PROFILE REPORT

Description   The skills profile report is one of the outputs generated from the skills update turnaround report. It contains a comparison of the individual's skill levels to the requirements of his/her current and/or next position, as determined by the skills matrix. The employee education turnaround report is another output generated from the skills update turnaround form. It serves as a skills development plan, allowing the manager to decide which skills need development* and indicate which of the related courses the employee should attend. By also completing a desired date for attendance on the form, the document serves as an education turnaround vehicle.

Core Skills All core skills (i.e., skills critical to the job) identified for a group are printed on the profile report.

Peripheral Skills A peripheral skill (i.e., project development) is printed on the profile report only if the individual has a skill level of one or greater.

HOW TO COMPLETE THE SIX-MONTH COUNSELING FORM

Purpose This form, completed by the first line manager, has two purposes. First, it includes an informal performance appraisal to allow the manager and the employee to discuss employee performance over the last six months. Second, it is used as a career counseling tool, enabling the manager and the employee to discuss the employee's career development.

Form Summary The form is divided into three parts, Performance counseling, career counseling and signatures. In Part I, Performance counseling, the employee's performance over the last six months is discussed, based on the objectives set at the previous review. In Part II, career counseling, the employee's short- and long-term goals are determined, career development objectives are

---

*Skills selected for development should consider both the needs of the project and the development of the employee.

established and, if necessary, job assignments are revised. In Part III, signatures, the employee comments on the review and the employee and the first line manager sign the form.

PERFORMANCE COUNSELING: HOW IT SHOULD BE IMPLEMENTED

Description   Part I of the form is used to comment on the employee's performance over the last six months.

Interim   The interim performance appraisal is based on the
Performance   objectives, both assignments and accountabilities, set
Appraisal   for the employee at the previous performance appraisal. The manager comments only on those objectives already accomplished or currently in progress. Performance ratings (fully adequate, above expectancy, etc) are not indicated. Rather, what is intended is a written discussion of the individual's performance, how well objectives are being met, what areas of deficiency need to be addressed, and the areas of strength that should be acknowledged. The discussion should be a counseling tool rather than a formal evaluation.

CAREER COUNSELING

Employee's   This area is used to indicate the employee's short-term
Objectives   (up to one year) and long-term objectives as defined by the employee and agreed upon by the manager. It should be completed at the review after discussion with the employee.

CAREER DEVELOPMENT OBJECTIVES

Description

In addition to performance, and employee's development within the present position and advancement to the next position are based on two criteria: improving skill proficiencies and assuming additional responsibilities associated with the present and/or next position. For this reason, career development objectives are really a composition of the employee education turnaround report and the career counseling form, which discussed position responsibilities.

Position Responsibilities

The area is used to define objectives relating to the additional responsibilities that the employee is expected to assume in his/her present position or in preparation for advancement to his next position. The objectives should be specific and, where possible, should include the work assignments through which the employee will assume the responsibility. The manager refers to the position description for the employee's present position and, if the employee is close to a promotion, the position description for the next position. These will help to determine what is expected of an individual at the employee's level.

Revised Job Related Objectives/ Assignments

This area enables the manager to modify the objectives and assignments set at the last performance appraisal. Modifications or additions to the job-related objectives/assignments or the accountability objectives may be due to several factors:

• The project requirements have changed since the last performance appraisal. A new job-related objective/assignment may be necessary.
• The quality of the employee's work perfor-

mance is below what was expected. A new accountability objective may be necessary.

- The career development objectives indicate a need for responsibilities other than those originally planned.

If the objective listed is new, the manager simply states the objective and its due date. However, if the objective is a substitution for one previously listed on the performance appraisal form, the manager states the revised objective and indicates the old objective that it replaces.

Employee Comments

This section is completed by the employee at the end of the counseling session. The employee is encouraged to indicate comments.

Next Counseling Date

This section is determined by the manager and indicates, to the automated career development system, the next career counseling date.

Signatures

After the counseling session, the manager and the employee sign the form on the lines provided.

CONDUCTING THE SIX-MONTH COUNSELING SESSION

Before the Session

The six-month counseling session is held after the six-month counseling form has beeen completed. The manager should arrange a date and time for the session with the employee at least two days in advance. The two days' notice gives the employee a chance to think about his performance over the past six months and his career aspirations, specifically his short- and long-term career objectives. The manager should arrange for a private room where there will not be any interruptions. At least an hour should be allotted for the session. Either before lunch or late in the day is recommended to allow the session to exceed an hour if necessary.

At the Session

Each section of the six-month counseling form is discussed in detail. The session is meant to provide the manager and employee the opportunity to exchange ideas regarding the employee's performance and career goals. It should serve as a counseling session, not a performance evaluation session.

Career Counseling

The employee's short- and long-term career objectives should be discussed. Those objectives that are mutually agreed to are entered on the form in the employee's objectives section. The career development objectives that the manager established are discussed. The manager explains that the dates for the education scheduled on the employee education turnaround report are estimated and are flexible. The employee will be notified of exact class schedules as they are determined. All the objectives are discussed and agreed to by the employee. The reasons for the revised job-related objectives/assignments (if there are any) are explained.

Employee Acknowledgment

The employee is encouraged to comment on the value of the session. Both the employee and manager then sign on the appropriate lines.

After the Session

The manager gives the employee a copy of the entire six-month counseling form for reference purposes and sends the original to his/her advisor.

Advisor Review	The advisor reviews the six-month counseling form to ensure uniform use of the procedures, and to make a general appraisal of the quality of the statements on the form. The advisor may contact the manager to request explanation of information on the form or suggest corrections/enhancements.
Education Review	The education department reviews the employee education turnaround report to ensure the appropriateness of the education chosen. The form is then filed in the education department and used to plan and schedule education during the year.
Introduction and Document Summary	This page provides a checklist of the documents used in the six-month counseling procedure.

DOCUMENT	PURPOSE	COMPLETED BY	AUTHORIZATION
Skills update	Update employee's skills profile in the automated career development system	Project manager, employee	N/A
Skills profile report	Provide a picture of employee's skills	Output of automated career development system	N/A
Employee education turnaround report	Provide tool for planning education	Project manager, employee	N/A

DOCUMENT	PURPOSE	COMPLETED BY	AUTHORIZATION
Six-month counseling form	Informally evaluate employee, and set objectives for career development	Project manager	Project manager, employee
Previous performance appraisal form	Supply manager with information on employee's last review	N/A	N/A

TECHNIQUES

Employee Preparation and Participation

Surprisingly, most employees are more self-critical and accurately self-reflective than managers expect. In order to ensure that the employee has given the session as much thought and self-appraisal as the manager has, we recommend that managers have the employee also complete all the forms of the session *prior* to the session. This ensures that the employee is prepared, has thought about his/her strengths and deficiencies, and is open to discussing his or her career. Employees who have gone through this exercise are the most participative at the session itself and contribute to a successful career analysis.

Intimacy of Process

It is critical that the career counseling session allow for an honest, intimate exchange between the manager and employee. The more open the session is, the more can be gained from it. It is therefore a session between the employee and his/her first level supervisor *only*. No other approvals, inputs or signatures are required. It is amazing how much more comfortable and open to constructive counseling employees are when this kind of environment has been established.

Other Options
Available from
Automated
System

The automated career development system offers many tools that can assist in the counseling session. At the manager's request, the following are available.

1. *Skills profile for next position.* If an employee is nearing a promotion, a profile can be called that compares the employee skill levels to those levels required for his/her *next* position. Concurrently, the manager would receive an employee education turnaround report that would address skill deficiencies of this new comparison.
2. *Employee education history report.* This lists all courses already attended by the employee, when they were taken and the skill level of expertise they addressed.
3. *The skills training relationship report.* This report can be used to show *all* available courses that will provide a particular skill level of expertise.

ADVANTAGES OF CAREER COUNSELING

The career counseling session process can result in tremendous benefits to both employees and corporation.

1. It is a most effective process for modifying performance. Because its non-threatening nature, performance counseling can readily take place. The openness of the session allows for maximum receptivity on the parts of both parties.
2. The session indicates to the employee that the organization cares about him or her; that it wants to see this individual developed; that it's concerned about his/her own career objectives. It allows employees to provide input to their own career plans and to play a major role in determining their career success.

3. For most companies who give out annual salary increases, the cost of their employees rises yearly. This process ensures that the benefit of this commodity also rises. Employees are consciously developed; i.e., they are given the skills and training that they need, to take on increased responsibilities. By moving up the career ladder, they are in fact worth more to the organization in their increased scope.

4. With the cost of education skyrocketing throughout the DP industry, it is even more important to ensure that education is not expended carelessly. By linking education directly into skills enhancement and career development goals, we are ensuring the most relevant, appropriate use of this media.

5. By providing the education department with five-year plans for employees, the education department receives a vehicle which allows for effective long-range planning (this factor is discussed in more detail in Chapter 8).

6. By providing the human resources (HR) department with career plans for employees, the process ultimately facilitates manpower planning and long-range succession planning. The HR area receives what ultimately creates a data base of career opportunities and anticipated career moves. It therefore can easily forecast what skills will exist in the future, what positions will be vacated and who will be skilled enough to move up in the organization.

7. DP professionals are greatly motivated by career progression and increased skills development. The career counseling process therefore is very appealing to them. It has been our experience that it (as a price of course of a large HRM system) has contributed to our controllable level of turnover and our ability to successfully attract from the outside marketplace.

WHAT WAS LEARNED

As with any system, we have had to modify, adjust and update this process along its maturity stages. We have learned a lot in that process, some of which is highlighted below.

- No one is born with the ability to do effective counseling. It is a skill that, like all others, must be taught. Our process is detailed enough so that it takes a manager through the required steps. However, for most managers, it is an unnatural process. Good, close individual training was a key to our successful implementation. Sometimes when we unexpectedly detoured into some departures from the process, the negative impact on the quality of these sessions was noticeable.

- Many of the components of this system were added on, perceived as further information needs were identified. What we have learned is that the larger the workforce, the more critical the need for a data base, especially one that is automated. Managers must be given the appropriate tools if they are expected to handle this process; i.e., education history, education available to address skill deficiencies, career ladder and job requirements, etc.
- Due to the constantly changing DP environment, the DP skills data base is always operating being "out of date." We have found that it is necessary for the HR department to review and update skills on an *annual* basis if it is to be relevant. Even position descriptions, if they are to reflect jobs appropriately, must be looked at regularly (every three years has proven adequate to us).
- As with all HR-related systems, administrative control is critical and must be accounted for in the establishment of this process. Follow-up with your managers to ensure that the forms are returned and that the sessions take place on schedule will be necessary in all but the smallest companies.
- The HR advisor has played a tremendous role around this process. By reviewing the counseling documents, the advisor performs a qualitative review and can follow up with managers (and staff) as necessary. In addition, the advisor provides an "ombudsman" role, resolving career-related disagreements between employee and manager, if they should occur. This impartial, yet informed and respected third party has often resolved career issues that most certainly deterred subsequent morale/productivity problems.

8
Education

In order to implement a skills enhancement delivery vehicle, a sophisticated education methodology is necessary as its support and implementation source. An education department must then be established, and staffed with high-level data processing (DP) education specialists. The new organization's primary responsibility will be to support all career development systems, understanding the various skills required and determining the development tools necessary to supply and reinforce the needed education. The new education function must also be equipped to develop and select augmenting courses offered by outside vendors which will fulfill the all-around needs of the DP department.

The new education function will be a most critical priority to DP managers considering a human resources (HR) management system approach. The reason is because it will also amount to the largest expense category. Here's why the costs will be high: first, the function must be staffed with high-priced, senior analysts, a ratio of about 1 per 150 users (DP employees); second, direct education expense (course development and implementation) can run as high as $1,000 to $1,500 per employee annually. Such an expensive commitment requires a system that ensures that education is:

- Cost-effective
- Skills-driven
- Business strategy-driven.

The following pages introduce the makeup of the education system and its associated procedures. Also included are the methodologies that allow these parameters to be addressed.

A GUIDE TO THE EDUCATION SYSTEM COMPONENTS

Are you ready to begin your own organization's in-house education system for the growing ranks of in-house DP staffers? Here is the step-by-step building process showing how to initiate that milestone process.

Education Skills Matrix

The first component used to establish the framework for the total in-house education system consists of implementing the highly functional education skills matrix. It's often regarded as the "backbone" of the process.

The education skills matrix (Figure 8-1) is a tool for managers to use in their education planning process. It ties into the skills and career development process by identifying specific courses that address each skill and skill level of expertise. It also provides recommended courses that address specific training levels of technical and managerial skills.

SKILLS CATEGORY	SKILL NO.	LEVELS 1	2	3	4
LANGUAGES	AB000				
COBOL	AB001	IBM7000 IBM9020	IBM8010		
IBM Assembler	AB002	IBM7025 IBM5050	AGS0007 IBM0048	AGS0002 IBM0010	
Neat/3	AB007	NCR0006	NCR1100 NCR0002 NCR0007 NCR0001		
Culprit	AB008		CUL0001 CUL0002		
Report Program Generator (RPGII)	AB009				

Figure 8-1. Systems and programming education skills matrix. Part I.

| SKILLS | | LEVELS | | | |
CATEGORY	SKILL NO.	1	2	3	4
IBM System 7 Assembler	AB010				
Macro Assembler	AB011		IBM9050		
PDP Assembler	AB012		DEC0017 DEC0010		
CICS Macro	AB013				
CICS Command	AB014	MCC1000	IBM5575 TCT0003		
DL/1 Programming	AB015		TCT0004 IBM8007	IBM8008	
Structured Code	AB016		ASI1600 IBM5000		
FORTRAN	AB017		DEC0014 IBM5025		
Program Language 1 (PL1)	AB018	IBM9060			
Basic—Plus	AB019	IBM9070	DEC0013 DEC0018	DEC0003	

Figure 8-1.   Part II.

By looking at the education skills matrix horizontally, it contains the course by category, skill number and the levels of proficiency. The levels of proficiency are defined as follows:

Level 0: Employee has *no* knowledge of subject matter
Level 1: Employee has *awareness* of subject matter
Level 2: Employee has had *moderate* use of subject matter
Level 3: Employee has had *heavy* use of subject matter
Level 4: Employee has *expert* knowledge of subject matter

For each skill level of proficiency within a skill, the matrix indicates the course—identified by course code—that will assist the individual in attaining that level. It is important to note that a level of proficiency cannot be achieved through formal education alone. This information must be assimilated and strengthened through practical on-the-job experience.

Education Course Descriptions

The education course descriptions (see Figure 8-2) support the education skills matrix. Organized by the course code used on the matrix, this component describes each course offering. It also details audience, media, length, course objectives, etc.

In addition, this component also provides a summary of the important features of each course. Each course description contains the following information:

- *Course name.* Code, type, vendor, tuition, length, vendor code.
- *Audience.* Indicates the individuals who would receive the most benefit from the course.

COURSE:	OS/VS DUMPS AND DEBUGGING COURSE
CODE:	AGS0001
TYPE:	In-House Seminar
VENDOR:	
TUITION:	N/A
LENGTH:	2 Days
VENDOR CODE:	
AUDIENCE:	Programmers
PREREQUISITES:	Basic COBOL and/or Assembler programming skills
DESCRIPTION:	This course provides information that enables the student to list and explain the major control blocks in an OS/VS dump. The student will be able to debug problem programs and successfully correct them.
OBJECTIVES:	Upon completion, the student should be able to discuss the following:

- System/370 data and instruction formats
- Base and displacement techniques of addressing
- Specific control blocks
- Abend dumps
- OC7 return code
- Specific dumps
- Data management blocks

Figure 8-2. Education course descriptions. Part I.

COURSE:	ADVANCED ASSEMBLER AND MACROS

CODE:	AGS0002
TYPE:	In-House Seminar
VENDOR:	
TUITION:	N/A
LENGTH:	10 Days
VENDOR CODE:	

AUDIENCE:	BAL Application or Systems Programmers
PREREQUISITES:	Basic Assembler Course, or a good working knowledge of BAL, OS/VS, JCL, and Utilities
DESCRIPTION:	This course consists of lectures and extensive workshop sessions designed for the experienced BAL programmer in an OS or VS environment. Student exercises include six to eight BAL programs which are coded and executed to utilize Macros and techniques covered in the course.
OBJECTIVES:	Upon completion, the student should be able to discuss the following: • All significant OS/VS Supervisor, data management macros, and related facilities • Control program logic at a sophisticated level • Data management and QSAM • Basic Sequential Access Method (BSAM) • Indexed Sequential Access Method (BISAM, QISAM) • Basic Direct Access Method (BDAM) • Basic Partitioned Access Method (BPAM) • The Supervisor program • Program management • Multitasking • Supervisor service macros • SVC and time supervision • Macro language • Debugging • Paging Supervisor

Figure 8-2.   Part II.

• *Prerequisities.* Any necessary prerequisite knowledge that an individual may need to benefit from the course. In some cases, there are no prerequisites for a course.
• *Description.* Each course is described in terms of topics and course format.
• *Objectives.* What the individual should gain from the course is stated.

Employee Skills Profile Report

As mentioned in previous chapters, the employee profile (Figure 8-3) lists those courses that are available to address the *individualized* needs of the employee, based on specific skill deficiencies.

Employee Education History (see Figure 8-4)

As an additional tool in the education planning process, managers receive the education history for their employee. This will show what additional courses the employee has already attended and what, if anything, he or she is currently scheduled for.

Career Counseling Form (see Chapter 7)

Last, the key component is the career counseling form. By assessing all the available tools, a manager can easily identify skill deficiencies, choose appropriate education, plan for the education and communicate that plan to both the employee and the education department through the same mechanism.

OBJECTIVES OF THE EDUCATION PLANNING PROCESS

The objectives of the education planning process procedure are to provide timely and appropriate education to support project needs, technological advances and business requirements. The procedure also supports an individual's career development by:

- Defining appropriate courses to assist the individual in attaining the next level of competence in a particular skill.
- Reviewing education turnaround report (see Figure 8-5) for applicability and effectiveness in achieving desired goals.
- Making education recommendations to management based on reviews of turnaround report plan.

At the same time, the education planning process also provides constant evaluation of the education presented to help assure its applicability and effectiveness.

```
                              CAREER DEVELOPMENT SYSTEM              REPORT      HRA3400A
                                SKILLS PROFILE REPORT                PAGE NUMBER        1
                                                                     RUN DATE 09/02/82

EMPLOYEE NAME                                              PAYROLL NUMBER  0000068079
PRESENT POSITION     SENIOR SYSTEMS ANALYST               SOC.SEC.NUMBER  111-62-7745
PROJECTED POSITION
DEPARTMENT           88000
LAST SKILL DATE      / /      NEXT COUNSELING DATE

                                                                          SKILL LEVEL
GROUP NAME           SKILL                                               INDV  RECM'D
                     NUMBER   SKILL NAME

HARDWARE
       CORE SKILLS   AA001    IBM HARDWARE & PERIPHERAL DEVICES             2

LANGUAGES
       CORE SKILLS   AB001    COBOL                                         3
                     AB002    IBM ASSEMBLER                                 3
                     AB014    CICS COMMAND                                  3
                     AB015    DL/I PROGRAMMING                              3

SYSTEM SOFTWARE
       CORE SKILLS   AC001    OS CONCEPTS                                   3
                     AC002    OS/VS CONCEPTS                                3
                     AC003    JOB CONTROL LANGUAGE                          3
                     AC004    UTILITIES                                     4
                     AC005    TIME SHARING OPTION (TSO)                     3
                     AC006    DUMP READING                                  3

ANALYSIS
       CORE SKILLS   AD001    FEASIBILITY STUDIES                           3
                     AD002    FUNCTIONAL SPECIFICATIONS                     3
                     AD003    AUDITS & CONTROLS                             4
                     AD004    PERT/GANTT CHARTING                           3
                     AD005    PROJECT LIFE CYCLE                            3
                     AD006    COST/BENEFIT ANALYSIS                         4
                     AD007    HIPO                                          3
                     AD010    USER LIAISON/DATA GATHERING                   3
```

Figure 8-3. Skills profile report.

IMHI ** STUDENT TRAINING HISTORY INQUIRY **   D 09/29/82 T 15:03:00
                                                                          PAGE: 1

COMPANY #/ PAYROLL #: 001 039206   EMPLOYEE NAME:
DATE: FROM   TO

COURSE NUMBER	COURSE TITLE	STU CCTR	CHGD CCTR	TYP	SUB CLASS DATE	EMPL STAT	TUIT COSTS	LIV/TRV COSTS
AB10000010	D.P. PROJECT MANAGMENT	00886	00886	I	11/20/81	CMP	0.00	0.00
AG50000080	V.S.A.M.-VIRTUAL STORAG	00886	00886	I	12/18/81	CMP	0.00	0.00
CPT0000010	PROJECT IMPLEMENTATION	00886	00886	I	10/01/81	PLN	0.00	0.00
DBD0000010	CICS DESIGN	00886	00886	I	03/17/80	CMP	104.00	0.00
DBD0000020	CICS CONCEPTS & FACILIT	00886	00886	I	03/10/80	CMP	56.00	0.00
DBD0000040	DATA BASE STRUCTURES AN	00886	00886	I	06/09/80	CMP	15.00	0.00
DBD0000070	CICS COMMAND LEVEL CODI	00886	00886	I	08/18/80	CMP	208.00	0.00
DBD0000100	IMS SYSTEM DESIGN	00886	00886	I	08/27/80	CMP	92.00	0.00
IBM0000010	DMS/VS APPL. DESIGN & C	00886	00886	I	02/26/80	CMP	0.00	0.00
IBM0000430	DB/DC DATA DICTIONARY	00886	00886	I	10/02/80	CMP	0.00	0.00
IBM0080080	DL/1 ADVANCED PROGRAMMI	00886	00886	I	04/01/82	PLN	0.00	0.00
MHI0000021	BASIC SUPERVISION-1	00886	00886	I	04/01/82	PLN	0.00	0.00

FUNCTION: KEY:
PRESS PF7 TO PAGE FORWARD
IMHI ** STUDENT TRAINING HISTORY INQUIRY **   ATTENTION

IMHI ** STUDENT TRAINING HISTORY INQUIRY **   D 09/29/82 T 15:03:21
                                                                          PAGE: 2

COMPANY #/ PAYROLL #: 001 039206 NAME:
DATE: FROM   TO   TOTAL TUITION COST: 475.00
                                TOTAL LIVING/TRAVEL COST: 0.00

COURSE NUMBER	COURSE TITLE	STU CCTR	CHGD CCTR	TYP	SUB CLASS DATE	EMPL STAT	TUIT COSTS	LIV/TRV COSTS
TCT0000030	CICS/VS COMMAND LEVEL P	00886		I	03/01/82	PLN	225.00	0.00

Figure 8-4.   Employee education history form.

```
                          CAREER DEVELOPMENT SYSTEM                                    REPORT  HRA1700A
                  EMPLOYEE EDUCATION TURN-AROUND REPORT                                PAGE NUMBER   1
                                                                                       RUN DATE

EMPLOYEE NAME
PRESENT POSITION                                        PAYROLL  NUMBER
DEPARTMENT                                              SOC.SEC. NUMBER
```

SKILL NUMBER	SKILL NAME / COURSE DATES	COURSE STATUS	MHT CRSE CODE	COURSE NAME	MEDIA TYPE	HRS	DAYS	TUITION COST	SKILL LEVEL INDV	SKILL LEVEL RECMD	CRSE ED LEVEL
AA001	IBM HARDWARE & PERIPHERAL DEVICES								1	3	
	__/__/__	__/__	ASI1401	MANAGING TIME	V	3.5					1
	__/__/__	__/__	ASI1402	WHAT CAN I CONTRIBUTE	V	3.5					1
	__/__/__	__/__	ASI1403	FOCUS ON TOMORROW	V	3.5					1
	__/__/__	__/__	DTK1201	DP CONCEPTS FOR MANAGERS - PART II 7-010	V	3.0					1
	__/__/__	__/__	DTK1202	DP CONCEPTS FOR MANAGERS - PART II 7-020	V	3.0					1
	__/__/__	__/__	DTK1203	SYSTEMS PROCESS 7-030	V	3.0					1
	__/__/__	__/__	DTK1204	THE SYSTEMS STUDY	V	3.0					1
	__/__/__	__/__	DTK1205	THE SYSTEM SPECIFICATIONS	V	3.0					1
	__/__/__	__/__	SRA1000	COMPUTING SYSTEMS FUNDAMENTALS	M	4.0					1
AB001	COBOL								3	4	
	__/__/__	__/__									
AB002	IBM ASSEMBLER								1	4	
	__/__/__	__/__	AGS0002	OS ADVANCED ASSEMBLER	I						3
	__/__/__	__/__	AGS0007	BASIC ASSEMBLER LANGUAGE WORKSHOP	I		12.0				2
	__/__/__	__/__	IBM0010	OS/VS ASSEMBLER INTERFACE SAM/BDAM H3783	P		10.0				3
	__/__/__	__/__	IBM0048	ASSEMBLER LANGUAGE WORKSHOP K3303	P		5.0	1130			2
	__/__/__	__/__	IBM5050	ASSEMBLER LANGUAGE CODING WORKSHOP K3303	M	4.5	5.0	760			1
	__/__/__	__/__	IBM7025	ASSEMBLER CODING TECHNIQUES	V	90.0					1
AB014	CICS COMMAND								2	4	
	__/__/__	__/__	IBM5575	COMMAND LEVEL CODING FOR CICS/VS	M	40.0	5.0	225			2
	__/__/__	__/__	TCT0003	CICS/VS STRUCTURE & PROGRAMING	I						2

Figure 8-5. Employee Education Turnaround Report

HOW TO PLAN AN EMPLOYEE'S
EDUCATION STRATEGY

The process to plan an employee's strategy begins when the project manager outlines the employee's education by developing a 12-month education plan and subsequently reviewing that plan during the year. The custom-tailored education strategy is developed at the respective employee's six-month counseling session. A complete description of the above-mentioned procedure appears in detail in Chapter 7. However, Chapter 8 deals with those aspects specifically relating to education. Meanwhile, the employee/manager counseling session remains critical to all subsequent career path growth.

At the management-initiated counseling session, the manager and the employee jointly review the skill deficiencies and the education course index. The education course descriptions—contained in an education catalog—are accessed as additional detailed information if required. Specific courses are selected and a classroom/work environment schedule is developed and mutually agreed to for the coming year.

Advisor Role

Once the counseling session is completed, the associated forms are sent to the HR advisor for review. As detailed in previous sections, the advisor next ensures uniform use of the procedures and provides a general appraisal of the quality of the utilization of the form. If necessary, the advisor will meet with the manager and/or employee to obtain more information to maximize the success potential.

Education Analyst Role

After advisor review, the form is sent to the education department. This is a critical step in the process. Next, an education analyst carefully reviews the plan to determine the appropriateness of education selected. Follow-up meetings with the manager will take place when required. The analyst's subsequent role is to ensure that selected education is required for development purposes and that matching of education and skill deficiencies is correct. Additionally, the analyst reviews for cost effectiveness. Can a cheaper alternative course be selected? Can a plan date be changed to take advantage of "local" or in-house offerings?

Education Scheduling Procedures

The employee education plan now is positioned to serve as the annual commitment to the respective employee and manager by the in-house education department. Scheduling will occur as requested during the year. Managers are subsequently sent enrollment applications—keyed off the plan—six weeks prior to each course date for confirmation or scheduling.

Education Plan Updating Procedure

Since DP projects must respond to both internal and external changes, those projects are often forced to change their direction. DP plans and strategy objectives are very rarely "stagnant" and annual plans are almost always modified. Because of that DP fact-of-life reality, the education plans always allow for flexibility and instructional modifications.

If last moment or suddenly unexpected changes are necessary, the manager indicates them on the respective employee's education plan and returns it to the education department. Scheduling then proceeds, using the modified plan.

THE PHILOSOPHY OF THE EDUCATION DEVELOPMENT PROCESS

During the past decade, a few key and distinctive philosophies and methodologies have been adopted in the in-house education mechanism. Those educational refinements appear in the subsequent pages.

The first methodology is the commitment to career pathing. In-house DP education is geared toward moving employees up the career ladder.

It is this management team's philosophy and experience that in-house-developed DP staffers are more productive than hires from outside company training programs. That's because in-house training is custom-tailored to the actual needs of the respective DP user.

In addition to providing education in support of the career development program, the education department runs a biannual training program. This program is specifically for people with no previous DP experience. Those who pass the rigorous screening will be comprehensively trained as programmers over a three-month period. The training is comprised of three months of extensive and formal DP classroom education, geared to the latest state-of-the-art technical environment. The trainees are closely supervised and taught how to apply their new technical expertise in a combination classroom/business environment. This entry-level DP training program is essential to the success of individual career development. Not only does the three-month training course develop future DP employees for the company, but its steady DP infusion of graduate trainees provides a constant upward job mobility movement throughout the entire department. There's an added bonus: Because many of the new trainees' assignments are in the more basic areas of DP, such as maintenance, more seasoned DP staffers are free to pursue more challenging assignments—and they can begin climbing up the career ladder.

Meanwhile, all DP/educational strategy yields a dual payback—its commitment to supporting the organization's business requirements. All HR department strategies are required to be in line with and complement the DP area's technical requirements and directions. The second paycheck is that it reduces DP employee turnover considerably below the turnover rates normally posted in the DP field.

Development, selection, and evaluation of all education offerings, meanwhile, follow a basic two-fold process. In order to maximize the abilities of the respective internal education staff's abilities—while capitalizing on the unique expertise available in the marketplace—we utilize both in-house education analysts and external consultants in what is regarded as a complementary process.

GUIDE TO THE EDUCATION ANALYST'S ROLE AND QUALIFICATIONS

It is critical that all in-house education analysts have heavy line experience in the DP field, plus significant education development expertise. Although the combination of such skills is very rare in the marketplace, it is well worth the difficulty it causes for staffing. The following are additional criteria essential to the education analyst's long-term success.

Career Development Support

This is one of the education analyst's most critical roles. Skills glossaries and definitions are modified regularly, to reflect current technology. Therefore, education course matrixes also must be constantly updated. This will require some course evaluation, course development and maintenance of the education catalog, consisting of course descriptions, matrixes and scheduling calendars.

Management Counseling

Analysts often provide ad hoc counseling to managers on education-related issues. This counseling often runs the spectrum from individual development issues to comprehensive needs analysis (e.g., generated from a thrust into a completely new technology impacting a significant number of DP projects).

Vendor Selection

Once completing an education needs analysis, the analyst determines the developer and/or instructor. If it is necessary to obtain outside expertise, multiple bids are requested and the analyst is responsible for vendor selection. The analyst relies upon many aspects in the decision, some of which may be:

- Expertise
- Previous experience at organization (including course and instructor critiques)
- Previous experience (references)
- Cost.

Course Tutoring

Though not used as instructors, the analyst can provide an excellent source of tutors. In support of both in-house and audio-visual self instruction, the tutor concept has proved most valuable. Follow-ups on course participation can solidify the expertise gained and ensure successful course completion.

Course Coordination/Scheduling

Based on annual education plan information—plus the knowledge of the DP area's business strategies—the analyst can determine the respective yearly education offerings and develop an annual schedule/calendar. The responsibilities continue into course coordination, ensuring that courses are implemented appropriately. This includes appropriate student enrollment, the selection of course materials and facilities, etc.

Education Evaluation

Heavy emphasis is placed on the quality of training and, therefore, significant effort is put into post-education evaluation. The entire area of quality assurance is the responsibility of the education analysts. This function is further described in subsequent pages of this chapter.

A GUIDE TO THE CONSULTANT ROLE
IN THE EDUCATION DEVELOPMENT PROCESS

Because the DP field changes so rapidly, it is highly important that the in-house education process be positioned to recruit external expertise required from a large pool of vendor resources to remain abreast of new technological developments. Experience has shown that it is virtually impossible to maintain a small DP permanent staff up-to-date and technically current and expert enough to provide that critically needed expertise. That's why we utilize education consultants for the development and teaching of in-house technical training. The next stage to begin the classroom training is fairly simple.

Based upon a needs analysis conducted by an education analyst familiar with the needs of the organization, a consultant will next develop the actual class. The selected consultant/teacher is someone who is an expert in the particular subject matter and best equipped to determine what expertise must be covered in the respective course.

Additional, "hands-on" experience has shown that it is beneficial to have this same consultant teach the respective course. This classroom continuity ensures that the same level of expertise will remain constant in the classroom and that all student questions can be answered immediately and knowledgeably.

In addition to the in-house staffing with highly qualified DP/consultant professionals, and ensuring that quality education is linked to required skills development, the following guidelines augment those processes presently in place.

Education Needs Analysis

All course development begins with a comprehensive needs analysis. Often, what persons or managers perceive as a need for education is really something else—e.g., a performance, environment, or staffing issue. The education needs analysis ensures that the development of the education product is based on an accurate understanding of the actual need.

Selection of Students

Since all of education is linked to skills, the selection of students merits a solid basis. Students are chosen because of their distinct skill deficiencies, and that relationship to the prescribed education offering predetermined by the education department. In addition, the education analyst also screens all student enrollments, ensuring that appropriate selection occurs.

Selection of Vendors

Since selection of both developer and teacher is from a large pool of resources (i.e., education consultant firms), the most appropriate resource can be chosen. By utilizing competitive bidding in the process, the action ensures that good price performance will be attained.

Tutoring

By supplementing education with tutoring—when required—the in-house education department, in effect, is subsidizing the process. In addition, its staffers can identify deficiencies on the part of a student or of the course itself and can identify the appropriate rectifying steps.

Post-Evaluations

This is a three-fold process. The education department conducts a post-evaluation of a student, instructor and class content. Post-course analysis focuses on various aspects determining course success. Questions to be posed, for example, are: Did students obtain the skills as defined? Were these in fact the skills needed for the job? Did they get a chance to utilize these skills on the job? Did it assist them in meeting the technical requirements of the job? Was the instructor effective? Did the course meet its stated objectives? Was the class well run?

HOW TO CONDUCT EDUCATION MEDIA COMPARISONS

In order to produce quality education, a variety of media are available, each offering unique benefits. Maximizing these benefits and applying them to the right situations is the key. Each media type does present its own particular drawback of sorts. The following is a "hands-on" rating and experiences of education media vehicles.

Personal Instruction Manuals (PI)

Although DP employees are certainly self-motivated and eager to learn new skills, self-instruction has not been 100 percent successful for in-house use. The medium, involving an individual and a manual as its only tool, does not generate enough attraction, staying power, reinforcement or retention. It is, however, the least expensive of the media and is only brought into play if funding is very low. If personal instruction manuals must be used, supplementing them with tutoring can improve on their effectiveness.

Audio-visual (A/V)

Certainly more entertaining than PIs, A/V is rated a notch above. A/V libraries, however, will require more education staff support than required by PIs. In order to ensure than the subject matter is relevant and addressing current technological issues, a staff must closely monitor all flow in and out of the subject tapes. And because technology changes so rapidly, it's best to have a "rotating" A/V library; i.e., new tapes coming in to replace obsolete subjects.

Many A/V firms offer this facility, meaning that tapes are "rented" rather than bought. If managed through a good scheduling process, this option can greatly reduce all associated costs. Tapes can be brought in at select times, students can be informed of their presence and then the tapes can be released as soon as they've been utilized.

A cautionary note: A/V rotation is not an easy task. It requires a significant portion of a senior education analyst's time. However, on the positive side, A/V can be utilized very cost effectively and can easily be adopted to address the needs of remote locations users. In all cases, the reinforcement of a tutor—and pre- and post-testing if possible—is suggested.

Computer Assisted Instruction (CAI)

Of all non-classroom instructions that we have used, CAI has certainly proved to be the most exciting. This self-instruction medium involves the student and the computer—the latter offering numerous interactive capabilities. Because the course is "taught" by the computer, an intelligent device (as opposed to a A/V tape), communication can take place continually between the student and the teaching device. The computer can ask questions and, more important, the computer will also generate a response based on the answer it receives. CAI, therefore, can pace the course specifically to the pace of the student. It can reteach concepts if necessary and it can speed through others if it appears that the student is ready to move on. Pre- and post-testing are inherent in the process and, therefore, an excellent monitoring device is available.

CAI courses can be purchased or self-developed. By calling upon the available in-house expertise, we have been able to develop CAI courses that are totally company-specific. Also, subject matters that are not addressed by any other available media can be developed by CAI. CAI does require a significant commitment. Computer time and terminals are required. Additionally, a small—but technical—

education staff must be assigned to CAI units for technical maintenance, course authoring support and general CAI coordination.

Seminars

This medium stands out as the best for extensive education when addressing a *number* of students. It is also, however, the most expensive. As previously mentioned in the chapter, in-house education analysts perform needs analysis—as indicated—to identify training needs. If it appears that the need requires a classroom method, outside available education is investigated.

If none prove satisfactory, the analyst will develop a request for proposal (RFP), extensively detailing the findings of the needs analysis and specifying the course outline and requirements. Multiple vendors are selected to receive the RFP and bid if so desired. Bids must include specifics about vendor references, specific instructor(s) who will be assigned to the courses (with resumes and referrals indicated), cost, training methodology to be utilized and specific course outlines. This process ensures that all seminars will address the respective user needs and are of high quality while offering good cost performance. Again, pre- and post-testing are utilized, where appropriate, as is post-course needs analysis, addressing whether or not the course in fact addressed the needs as originally defined.

PAYBACK TIME AND THE BOTTOM LINE:
WHAT WE HAVE LEARNED
FROM EDUCATION CAREER DEVELOPMENT

A lot of time, money, energies and strategies were expended to produce the all-encompassing HR system for the DP environment. The following is a summation of our corporate team experience.

Benefits

The education/career development philosophy has resulted in significant benefits from cost, quality and HR viewpoints. Here's how the benefits were accomplished:

- Education is directly tied to skills development. This means that once a skills deficiency is identified, the appropriate education is employed to directly deal with that deficiency. It also guarantees that all education is directly geared toward the respective company's DP technological directional thrust.

- Courses are subsequently developed appropriately and specifically for these new directions as they initially come into play.
- Students are selected for course attendance based on specific skills development needs, ensuring that appropriate student selection occurs. This is a critical step in the education process. Education courses—no matter the quality—are of little benefit if they are filled with inappropriate students.
- Education is cost-effective. Vendors, when necessary, are selected based on multiple bidding and price/performance, is the bottom-line driving force for selection.

Education Must Be Linked to Work Objectives

The timing of education is critical. Training must take place close in time sequence providing the students the immediate ability to use the newly learned skills on the job. Education planning—if based on anything but short-term horizons—can be detrimental. Course content is easily forgotten if not used by the student within one to two months of instruction.

Need to Keep System Current

Since our education system is tied directly to skills, and since DP skills are changing continuously in the marketplace, the entire system's components must be examined on a regular basis and upgraded to reflect current technology. Every 12 months—at a minimum—the system should be updated. The crucial updating process should be done by education and DP analysts who themselves are current in the field.

Impact on Turnover

Although turnover is the result of a multitude of factors, we believe that our education program has had a direct impact on keeping our DP turnover down at a manageable level. Based on attitude survey and exit interview data, we are firmly convinced that the programs

```
                                                                MM/DD/YY
    TRNG              CORPORATE ADMINISTRATIVE SYSTEM            HH:MM:SS
                            TRAINING MENU

               DESCRIPTION                           FUNCTION
                  TRAINING COURSE MAINTENANCE        TCRM
                  TRAINING COURSE INQUIRY            TCRI
                  TRAINING CLASS MAINTENANCE         TCSM
                  TRAINING CLASS INQUIRY             TCSI
                  EMPLOYEE TRAINING MAINTENANCE      TMTM
                  EMPLOYEE TRAINING INQUIRY          TMTI
                  SCHEDULED TRAINING CLASS INQUIRY   TSCI
                  TRAINING CLASS PARTICIPANTS INQUIRY TCPI
                  LAST NAME INQUIRY                  TENS
                  EMPLOYEE TRAINING HISTORY INQUIRY  TMHI

                                   SELECTION:_____




    FUNCTION:             KEY:
    PRESS PF7 FOR ADDITIONAL SELECTIONS
```

Operator enters:
  TCRM

```
                                                                MM/DD/YY
    TRNG              CORPORATE ADMINISTRATIVE SYSTEM            HH:MM:SS
                            TRAINING MENU

               DESCRIPTION                           FUNCTION
                  TRAINING/SKILLS RELATIONSHIP MAINTENANCE  TSRM
                  TRAINING SKILLS RELATIONSHIP INQUIRY      TSRI








                                   SELECTION:_____




    FUNCTION:             KEY:
    PRESS PF8 FOR PREVIOUS SELECTIONS
```

Figure 8–6

```
 1        PI10 TCRM ** TRAINING COURSE MAINTENANCE **          D       T
 2        MODE:
 3        TRAINING COURSE NUMBER:                  DATE LAST UPDATED:
 4        COURSE TITLE:
 5        GRADE RANGE FOR COURSE ELIBIBILITY:  FROM       TO:
 6
 7        COURSE DURATION:                   INITIATION DATE:
 8                        DAYS:              COURSE TYPE:
 9               OR HOURS:                   COURSE SUBTYPE:
10        VENDOR COURSE NUMBER:              VENDOR NAME:
11
12        COURSE SUMMARY:
13
14
15        COURSE FLAT COST:                  TUITION COST/STUD:
16        PROJ. LIVING COSTS:                PROJ. TRAVEL COSTS:
17
18        PASS PERCENTAGE:                   MAX STUDENTS:
19        APTITUDE TEST ID:                  MIN STUDENTS:
20        APTITUDE PASS LVL:
21        INACTIVE INDICATOR:                INACTIVE DATE:
22
23        FUNCTION:              KEY:
24        SUPPLY MODE AND COURSE NUMBER / PRESS ENTER
```

Operator enters:
    Mode   A (new course) (C, I, R)
    Course #   MHT0100112
         (10 chars.)
System responds:
    Date last updated   today's date
    Initiation date   today's date
    Inactive indicator   N
    PLEASE ENTER DATA
Operator enters:
    Title   XXXXXXXXXXXXXXXXXX
    Grade range   014–020 (not required)
    Course type   C, P, G, H, I, M, Q, R, Z — (clerical, prof.,
         supervisor)
    Subtype   M, V, T (self-study — prgrmd instruction,
         audio-visual, IIS — enter hours)
         I, P, R, L, C (internal, external, school-
         enter days)
    Days or hours   0001-9999
    Vendor #   Optional — no editing
    Vendor name   Required — no editing
System responds:
    PLEASE PRESS PF4 TO CONFIRM UPDATE
Operator presses PF4
System responds:
    SUCCESSFUL UPDATE/PRESS ENTER FOR NEXT SCREEN

Figure 8–7

```
1    PI11 TCSM ** TRAINING CLASS SCHEDULING MAINT **      D       T
2    MODE:
3
4    COURSE NUMBER:
5    CLASS DATE:           ENTER 'Y' TO OBTAIN FILLED SCREEN (ON ADD):
6
7    ─────────────────────────────────────────────────────────────────
8
9    CLASS LOCATION:
10
11   CLASS INSTRUCTOR:
12
13   CLASS START TIME:     MAXIMUN NUMBER OF STUDENTS:
14                         MINIMUM NUMBER OF STUDENTS:
15   SCHEDULED
16   COMPLETION DATE:
17   ACTUAL                NUMBER OF STUDENTS ENROLLED:
18   COMPLETION DATE:      NUMBER OF STUDENTS PLANNED:
19
20   CLASS CRITIQUE SUMMARY:
21
22
23   FUNCTION:            KEY:
24   PLEASE SUPPLY MODE, COURSE NUMBER, AND CLASS DATE
```

Operator enters:
    Mode   A (C or D)
    Course #   MHT0100112
    Class date   mm dd yy
System responds:
    Please enter data
Operator enters:
    Location (R)   New York
    Instructor   Joe Jones
    Start time   0900
    Completion date (R)   mm dd yy
System responds:
    SUCCESSFUL UPDATE/PRESS ENTER OR PF3
Operator presses ENTER
System responds with EMPLOYEE TRAINING MAINTENANCE screen.

Figure 8–8

```
1    PI12 TMT ** EMPLOYEE TRAINING MAINTENANCE **        D      T
2    MODE:
3    COURSE NUMBER:
4
5    CLASS DATE:                        COMP NO/PAYROLL NO:
6
7    ENTER 'Y' TO RECEIVE FILLED SCREEN:
8    _____
9
10   GRADE RANGE:           TO        MAX STUDENTS:   NO. ENROLLED:
11
12   (AT TIME OF CLASS) EMPLOYEE'S JOB GRADE:
13   _____
14
15   CLASS STATUS:          CHG COST CTR:       COMPL/CANC DATE:
16
17   CLASS LOCATION:
18
19   CLASS TUITION:         LIVING COSTS:       TRAVEL COSTS:
20
21   CLASS RATING:          CLASS DURATION:
22
23   FUNCTION:              KEY:
24   PLEASE ENTER REQUIRED DATA AND PRESS ENTER
```

Operator enters:
    Mode   A (C or D)
    Course #   MHT01001122
    Class date   mm dd yy
    Payroll #   001/023166   001/969696
                            001/999911   015/999923
    Recv filled screen   Y
System responds:
    (Class data is filled in)
    PLEASE ENTER DATA
Operator enters:
    Class status   Required — PLN, ENR, COM, CAN
    Class rating   Optional — 1-5
System responds:
    PLEASE PRESS PF4 TO CONFIRM UPDATE
Operator enters PF4
System responds:
    SUCCESSFUL UPDATE — PRESS ENTER OR PF3
    ENTER will cause TCSM screen to be displayed — operator can schedule next class

Figure 8-9

```
PI14 TSCI ** SCHEDULED TRAINING CLASSES INQUIRY ** D      T

                                                      PAGE:
COURSE NUMBER:
_____
SEL      CLASS          MAX          ENRLLD       CLASS LOCATION
         DATE           STU          STU

  _      _____       _____       _____     _____
  _      _____       _____       _____     _____
  _      _____       _____       _____     _____
  _      _____       _____       _____     _____
  _      _____       _____       _____     _____
  _      _____       _____       _____     _____
  _      _____       _____       _____     _____
  _      _____       _____       _____     _____
  _      _____       _____       _____     _____
  _      _____       _____       _____     _____
  _      _____       _____       _____     _____


FUNCTION:            KEY:
PLEASE SUPPLY COURSE NUMBER/PRESS ENTER
```

Operator enters:
        Course #   MHT01001122
System responds:
        Lists all scheduled classes
Operator enters:
        Y
System responds with TCSI screen showing all data on class selected.

Figure 8-10

```
 1          TCSI ** TRAINING CLASS SCHEDULING INQUIRY **     D        T
 2
 3
 4     COURSE NUMBER:
 5     CLASS DATE:
 6
 7     _____
 8
 9     CLASS LOCATION:
10
11     CLASS INSTRUCTOR:
12
13     CLASS START TIME:       MAXIMUM NUMBER OF STUDENTS:
14                             MINIMUM NUMBER OF STUDENTS:
15     SCHEDULED
16     COMPLETION DATE:
17     ACTUAL                  NUMBER OF STUDENTS ENROLLED:
18     COMPLETION DATE:        NUMBER OF STUDENTS PLANNED:
19
20     CLASS CRITIQUE SUMMARY:
21
22
23     FUNCTION:               KEY:
24     PLEASE SUPPLY MODE, COURSE NUMBER, AND CLASS DATE
```

Operator presses ENTER
System responds with all data on class selected.
Operator presses PF5 to return to selection screen.

Figure 8–11

```
1   PI16 TCPI ** TRAINING CLASS PARTICIPANTS INQUIRY ** D        T
2                                                             PAGE:
3   COURSE NUMBER: _____
4   CLASS DATE (OPTIONAL):_____   STATUS (OPTIONAL):
5      OR QUARTER: ___ AND YEAR (OPTIONAL): ___
6                                   NO. ENROLLED ___ NO. PLANNED ___
7   ─────────────────────────────────────────────────────────────
8   EMPLOYEE         EMPLOYEE NAME     EMPL  COST CTR/  JOB     START
9   CO NO/PAY NO                       STAT  SECTION    GRADE   DATE
10  _____       _____     ____  _____  _____   ____
11  _____       _____     ____  _____  _____   ____
12  _____       _____     ____  _____  _____   ____
13  _____       _____     ____  _____  _____   ____
14
15
16
17
18
19
20
21
22
23  FUNCTION:            KEY:
24
```

Operator enters:
            Course #   MHT0100112
System responds:
            Lists all employees registered for the Training class
Number enrolled and planned are only displayed when a particular class date is requested.
Status — will show only those students who have COMpleted the course or who are ENRolled, etc.

Figure 8-12

```
 1
 2        TSRM * TRAINING/SKILLS RELATIONSHIP MAINTENANCE * D       T
 3                                                                   PAGE:
 4      TRAINING COURSE NUMBER:      COURSE TYPE:   COURSE SUB-TYPE:
 5      COURSE TITLE:
 6
 7      MT        SKILL       DESCRIPTION            EXPECTED PROFICIENCY
 8      CD      TYPE/CODE                            ACHIEVEMENT LEVEL
 9      =         =  =     ================             =
10      _         _  _     _____            _
11      _         _  _     _____            _
12
13
14
15
16
17
18
19
20
21
22
23      FUNCTION:              KEY:
24      ENTER TRAINING COURSE NUMBER
```

Operator enters:
    Course #   MHT0100112

System responds:
    Lists existing skills
    ENTER MAINTENANCE DATA — LAST PAGE OF RELATED SKILLS

Operator enters:
    Mode   A, C, D
    Skill type   (not entered)
    Skill code   DPAD0100, -0150, -0151
                                    DPPG0100, -0110, -0130
    Description   (not entered)
    Prof. level   1–7

System responds:
    Type and description are displayed
    DEPRESS PF4 TO CONFIRM UPDATE

Operator enters:
    PF4

System responds:
    UPDATE SUCCESSFULL

Figure 8–13

have been favorably received and appreciated by all staff ranks, including senior-level management.

Impact on Employee Development

The methodologies described in these previous pages have been evolving for over a decade. Within that decade, some 400 trainees—who began at the bottom of the system's career ladder—moved along the career ladder successfully. The same upward training and mobility was also accorded their replacements, who assumed their former low-end career ladder positions.

Need for Automated System

As the in-house user population grew, so did the respective course offerings. These two factors led to a significant growth in the amount of data next needed to maintain, update and to report on. It would require additional administrative support. As a result, an automated system was produced to handle skills maintenance, education course data, employee education history and education planning and scheduling. Currently, revisions to that system are being designed to delivery on-line inquiry and update capability. Some of the screens from that system are displayed in Figures 8–6 through 8–13.

There has never been any doubt that all of the previous programs described were not worth the effort. The HR system milestones are easily justified by providing expense control, producing high-quality in-house education and delivering the technical/human resources clout to meet all DP challenges, plus providing back-up overall strong development and retention devices.

9
Valuing the Human Resource

"Instead of the single "bottom line" on which most
executives have been taught to fixate, the Third Wave
corporation requires attention to multiple bottom
lines. . . .
"Faced with this new complexity, many of today's
managers are taken back. They lack the intellectual
tools necessary for Third Wave management. . . ."
Alvin Toffler
Futurist/Author

SCENARIO

The growing complexity of organizations, increased sophistication of goods and services offered, specialization of staff employed and the unrelenting pace of change are taking their toll on the modern-day management process.

Today's manager, operating in the absence of planned and relevant training and lacking access to sophisticated tools, finds him/herself involved in all areas of non-management condition work. This counterproductive "working" manager syndrome effectively relegates the embattled manager to operate in a strictly react mode which, when coupled with the associated pressure, leads to automatic "crisis management." As the onslaught of "crisis management" work comes across his desk, anticipation and planning flies out the window, imprisoning the manager.

This servitude increases frustration level of the manager who is occasionally shaken out of this work-driven transfixed state. Each time this happens, the manager recognizes the dilemma and earnestly resolves to break out of this self-restrictive work mode. This resolve,

256

however, normally becomes subordinated to the work needs of the time and ends up like most hell-bent intentions made under fire. It is a vicious circle. Managers are forced to become fixed in their perspective and extremely artful in asking questions to support predetermined and survivorship (or work-reducing) answers. This survival mode minimizes the time/problem and/or provides managers with the highest degree of comfort. In addition, the embattled manager does not have the time to spend with his or her employees additionally serving as a career counseling guru. Besides, that action visually receives the lowest priority reducing feedback and reinforcing one-way communication. The resultant communication tends to be terse, impersonal and unexplained, as if it was a test of some sort that the employee must take in order to continue working for this manager. Like the orchestra leader, the manager, to be effective, must be "out in front" of the respective area of responsibility in order to orchestrate and manage both the day-to-day process and the introduction and adoption of change to that process.

Today's successful managers must be part chameleon to anticipate, sense and modify their style of management to fit the varying demands of work situations they encounter. The effective manager does not consistently manifest a particular set of traits or skills (mechanistic) but reacts to the necessities born out of perceived differences.

Whether Americans believe management is an art, a science or both, the health of the nation's management today is of grave concern to all who examine it closely. Meanwhile, the anxiety level of many managers is running very high, adding to the belief that the management process is becoming less effective. Unfortunately, this blemished observation is occurring at a time when an effective management process is the *crucial stabilizing* element required, in order to successfully manage the integration of the "change" itself into the existing process.

With the increasing and unrelenting demand for specialization, it is projected that, in the data processing (DP) industry alone, there will be one qualified person for every five jobs available in the mid-1980s. A natural consequence of this tight marketplace is the increasing costs—recruitment, salaries, etc.—associated with rapid expansion of demand and a slower growth of human talent.

In varying degrees, escalating costs force organizations to seek optimal combinations of skills, subject to project and budget constraints. Thus, organizations will have to staff positions with new hires who have not received fully adequate education, training and experience to prepare them for these new jobs. Additionally, appointments to management-type positions will have to be made from the existing staff pool or from less experienced new candidates. It is strongly anticipated that by appointing such educationally deficient candidates to management jobs may ring the death knell for both the organizational group and for the quality and timeliness of the products planned. Here's why:

Such newly appointed managers—lacking training, experience, availability of tools, upper management support or any combination of these elements—will tend to embrace this new position with great reluctance.

On the one hand, they may not want to appear negative by refusing the promotion. But they may also feel insecure in this new milieu which can only serve to stimulate survival instincts. There is a tendency for workers in such a dilemma to revert back to doing what they know best and therefore to work only on those aspects of their responsibility with which they are familiar.

Normally, this attitude is to the detriment of the job's other needs. This preoccupation with lower-level activities tends to reduce the "challenge and decision-making opportunities in the area" for their subordinates, thus demoting them one level.

The synergy and dynamics of the group enter into a slowly downward spiral, requiring dramatic change to arrest and reverse the downward action. Further, subordinates hired by this manager tend to be on the light side of the position requirements. These "light-side" subordinates usually increase the manager's comfort zone and decrease his/her anxiety level in the work environment. Rapid organizational growth has also placed in management employees who are desirous of a managerial position but who have received little or no formal training in the discipline. These corporate newcomers are really frustrated technicians who can't say no when a promotion is offered—and they're capable of reversing all of the forward momentum garnered since the industrial revolution.

Unfortunately, in today's increasingly complex work environment, the classic organizational structure does not provide the most effective way to harness the energies of the human component toward tangible goals. It has been proven that the "Mongolian Hordes" approach does not work (i.e., doubling the staff does not halve the delivery time). Is there a solution left to help make things work again? There is a mechanism on the corporate horizon that may help the user in the new mandate for "work smart" change. And it begins deep within the organization.

The contemporary reward mechanism (project-based, not people-based) employed by typical corporations (both official and non-official status) modifies the behavior of all employees. This behavior is then copied by the would-be managers, sometimes to the detriment of others, the organization and themselves.

The most frightening aspect of this self-destruct scenario is that management—not in complete control, but in a controlling position—is setting the pace, developing and training subordinate resources to be the future supervisory resources of the company both by courses, jobs and its own demonstrated behavior. Thus, observers note that if you believe in that old adage, "you are what you eat," then you will also have to support the notion, "corporations are what they reward, train and tolerate."

This condition then raises the questions about the stewardships of management and whether managers are actually responsible for the resources placed in their hands. Are they really accountable for managing these resources like a business, given that employees represent a "valuable" company resource entrusted to the manager?

By examining the budgets for DP departments, corporate observers see the increasing shift in allocation of funds from hardware/software products to employee-associated costs. This ratio is currently in the 60 to 70 percent range and is anticipated to climb to 80 percent in the not-too-distant future.

If the nation's corporate leaders today accept the notion that a human resource is a highly "expensive item" and, like a piece of high-technology equipment used to provide the respective company with full profit yield potential, then the "human resource" takes on a stronger investment-like character. The contemporary manager, therefore, automatically assumes the equivalent of a de facto portfolio investment manager, controlling projects, project profiles, people and development costs. The destiny of the organization's short- and long-term economic future may be weakened or strengthened, depending on the human resources decisions made. But those choices should not be made or determined by those not operating in the human resources mainstream.

Meanwhile, as the operations on which these resources are employed continue to produce income resources for the organization, then the associated costs and margins resulting from "human resources decisions" becomes extremely crucial. This key marketplace observation is not new but, for some reason, the corporate manager has been insulated from personally adopting this corporate lifeflow philosophy.

Relevant information on the investment cost of resources has always been available. What has always been lacking is the subsequent synthesizing process which would allow a cost benefit approach to be undertaken toward acquiring, retaining, developing and, more important, utilizing these costly human power and brain power resources.

For the 1980s manager who plays to win by managing more effectively, that manager must be highly aware of the cost/profit consequences of human resource decisions. This contemporary leadership trait involves mature, business-like judgments, made to balance project and project assignment needs with career development plannings for employees. It also involves implementation of a process to measure, in a timely fashion, all changes to the portfolio of investments under that manager's control.

Hardware investment measurement is a major priority. Hardware cost reduction will, in addition to enabling companies to buy their first computer, allow existing users to modify, enlarge and/or reconfigure their current equipment.

Subsequently, the demand for skilled staff to operate and develop systems will significantly increase. As a result, the over-optimistic momentum in the budgeting and project planning cycle will also continue for some time, increasing/reinforcing the human resources demand curve.

The as-to-be-expected shortfall situation will place an increasing emphasis on the quick-fire need to be able to implement sound investment-type decisions directly related to human resources. The cost of specialized people resources will increase and there will be a natural adjustment in the mix, duration (profile) and therefore cost/benefit of projects initiated.

These pressing manpower and economic priorities—coupled with the current productivity issues—make it imperative that contemporary managers be measured on their all-around effectiveness managing key organizational resources. The traditional and now highly-antiquated mechanical approaches currently employed must be revised and supplemented with other measures that reflect the true value of the human resource to an organization in a meaningful way while also showing how this value can be improved and measured.

The modern corporate leader's objective, therefore, is to fully explore this major organizational fact-of-life reality and subsequently produce new basic tools to aid the frontline manager and the corresponding organization to more effectively utilize this costly, depletable and highly mobile resource, entrusted to the manager's care.

The most important assets today in any organization are its human, financial and physical assets. Corporations are now acknowledging that survival and success in a technologically and socially complex society depend on the quality, condition and contribution of the human assets employed. Like any asset, the human resource represents a risk assessment and a corresponding investment by the corporation, in order to possess the right to receive future economic benefits. In addition to the initial "capturing" cost/investment by a company, it also has to protect its investment by continuing to develop, maintain and maximize the condition of this asset. Companies must provide continuous, recurring learning opportunities to their working population (human assets) through the creation of comprehensive, formal and informal learning structures and activities. Otherwise their internal knowledge banks and human resources supplies will turn into huge pools of stagnant water reserves.

Organizations, meanwhile, have invested large amounts of money in a variety of mechanisms and processes to increase the level of control and effective utilization of the organizational physical resources. Sadly, the now largest, most expensive and vital resource to an organization's future—its people—has been neglected in this regard. This puts additional strains on the management process, which is already stretched to its limit.

The 1980s DP/human resources leader knows where to find and then how to implement that winning human resources strategy. He or she has heard of the Hasbis 1973 definition which is highly relevant:

"Human Resources are the energies, skills, talents and knowledge of people which potentially can or should be applied to the production of goods or the rendering of useful services.''

It is the only winning definition used in the 1980s corporate marketplace—and the message will stand up against the future test of time.

COMPONENTS OF THE WINNING HUMAN RESOURCES STRATEGY FOR THE 1980s

Entrusted to management, "valuing" the company's human resources will increase management's realization of the tremendous opportunity, loss or gain that could/did/will occur through either effective or ineffective management of this key resource.

To help make this strategy successful is the inherent process that managers will gain additional economic perspective on the accountabilities of their roles. This increased managerial awareness role— magnified by a "valued" approach—should help to resolve and remedy the accountability/responsibility inbalance that apparently seems to be vocalized increasingly by larger numbers of managers.

Here's how the basic tenets of these valuations are lined up:

1. The identified tools and components associated with the "human resources" winning strategy can be quantified, and are readily available to be generated in a cost-effective manner.
2. An objective measure of each of the components selected can be derived. Subsequently, such a measure can be applied in a consistent manner across the organization and over which the manager has an acceptable level of control.
3. A reporting format—a human resource accounting (HRA) report—can be designed that effectively portrays these findings.

Properly arranged, this pivotal information will enable management to gain a clearer understanding of:

1. The initial period start-up cost (i.e., salary, benefits, agency fees, etc.) of the human resources value entrusted to a manager's control.
2. The "other" values available to further increase the total value of the manager's human resources (i.e., team awards, education, project assignment).

3. The internal changes in value over the period resulting from the manager's "development" activity and/or inactivity, with respect to the "human" resource.
4. The external changes in value over the period resulting from turnover, project allocation, recruitment, etc.
5. The end of period value and condition of the human resources entrusted to the manager's care.
6. Comparison against predetermined and budgeted plans in the areas of performance distribution, etc.

The components and measures selected must stand the test of relevancy, and must be under control of the manager. They must appear as useful and natural sense indicators associated with the job. In some cases, values can be computed to reflect the measure sought while others will have to be factors or comparisons against a plan or organizational norm. The items explored need to be implemented and constantly changed as on-going experience dictates fresh evaluation following the initial pilot's development.

The more obvious components that automatically come to mind are explored in the following pages together with some careful examinations behind measurement rationale.

TURNOVER: IT CAN BE A POSITIVE VALUE KEPT WITHIN RANGE

Turnover is inevitable and—if properly controlled—it can also be healthy for any organization, especially where large specialized populations are employed.

A department of reasonable size, for example, develops its own culture, norms and values, mirroring the quality of leadership in the department and its perceived role in the organization. The existence of standards, usage of state-of-the-art techniques, degree of development activity and organizational morality reinforce and subsequently normalize this subculture. In the case of a DP department not perceived by its "rank and file" to be a vital contributing member of the corporation, the resultant look from within produces gloom and the net worth of the people declines, as does the subsequent quality of work produced and all internal decisions made. Consequently, mediocrity settles in and flourishes, in turn breeding decreasing levels of mediocrity. The gloom/stagnation environment

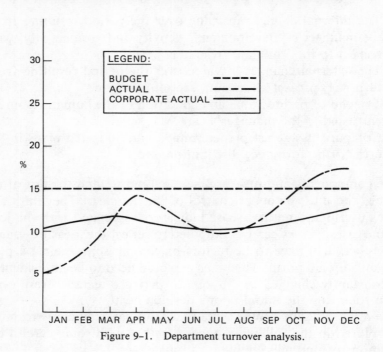

Figure 9-1.   Department turnover analysis.

works heavily against the best interests of the parent organization. Turnover will serve as the hero of the new financial quarter.

Turnover provides the means to inject new life, ideas and vigor into a group where new relationships are formed and old ones weakened. The renewal process begins with the first resignation. To ensure objective information is available concerning exiting employees' reasons for leaving, meaningful exit interviews must be conducted by an independent group. This group then forwards the terminating reasons to management together with its independent judgment regarding problems and/or trends that require management attention (see Figures 9-2 and 9-3). Figure 9-2 compares the current department turnover rate with the existing corporatewide turnover rate by reason classification. In the following examples, the employees turnover classifications are:

Good/good = Good performer for a good reason
Good/bad   = Good performer for a bad reason
Bad   = Unsatisfactory performer

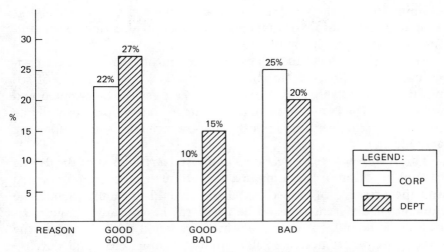

Figure 9–2. Department turnover analysis by reason classification.

A good reason, for example, is when the corporation could not provide the job-market experience or upgrading sought by a deserving employee. A bad reason example is where the corporation might have met the employee request but for some reason failed to do so.

The most significant class—requiring significant follow-through

	POSITION									
	ASSOC. PGMER.		PGMER.		A/P		BUS. ANAL.		TOTAL	
REASON	#	%	#	%	#	%	#	%	#	%
1. ～～～～	XX	XX.X	XX	XX.X	XX	XX.X	XX	XX.X	XXX	XX.X
2.										
TOTAL	XXX		XXX		XXX		XXX			
%	XX.X		XX.X		XX.X		XX.X			
BASE	XXX		XXX		XXX		XXX		XXX	
CONSULTANTS	XX		XX		XX		XX		XX	

Figure 9–3. Department turnover analysis by position and reason code.

examination—is the good/bad category, which can be construed as a highly valid measure of management concern/attention to the full-time job needs of the employee.

Meanwhile, a level of turnover based on projected market conditions, geography, development activity (new systems), use of sophisticated hardware and software etc., can also be determined and quantified. The resultant projected turnover rate would normally be the same as the ones used in both manpower planning and budgeting activities.

This turnover-rate projection—employed as function of the degree of sophistication of the company, size of the departments concerned and the presence of skilled resources—would normally dictate the number of different rates to be used. In the case of a large engineering company, for example, observers might wish to stratify the engineers into trainee, associate, junior, senior, etc., and develop separate turnover rates for each position.

A useful comparison against the respective organization's turnover rates would be the industry projections obtained from trade journals. It should be remembered that the projecting, collection and measuring of data would occur *throughout* the year. The analyzing of the results, reviewing across-the-board rate adjustments and evaluating other pertinent measurement/comments, would be made at the end of the year concerned.

These operating results for the year would provide further data for fine-honing the next year's estimates and budgets (see Figure 9–1). Figure 9–3 further refines the turnover rate to reflect the activity by both position title and corporate reason. In addition to the various totals and percentage, the actual base of employees used to measure turnover is included together with the number of consultants employed in similar positions.

The value would take into account the direct and indirect savings from reduced levels of recruitment (see recruitment section) and are coupled with turnover costs. These latter costs would comprise:

- *Direct education costs.* Industry averages indicate that eight to ten days of planned education are provided to each employee per year. It has also been observed that a large number of employees request and attend education, and that resignations then quickly follow. In such cases where a course was attended during the last three months the total course cost then should be used; otherwise, 50 percent of the average yearly employee education cost should be used. If this information is automated, the 50 percent criteria can be further refined down to satisfy management's desire for more exacting information.

- *Education/salary cost.* An employee's salary paid while enrolled in a course is another direct cost of turnover. The average annual salary for the position should be used to calculate the wages paid while on the course: the greater of 50 percent of average yearly number of days times daily salary rate, or the total number of days spent on course during the last three months multiplied by the daily salary rate for the position.

- *Work out resignation time.* In the majority of cases, the employee who has resigned and is working until his last day tends to spend increasing amounts of time in preparing for the new job. The average length of this stay would be in the two to four weeks category, depending on the industry concerned and company policies. During this time period, the terminating employee tends to heavily socialize with other employees. The salary/ overhead value for this period is therefore considered an expense to reflect the unproductive time. Not only is the terminating employee's time unproductive but so is the time of those employees who are also engaged in the socializing as they are also distracted from working. For this powerful reason the terminating employee's salary for the period is doubled.

- *Knowledge costs.* The departing employee leaves with an insider's knowledge of the company, its makeup, its power basis (who to go to in order to get things done), its culture, standards, products, services, customers and people. This as function of the position being vacated directly reflects a lost opportunity cost to the organization. It is conservatively estimated that this manpower cost would approximate two to five months' salary and is akin to the "acculturation" cost of a new employee getting up to speed.

The recruitment elements might include the difference between the actual cost of recruitment and the estimated cost of recruiting to replace the "quantified acceptable level" of turnover. (Recruitment cost to include agency fee, assimilation, associated education costs, etc.)

Turnover kept below this "quantified acceptable level"—factored by resignation reasons—could be easily translated into a positive value to the manager's credit. Turnover kept within range of the "quantified acceptable level"—factored by resignation reasons—should be translated into a positive value to the manager.

A typical depiction of these costs is provided in Figure 9-4, which represents the total cost of terminating employees less the "quantifiable acceptable level." The net difference would then be carried through to the summary statement depicted in Figure 9-8.

Turnover above the "quantified acceptable level"—factored by resignation reasons—should be translated into a negative value to the manager.

Measures of turnover should be planned around job family, job title or even department based on the confidence level the organization wishes to achieve.

This, of course, assumes that the quantified acceptable level is a range representing those employees quitting the organization for reasons other than those under direct control of the manager (i.e., spouse relocating, joining armed forces, etc.).

Those employees who quit, due to dissatisfaction with their manager and where it is objectively assessed their reasons are valid, should be automatically credited to the manager. Further, this value should be factored up as a function of the performance of the employee.

A high performer represents a larger potential loss to an organi-

RESIGNATION TYPE	EMPLOYEES	EDUCATIONAL COST	SALARY COST	RESIGNATION TIME COST	KNOWLEDGE COST
GOOD/GOOD	XX	XXXX	XXXX	XXXX	XXXX
GOOD/BAD	XX	XXXX	XXXX	XXXX	XXXX
BAD	XX	XXXX	XXXX	XXXX	XXXX
TOTAL COST	XX	XXXXX	XXXXX	XXXXX	XXXXX
LESS: BUDGETED	XX	XXXXX	XXXXX	XXXXX	XXXXX
	XX	XXXXX	XXXXX	XXXXX	XXXXX

Figure 9-4. Department turnover analysis by turnover cost.

zation than a standard performer. Assuming a replacement needs to be hired, the associated recruitment expenses should be added and then adjusted when a replacement is found.

RECRUITMENT: HOW TO MEASURE DIRECT AND INDIRECT COSTS

The cost of manpower recruiting, delays in hiring and successfully integrating a new employee into the job varies with the type of employee hired and the area and type of job the employee is hired for. From a management measurement perspective, an acceptable time-frame to acquire employees from the marketplace for standard types of resource (i.e., analyst, Cobol programmer, etc.) can be quantified (possibly over a range of weeks). There's even a suggested measurement-posting system, which is as follows:

- Managers taking less than standard time should be given a " + " value.
- Managers taking standard time should be given a smaller " + " value.
- Managers taking more than standard time should be given " − " value.

Coupled with this measurement are the direct and indirect range of costs of recruitment to the organization. Cost have been estimated in the past using various methods and depending on the position as:

- Agency fee—$4,000–$9,000
- Salary adjustment—$1,000–$7,500
- Start-up time—(project delay = $5,000–$15,000)
- Education, equipment, investment cost (including salary and education cost)—$1,000
- Orientation familiarization with the organization—$3,000–$12,000

It is assumed that the need to recruit is not in question and that the service support required by the manager in order to effectively hire is in place and responsive.

This leads to the factors and conditions under the manager's control, namely:

- Timeliness—how long it takes to hire a candidate into the organization.
- Quality—the quality of the hiring decision (i.e., did the employee resign within 12 months or was his or her performance unsatisfactory?).
- Source of resource—where initially obtained directly affects the cost component.

These costs are then translated into expense (opportunity) costs measured in terms of months and salaries as follows:

Position Type	Average Cost in salary months	Average Cost
Programmer	5 months	$9,000
Analyst	15 months	(salary costs) $45,000
Manager	24 months	$70,000

Managers using mobility/promotions/trainees—both management and DP—stretching people to fill needs should be given a " + " value.

This internal-recruiting avenue is a two-edged sword depending on the quality and leadership bases of the existing management making the decision. If the job candidates from within the corporation are placed/promoted into the open jobs—and are perceived to be good by their peers and subordinates—they will be successful.

Those employees will also have the support of their peers, because their competence has been proven. Additionally, the internal identification with the respective corporation will be increased for both the newly promoted person and the other colleagues. The move will increase the loyalty factor and thereby bolster productivity. This resultant feeling of equity, exercising fair play and displaying open morality surrounding the promotion, provides the selected individual the strongest leadership power base there is—namely, emergent power base.

Conversely, if the wrong person is placed in one of the open positions, a volatile catalyst will erupt and will lead to lower productivity and eventually generate higher turnover.

Managers recruiting applicants from a "finder's fee" or "employee referral program" and other referrals should be given a " + " value. (It represents the possible difference between the cost of stan-

RESOURCE TYPE	# OF RESOURCES SOUGHT	ELAPSED MONTHS ACQUIRE	AVERAGE # MONTHS	STANDARD SET # MONTHS	VARIANCE	RESIGNED WITHIN 12 MONTHS	MOBILITY	PROMO WITHIN	FINDERS FEE	AGENCY	REFERRAL	BASE POPULATION	CONSULTANT POPULATION	REDUCED CONSULTANTS
ENTRY LEVEL	XX	XX.X	X.X	X.X	(X.X)	XX					X	XX		
ASSOC. PGMER.														
PROGRAMMER	X	XX	X.X	X.X	.	X	X	X	X	X	X	XX	XX	X
PROG/ANAL														
BUS/ANAL														
TOTALS	XXX	XXX	X.X	X.X	X.X	XX	XX	XX	XX	XX	XX	XXX	XX	XX
COST BY SOURCE							X.X	X.X	X.X	X.X	X.X			
PERCENTAGE OF SOURCE							X.X%	XX.X%	.X%	X.X%	XX.X%			

TIMING | QUALITY | SOURCE

QUALITY COST

XX POSITIONS RESIGNED
*   REPLACEMENT, COST = $XXXXXX.XX

Figure 9-5.   Recruitment time, quality and source analysis for department.

dard recruitment that would have been incurred and the "finder's fee" awarded). However, it is felt that varying the amount of the fee would not strongly influence a manager to increase his or her use of this mechanism. The main reason to use or not use this service is the regard in which the manager views the corporation and whether that manager feels he or she would be doing a friend a disservice or not.

A manager converting a consultant contract to a full-time employee should be given a " + " (value/factor). This represents the possible difference between the commission paid to the release consultant, if applicable, and the cost of the agency fee. It also includes the cost of production time lost by a new employee until brought up to speed and incorporating the additional cost of manpower assistance provided to the new employee.

Conversely, a manager who converts a full-time position into a consulting contract should be given a " − " (value/factor) if the position calls for a standard type of resource.

As a follow-up, a measure to indicate the quality of a manager's hiring decision should also be examined. The employee's tenure (termination reason if less than n months) coupled with performance on the job, may also be included (see Figure 9–5).

EDUCATIONAL ALLOWANCES: HOW TO DETERMINE THEIR VALUE

Education allowance is targeted and budgeted for the year as n days per employee, and is moderated by employee development plans, future projects/responsibilities and past education.

This overt type of financial investment in an employee will cause the "value of the education received" to be "added" to the earlier value placed on the employee at the beginning of the year.

It is easily assumed—and readily supportable—that any such employee investment is expected to increase that employee's potential income earning ability for the corporation. That same investment can also be handled in such a way as to minimize a potential loss situation.

The "value added" of education—in order to be realistically reflected on the employer's books—must be reinforced by relevant project work or assignment. If this doesn't happen, the manager should then be charged with the entire educational cost. Because education usually tends to have a limited half-life of approximately

RESOURCE TYPE	# RESOURCES	BUDGETTED			ACTUAL			VARIANCE		
		DAYS	AMT.	AMT./DAY	DAYS	AMT.	AMT./DAY	DAYS	AMT.	AMT./DAY
ENTRY LEVEL										
ASSOC. PROGRAMMER										
PROGRAMMER	XX	X	$XX.X	$XX.X	XX	$XXXXX	$XXX.X	(X)	($XX.X)	($XX.X)
PROG/ANAL										
BUS/ANAL										
TOTAL	XX	XXX	$XXXXX.X	$XX.X	XXX	$XXXX.X	$X.X	(XX)	($XX.X)	($XXX)

Figure 9-6.   Educational Analysis.

three months—if not reinforced by practical application—a large number of dollars could potentially be misused because the educational process did not migrate from a knowledge base to a skill base.

When education is treated as a highly visible employee reward, there is a direct feedback tendency for that respective employee to review the current organization, methods and practices more favorably in the light of new learning. At the same time, when obvious existing practices are not perceived to be helpful to an organization, questions are raised and recommendations offered. Management's usual steadfast unwillingness to change or at least discuss the respective employee's suggestions plants the negative seeds of discontentment and/or nurtures the counterproductive feeling of frustration and unhappiness in the employee. This process easily takes its toll on employee ranks and could be one of the keystone reasons for depressing laissez-faire attitudes and dismal decreasing productivity records throughout the nation's corporate and industrial sectors.

After all is said and done, the rest is left to the use of the budget, measured with the following results:

- *Under-spending*. Should this condition occur, the resultant potential under-developing of people will be given a " − " value. It is recognized that in special circumstances, this "under-spending" fact could also generate a " + " (value/factor).
- *Over-spending*. This condition has indicated the potential lack of planning and control (unless valid) and should be given a " − " value.
- *Cancelling*. Last-minute cancelling, no shows and not turning in an evaluation should be given a " − " factor.
- *Unrelated training*. An " − " value/factor should be applied for training given that is not related to current job assignments, job assignments within three months of completion of training or project career goals (see Figure 9–6).

CONSULTANTS: HOW THEY FIT
INTO THE GRADING GUIDELINES

Consultant usage is becoming more of a misnomer than originally intended. Historically, the services of a management consultant were purchased due to the specialization/expertise and broad knowledge of solutions consultants provided. However, due to the differential in salary versus consultant fees, many bonafide employee analysts and programmers quit their employers and decided to go into business for themselves by renting their expertise back to companies. This type of resource exchange should be termed a "contract" person and not a consultant.

Most corporate decision-makers generally support the honored philosophy of using consultants for "peak" work demand periods. The assignments are usually highly technical—but short-term—or required specialized needs and can also be highly monotonous work. But the reality is that the consultant is a professional and, although well-paid, the typical consultant will not normally tolerate being under-employed as a "drone" for any significant period of time. If consultants create longevity records at any work site, someone should question their pedigree, current assignment and billings. They're really running up quite a tab.

Assuming the existence of a stated guideline or policy, a manager bringing in more consultants—without expressed permission—than guidelines allow should be given a " − " (value/factor).

Conversely, managers who employ less than guidelines allow should be given a " + " (value/factor).

Managers who continually extend consultants' contracts should be given a " − " (value/factor). The follow-up question to pose is why there is no replacement training of in-house employees or recruiting of full-time positions to fill those positions. The question must not be skirted as has been the custom throughout the nation's hiring sector.

Managers should be given a " + " (value/factor) if they accomplish the task with low consultant usage or document decreased usage (i.e., early termination of a consultant contract).

Whatever is said about consultant usage, there are advantages and disadvantages that must be dealt with. Other costs to the corporation using consultants are:

- A lack of continuity if the consultant leaves.
- The loss of knowledge.
- Loss of competitive edge on future developments.
- The possible morale problem on existing employees.

PERFORMANCE REVIEW: A REWARD
FOR EXPANDED EFFORTS

The real-life factors affecting an employee's on-the-job motivation and concurrent performance are to a large extent under the control of that worker's manager. The resultant employee productivity is based upon that individual's perceived "risk analysis" of the allocated work. If the employee perceives the task will be successful, then the resultant positive exposure should attract a good performance rating and thus be rewarded accordingly. Employees therefore expend the work effort (motivation) accordingly. Conversely, if employees feel there are insurmountable impediments, they approach the task with little or no enthusiasm. Here's how to rate that situation accordingly:

Managers get a " + " (value/factor) if their performance distribution of employees is reflective of announced targets and they have submitted all reviews in a timely fashion. Conversely, a " − " (value/factor) should be awarded where reviews are *not* submitted in a timely fashion.

Managers should receive a " + " (value/factor) if they were instrumental in achieving "desirable" turnover. This would include satisfying *all* the requirements (policies/practices/communications) in a quality fashion to the benefit of both the company and the employee.

Absenteeism, lateness and overtime should be controlled and measured against budget and/or a "standard" (norm) for the group. Positive and negative values/factors should be calculated based on (performance and remedial action initiated) against plan/norms.

It should be stressed that clearly-visible actions and behavior by management will, to a large extent, either increase/decrease the employees' perception of the probabilities of rewards for effort expended.

Other areas would include those below.

Salary Guideline Objectives

Manager receives a " + " (value/factor) if his/her resources are equitably rewarded (i.e., same resource types with similar performance and experience are paid close to market value and each other).

		PERFORMANCE											
	A		B		C		D		E		TOTAL	
	#	%	#	%	#	%	#	%	#	%	#	%
CORRORATION	X	X.X	XX	XX.X	XX	XX.X					XXXX	XXX
DEPARTMENT	X	X.X	XX	XX.X	XX	XX.X						
TARGET	X	X.X	XX	XX.X	XX	XX.X						
VARIANCE	X	X.X	X	X.X	X	X.X						
LATE SUBMISSIONS			X		XX							

Figure 9–7. Department performance statistics.

Project Completion Guidelines

Manager gets a "+" or "−" (value/factor) for completion/non-completion of projects and/or production quotas accomplished within time/cost targets and completed within standards set for employee/consultant profiles.

Years of Service Guidelines

Manager receives a "+" (value/factor) for retaining the services of a skilled employee resource for the determined period. This (value/factor) must be on a sliding scale yardstick and includes the function of both years of service *and* performance during the period.

This component and career development/mobility activity must be in harmony to correctly value and encourage the desired behavior of supervising employees; (i.e., good performers *who do not want to advance* and are deemed valuable in current position), are not penalized for their current status.

On this last significant point, across-the-board employee retention at numerous levels is an impossible objective to achieve. Managers, therefore, should ensure that such highly paid employee resources are efficiently deployed and the maximum productivity yields are generated while they're still part of the work-team effort.

Environmental Impact Guidelines

If, in the perception of the employees, the current organization is beyond salvage, any attempt to introduce the previously stated measures would be impossible. And it means going back to the corporate basics—revamping with a new cadre of the "play-to-win" managerial breed. It's not an impossible task. And when those new frontline managers are ready for their first evaluations, grade those resources accordingly.

Always keep in mind that there is no substitute for a good manager. Start with an "average" individual equipped with average memory and common sense, and having a management-type education, and that candidate should accomplish and perform a non-complex assignment reasonably well. This presumes the decision-making process will be primarily in the areas of performance expertise with a reasonably high incidence of recurrence.

A knowledgeable manager must, therefore, review past experiences, extrapolate on the problem and subsequently provide a reasonable, workable solution. These new solutions would invariably become fact, would work and would result from judgment calls in areas where there were no precedents.

In order to successfully integrate such a human resource measurement mechanism into an organization, the head manager must not only let it be known what is expected but must be also visibly reinforce that strong desire for this workplace tool.

In order for this tool to be timely and effective, raw data must be gathered, recorded and analyzed for reporting purposes. If the organization already has a human resources group, the majority of information can be gleaned from its existing records. If no such in-house group exists, the measurement criteria used will have to be reduced to primarily deal with readily available information only.

THE FUTURE OF THE MEASUREMENT PROCESS: WHERE IT STANDS

In addition to providing a well-rounded perspective of the manager's abilities, this information may yield improved decision-making opportunities at recruitment time. That insight includes evaluating the potential loss of a competent, skilled resource to the corporation, and accordingly determining that employee replacement costs—plus project delay costs—could cost the respective corporation an amount ranging from \$9,000 to \$$N$,000.

Knowing the true hidden costs, it would greatly benefit the affected organization to be able to retain the services of the terminating employee for up to one more year by offering a bonus of \$$N$. This would have direct impact on the continuity of services and decreased expenses (direct and indirect), while also ensuring that the void would be covered by succession planning.

In other related manpower strategies, when comparing two candidates, their value should be based on previous positions/education. That means hiring the candidate who already has taken company-approved courses.

Using the "no-nonsense" managerial valuation techniques, group heads can review respective individual growth in asset value as a function of services expensed away during the year's course. The

	ACTUAL # OF EMPLOYEES	ADJUSTED ACTUAL	P.A.R.	SALARIES	EDUCATION	LONG TERM	PERFORMANCE DISTRIBUTION	CONSULTANT COST	%
INVESTMENT BASE JANUARY 1, 19XX	XXX	X/(X)	XXX	$XXXX.X	$XXXX.X	$XXX.X	$XXXX.X	$XXX.X	XX.X%
ADDITIONS									
NEW HIRES	XX			XXX.X	XXX.X	XXX.X		XXX.X	X.X
MOBILITY IN	XX			XX.X	XX.X				
MERIT				XXX.X					
PROMOTIONS				XX.X					
BUDGET					XXX.X			XX	
TOTAL	XX	XX	XX	$XXXX.X	$XXXX.X	$XXX.X	$XXX.XX	$XXXX.X	XX.X%
LESS									
BUDGET				($XXXX.X)	($XXXX.X)				
MOBILITY OUT	(XX)		(XX)	(XXX.X)	(XXX.X)			($XXXX.X)	X.X%
TERMINATIONS									
– GOOD/GOOD	(X)			(XX.X)	(XX.X)				
– GOOD/BAD	(X)			(XX.X)	(XX.X)				
– BAD	(X)			XX.X)	XX.X)				
TOTAL	(XX)		(XX)	($XXX.X)	($XXXX.X)			($XXXX.X)	X.X%
ADJUSTED BASE	XX	XX	XX	$XXXX.X	$XXXX.X	$XXX.X	$XXXX.X	$XXX.X	XX.X%

Figure 9–8.   Changes in human resource values during the period from January 31, 19XX to December 31, 19XX.

"return on investment of projects" can be reviewed, including the prescribed level of staffing planned for, real level allocated and the resulting variance obtained for both reasonableness and in actual dollar terms.

The actual implementation of these measures and—more important—the actual process by which they are obtained will appear to produce a more objective method of reaching a subjective measure of performance.

For the longer term, these measures will become more complex, based on their interrelationships, but these measurements will be easier to both produce and understand because of the existing generation of other subordinate-type data. Once an automated "manpower planning model" is in existence—and the use of regression analysis becomes everyday usage—the subsequent measures base format will be automatically produced.

This chapter has theoretically explored the types of components and measures that naturally come to mind given the objective and nature of the process. We are currently reviewing each of the aforementioned components and "acid testing" them for applicability. Meanwhile, this in-depth review will, in addition to examining the direction and thrust of each component, also attempt to define the measurement process as well as the measures themselves.

Index